Toward
a New Economics

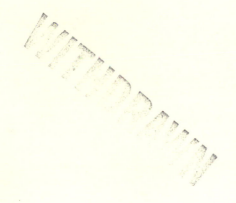

Toward a New Economics

Essays in Post-Keynesian and Institutionalist Theory

Alfred S. Eichner

M. E. SHARPE, INC.
Armonk, New York

Copyright © 1985 by M. E. Sharpe, Inc.

Library of Congress Cataloging in Publication Data

Eichner, Alfred S.
  Toward a new economics.

  1. Economics—Addresses, essays, lectures. 2. Keynesian
economics—Addresses, essays, lectures. 3. Institutional economics—
Addresses, essays, lectures. I. Title.
HB171.E35   1985   330   84-27724
ISBN 0-87332-326-2
ISBN 0-87332-327-0 (pbk.)

Design by Angela Foote

Printed in the United States of America

To my friends
Len Forman, Eli Ginzberg, Aaron Warner, and Mike Sharpe,
without whose support, intellectual and financial,
the work represented by these essays
would not have been possible

CONTENTS

Preface *viii*

1. Introduction *3*
2. The Megacorp as a Social Innovation *10*
3. Micro Foundations of the Corporate Economy *28*
4. An Anthropogenic Approach to Labor Economics *75*
5. The Demand Curve for Money Further Considered (*with Leonard Forman and Miles Groves*) *98*
6. Stagflation: Explaining the Inexplicable *113*
7. The New Paradigm and Macrodynamic Modeling *151*
8. Post-Keynesian Theory and Empirical Research *176*
9. Reflections on Social Democracy *200*

References *219*

Index *231*

Preface —————————————————

Two considerations have prompted me to bring out this collection of essays. The first is that it has taken longer than anticipated to complete the textbook which I had hoped would be the more immediate follow-up to *A Guide to Post-Keynesian Theory*. It will probably be at least two more years before *The Macrodynamics of Advanced Market Economies* appears, and in the interim there is a need for a more sophisticated treatment of the theory outlined in the *Guide*—something the more advanced student, and indeed the already established economist, will find useful.

The second consideration is that, upon rereading the articles and unpublished papers from which the collection is drawn, I could see that there was an underlying theme which tied the various pieces together, and indeed was of such importance that it deserved to be highlighted. That theme is the need to abandon the supply-and-demand framework of the orthodox theory if a realistic model of the U.S. and other advanced market economies is ever to be constructed. Indeed, it can be argued on the basis of the essays contained in this collection that supply and demand curves, with price as the common explanatory variable, play the same role in economic analysis that a belief in Divine intervention plays in scientific work in general: it is an extraneous element which obscures the factors actually at work.

The proof that the U.S. economy can be modeled more realistically by abandoning the conventional supply-and-demand framework will be found in the following essays. Here all I would plead is that this notion, so outrageous to those steeped in the orthodox theory, not be dismissed out of hand—without waiting to see what sort of case can be made on its behalf.

Much credit goes to a number of persons for the essays that have been brought together in this volume. The critical support I have received from Len Forman, Eli Ginzberg, Aaron Warner, and Mike Sharpe is reflected in the volume's dedication. In addition, I would like to cite the intellectual debt I owe to, among others, William Casey,

C. Wright Mills, Gardiner Means, Alfred Chandler, Joan Robinson, Wassily Leontief, and Luigi Pasinetti for the direct personal influence they have had on the development of the ideas reflected in these essays. I would also like to thank Dick Bartel for inviting me to write the paper on which essay six is based and then helping to edit that paper; Philip Arestis for inviting me to give the paper on which essay seven is based; and Mario Seccareccia and Jacque Henry for inviting me to give the paper on which essay eight is based. Finally, I would like to acknowledge the debt to my wife, Barbara Eichner, both for her contribution to the development of my ideas about human development and for the strong moral and other types of support she has given me over the years.

Alfred S. Eichner

Toward
a New Economics

1

Introduction

The essays that have been brought together in this volume are directed toward those who, whether long-time students of economics or only now just completing their graduate training, are reluctant to turn away from the orthodox theory, as represented by the neoclassical synthesis, because they believe there is nothing better to put in its place. The thrust of the essays is that there is, indeed, something better.

That something better is based on a set of ideas developed by economists working outside the mainstream of the discipline. In recognition of the fact that its core derives from the efforts by several of Keynes' closest associates at Cambridge University, in the years following his death in 1945, to go beyond just the principle of effective demand in describing the dynamics of an advanced market economy, this set of ideas has been labeled post-Keynesian. But it could just as well be termed post-classical, or even post-Marxist, since it also picks up where the classical mode of analysis left off following the marginalist revolution in the 1870s. Indeed, it could well be described as institutionalist since an important characteristic of the theory is the prominent role it ascribes to the dominant institutions of the twentieth century—in particular, the large multinational corporation, trade unions, and credit money. The purpose in bringing these essays together in one volume is to present this body of post-Keynesian theory as an integrated whole, thereby demonstrating that it is just as comprehensive and coherent as the neoclassical synthesis, the dominant theory in economics today, while at the same time being far more applicable to economic systems like those of the United States and the other OECD (Organization for Economic Cooperation and Development) countries.

The precise ways in which post-Keynesian theory differs from the neoclassical synthesis will be brought out in the following essays. What needs to be understood, even before turning to that subject, is why an economic analysis is almost certain to go astray when it is based on the orthodox theory. Only by understanding where and how economics has gone wrong will it be possible to put the discipline back on a progressive path of development and, once there, prevent it from being sidetracked again. What follows in this introductory essay is not a wide-ranging critique of economics—that can be found elsewhere (see, for example, Eichner, 1983a; Robinson, 1972; Ward, 1972; Hicks, 1974; Bell and Kristol, 1980; and Thurow, 1983)—but rather an attempt to point out the one flaw that invalidates virtually the entire body of orthodox theory. Indeed, the need to purge economics of that fundamental error is the principal theme of this first essay, tying together several strands of the argument to be found in the essays that follow.

* * *

One of the few objections Roy Harrod raised, when he was shown an early draft of *The General Theory*, was to Keynes' argument that it makes no sense to consider the interest rate as the price that equates the supply and demand for savings. Harrod wrote that while Keynes might be justified in arguing that the classical theory was incorrect, he should not say that the theory makes "no sense." As Harrod explained more fully in a subsequent letter:

> You may wonder why I lay such stress on a point that merely concerns formal proof rather than the conclusions reached. I am thinking of the effectiveness of your work. Its effectiveness is diminished if you try to eradicate very deep-rooted habits of thought unnecessarily. One of these is the supply and demand analysis. I am not thinking of the aged and fossilised, but of the younger generation who have been thinking perhaps only for a few years but very hard about these topics. It is doing great violence to their fundamental groundwork of thought, if you tell them that two independent demand and supply functions won't jointly determine price and quantity. Tell them that there may be more than one solution. Tell them that we don't know the supply function. Tell them that the *ceteris paribus* clause is inadmissible and that we can discover more important functional relationships governing price and quantity in this case which render the s. and d. analysis nugatory. But don't impugn the analysis itself. (Moggridge, 1973, XIII, pp. 533–34.)

Keynes nonetheless held to his position. As he later wrote Harrod:

> I still maintain that there is "no sense" in the view that interest is a price which equates saving and investment. . . .Perhaps the clue is to be found

where you allege that I am doing great violence to the accepted and familiar when I maintain that "two independent demand and supply functions won't jointly determine price and quantities," for my whole point is that the functions in question are *not* independent. (Ibid., p. 338.)

Harrod was quite correct in warning how difficult it would be to persuade economists, the young as well as the old, to abandon the supply and demand framework on which, almost without exception, they have cut their intellectual teeth. If anything, economists have become even more committed to that framework as a result of the neo-Walrasian counter-revolution, based on "general equilibrium" models, which *The General Theory* sparked.

Harrod was nonetheless wrong in urging Keynes to avoid a direct attack on the conventional supply and demand framework. What, in hindsight, can be seen with greater clarity is that it was precisely the retention of that framework as the micro foundation of the neoclassical synthesis that has ultimately defeated Keynes' larger purpose. It is that framework that suggests that inflation can occur only as the result of excess demand and that therefore, in order to combat the rise in prices, the Keynesian policy levers need to be thrown into reverse so as to make them the instruments for raising, rather than lowering, the unemployment rate.

Keynes had, in fact, put his finger on the essential flaw in the orthodox theory, micro no less than macro, when he told Harrod it makes no sense to argue in terms of supply and demand if the two factors are not independent of one another. This is precisely the point of essays three, four, and five which follow. In the usual way of delineating the subject matter of economics, these essays fall under the rubric of price theory, labor economics, and monetary theory. Within the framework of *The General Theory* itself, however, they are concerned with the three principal types of markets which serve to regulate the economic system's real and monetary flows. These are the markets for goods, labor, and credit (or finance) (Chick, 1983).

In *The General Theory*, Keynes denied, though only implicitly, that for the economy as a whole to be in "equilibrium" it is necessary for supply to be equal to demand in each of these three types of markets. Rather, all that is necessary is that aggregate savings be equal to aggregate investment. Still, Keynes failed to make the point as strongly or as explicitly as he might have—if indeed he realized the full import of defining the equilibrium condition in the way he did. The closest he came to an explicit statement was when he explained why "full employment" could not be achieved through wage cuts. But even then he avoided attacking the notion of a separate supply curve for labor, basing his argument instead on the depressing effect wage cuts are likely to have on the "marginal efficiency of capital." As for the interest rate, little of the argument made to Harrod in private found its way into *The General Theory*.

What Keynes should have made clear, and what essays three, four, and five bring out in the course of presenting a post-Keynesian alternative to the standard price theory, labor economics, and monetary analysis, is that in each of the three principal types of markets, the supply is not necessarily independent of the demand. Rather, the demand determines the supply, making the one a function of the other.

In the goods markets, at least when the goods are industrial products, it is the level of aggregate demand that determines the supply, once the necessary plant and equipment have been installed and a labor force recruited. Even over the longer run, it is the final demand vector, in conjunction with the set of fixed technical coefficients, that determines the quantity produced, and hence supplied, by each separate industry.

In the labor market, it is again the level of demand, in this case the demand for each firm's output, that determines the number of employment opportunities, and hence the number of individuals who will receive the on-the-job training needed for the development of a skilled labor force.

In the credit markets, it is the demand for new loans that determines the increase in bank deposits and hence any growth in the means of payment.

For each type of market, then, it is the demand that determines the supply. Moreover, and this is the critical point, it does so *independently of the price prevailing in that market*.

It will immediately be clear to anyone who has studied economics how radical a critique this is of the orthodox theory. What it implies is that virtually the first thing economists are taught—namely, to specify a supply curve which is separate and independent of the demand curve—is wrong in almost every case.

It may be the correct way to analyze the situation in certain commodity markets, those which have not yet been organized into a producer's cartel or stabilized through some type of government intervention. It may even be the correct way to analyze the shape-up which occurs almost daily in urban ghettos around the world for casual jobs requiring unskilled labor. But these are the exceptions. For the most part, a separate supply curve does not exist. To support the contention that it does, economists are forced to invent stories that are caricatures of reality—such as the story that industrial firms are subject to decreasing returns when they expand output or the story that workers who cannot obtain jobs are merely exercising their preference for leisure.

This is not to say that supply and demand have no place in economics as analytical categories. It is often useful to separate the factors influencing the quantity supplied from the factors operating on the demand side—as long as one does not assume that the two will automatically be brought into balance with one another through a change in the market price. It is the latter error, one that permeates the entire body of orthodox theory, that has led to the present intellectual bankruptcy of economics.

Why it is essential to purge economics of this error will become clear in essays six and eight. One reason is so that the underlying causes of the secular inflation which has afflicted the world's advanced market economies in the post-World War II period can be properly understood and an effective remedy, one that does not transform the problem of rising prices into the far more serious problem of stagnation, can be devised. Essay six shows how stagflation, which the orthodox theory cannot account for within a supply and demand framework, is easily explained by the alternative body of post-Keynesian theory. It also indicates the types of public policies which, as complements to the more conventional fiscal and monetary policies, will have to be implemented to bring the problem of inflation under control.

The other reason for purging economics of the conventional supply and demand framework is so that economics can finally be raised to the level of a scientific discipline. Essay eight, after noting that the conventional theory fails to meet any of the empirical tests that characterize a scientific body of knowledge, indicates how the post-Keynesian alternative can be used to free empirical research from its present conceptual straitjacket, enabling both the theory and the empirical research to advance in tandem with one another.

Essay seven meanwhile shows how the various elements of post-Keynesian theory, including those covered in essays three, four, and five, can be combined into a single macrodynamic model, one that lends itself both to improved empirical research and to better public policy. This entire group of essays is less concerned with pointing out the defects of the orthodox theory than with providing a positive alternative. Thus essay three indicates what can be substituted for the orthodox theory of the firm, essay four describes what can be used to replace the conventional model of the labor market, essay five offers a different way of analyzing the money and credit markets, and essay seven presents a macrodynamic model of the American economy to supersede the standard Hicks-Hansen LM-IS model. In each case, it is argued that the alternative body of post-Keynesian (and institutionalist) theory is no less coherent and comprehensive than the orthodox theory, does not run counter to what can be observed of the real world, and avoids positing a supply curve that is independent of demand. It is in this last way that the alternative body of post-Keynesian theory avoids the fundamental error that has largely invalidated the orthodox theory, especially the "general equilibrium" model which serves as the micro foundation of the neoclassical synthesis.

One last situation in which the orthodox supply and demand framework applies can be identified. This is a situation in which the mechanisms that have been put in place to soften what would otherwise be a socially unacceptable outcome of the market process have broken down. The characteristic institutions of the twentieth century—the large multinational corporation, trade unions, and credit money—are precisely these types of mechanisms. They have evolved over time as a way of insulating at least certain groups in society from the harsher effects which a sudden change in supply or demand conditions can produce within a commodity type of market, and they need to be understood as such, not as some perversion of an ideal form of economic organization. This is precisely the point essay two attempts to make in describing the historical evolution of the large multinational corporation, or megacorp. The essay suggests that the megacorp emerged toward the end of the nineteenth century as a protective response to the ruinous competition among firms that was threatening to destroy the entrepreneurial class directing the industrialization of the United States. It can be argued that trade unions and credit money emerged as institutions for similar reasons—though not necessarily to protect the same groups.

The dysfunctional nature of commodity markets in an economy undergoing industrial development is, however, only one of several themes developed in essay two. More broadly, it attempts to explain the dynamics of institutional innovation, using the megacorp as an example. At the same time, it offers an institutionalist framework for integrating the social sciences, one that can be viewed as an alternative to the better known Marxian theories of societal development. Finally, it is meant to indicate the broader social context in which any economic analysis, post-Keynesian or neoclassical, needs to be carried out. In this respect, it serves as a further introduction to the more narrowly focused essays on economic theory which follow.

Essay nine, the last of the essays included in this volume, brings the discussion full circle by pointing out the broader policy implications of a post-Keynesian perspective on the world's economy. Here the argument is that, just as economic theory needs to be reconstructed along post-Keynesian lines, so the types of social democratic policies that Keynes' ideas have inspired in the past need to be supplemented so as to make them more appropriate to the contemporary economic situation. High on the list of this post-Keynesian agenda for political action is the creation of a new international order as a substitute for the system of flexible exchange rates which has replaced the Bretton Woods arrangement, and the establishment of some form of indicative planning, with an incomes policy as the key component so as to avoid having to rely solely on monetary and fiscal policy to control inflation.

* * *

Since ingrained habits of thought are not easily altered, economists will not find it easy to abandon the supply and demand framework of the orthodox theory. In this regard, Harrod knew all too well what he was talking about. Nonetheless, until economists do abandon that framework, they cannot hope to make any real progress in understanding how an advanced market system like that of the United States and the other OECD countries actually works. Contrary to what some would argue, it is not enough merely to modify or alter the way the supply and demand curves are specified to cover the particular market situation. The curves themselves need to be abandoned as a way of trying to understand how the economic system works. That is the harsh truth economists must face if they want to make their discipline both intellectually respectable and a useful guide to public policy.

On the other hand, economists need not fear that there is nothing better to put in place of the orthodox theory. There is, in fact, a body of theory that is just as coherent and comprehensive as the neoclassical synthesis while at the same time being far more consistent with what can be observed of the real world. By replacing the conventional supply and demand framework with this other paradigm, economists will no longer have trouble explaining the dynamics of an advanced market economy like that of the United States. That is the prospect that should enable economists to face up, at last, to the truth about the orthodox theory.

2

The Megacorp
as a Social Innovation

History can be seen as the process by which human beings have developed the tools called social institutions, not just to give themselves some control over the forces of nature but also, even more generally, to enhance the options available to them over their lifetime. From this prespective, to understand history one must be able to comprehend the nature of social institutions, including their very real limitations as enhancers of individual options.

This essay consists of two parts. In the first half, a conceptual framework for understanding the institutional structure of a society is presented, with the historical experience of the United States used to show how social development depends on institutional innovation. In the second half, the process by which the megacorp emerged as the dominant type of firm within the U.S. economy is examined in detail to see what further light the same conceptual framework can shed, in this particular instance, on the determinants of institutional innovation.

* * *

In attempting to understand the role played by social institutions, the student of history will find himself up against the intellectual poverty of the sister discipline of sociology. Among contemporary sociologists only Talcott Parsons has attempted to provide a general theory of social institutions; yet in deliberately choosing concepts without any real-world counterparts except as figments of that reality, and by refusing to specify any behavioral models to accompany his schema, Parsons has made his work unusable for historians.[1] It is for this reason that Ginzberg and Eichner, coming out of institutional economics rather than sociology and building on their work as part of the Conservation of Human Resources Project at Columbia University, have attempted a different approach to the study of social institutions.[2] It is an approach that views historical development in terms of the interaction among four institutional dimensions—the normative, the political, the economic, and the anthropogenic, or human developmental.[3]

The normative dimension of society consists of all values, or implicit assumptions that underlie the behavior of individuals in the course of everyday life. To say hello when greeting acquaintances on the street, to be at work on time, not to steal from one's neighbors—these may all be part of the normative structure, or value orientation that characterizes a particular society. Values of this sort, which have important implications for the way in which society functions, can be distinguished from mere preferences—such as for shiny yellow sports cars, Mozart concertos, and Chinese cooking—that bear only on which specific options are exercised, not on the range of options available.

It can, of course, be questioned whether values, as just defined, have any existence separate and distinct from the behavior of either the individuals or the institutions that make those values manifest. And indeed, the value orientation of a society is in a certain sense basic to the way in which all other social institutions function. In the broadest sense, an institution is merely a habitual way of doing things (Berger, 1963). But this only means that the four dimensions coexist, not that one dimension can be subsumed under the others. Just as a particular point on a cube exists along the scalar dimension of width as well as the scalar dimension of length, so a particular social phenomenon—say the belief that government should be organized along parliamentary lines—can be viewed as part of the value orientation of that society as well as part of the same society's political structure.

What makes it necessary to consider the value orientation separately in its own right is the fact that part of the value orientation of any society deals with values themselves, that is, with the process by which certain values come to be legitimated and accepted. Since values represent the implicit assumption upon which human behavior is predicted, some such process is essential for consistency and coherence of behavior, if for no other reason. Whether in fact the assumptions that values represent are true is not an unimportant question, for it will determine whether the behavior predicted upon those values, or assumptions, will be appropriate to the actual situation that exists. It is therefore useful to know how appropriate a given value orientation is, the basis for determining this being the scientific method that has gradually developed over the last 500 years as the yeast of Western civilization (McNeil,

1963; Kuhn, 1962). The more appropriate the value orientation of a society, the greater will be the options—in an existential sense—of the individual members of that society.

It was along this institutional dimension that the original settlers of what is now the United States gained an early advantage over other societies. Not that the Puritans and other first Americans were more "scientific" than their European brethren. Far from it. Rather it was that the combined effect of the challenges posed to prevailing beliefs by the harsh realities of the New World and the differential nature of those who came and survived in the colonies created a ferment in values which has continued to the present day. Almost from the very beginning Americans were known to be more pragmatic about what they would accept as true, and this has led to a value orientation even more dynamic than that found in the Anglo-Saxon lands from which the colonists came. The result was to give the Americans one leg up on the process of societal development.

The second institutional dimension of society, the political, encompasses all the social institutions that serve to resolve the conflicts inevitably arising among the various members of any society. Since the resolution of conflict involves making a decision, choosing one alternative over another, the political dimension is the one in which societal decisions are made.[4] This political dimension of society includes not only that portion of the value orientation that consists of political beliefs and therefore defines the parameters of political activity, but also the actual organizations through which societal decisions are made. These political organizations, in turn, include both the formal bodies which constitute the "government" with its monopolistic exercise of coercive power, and the informal bodies through which coalitions are successfully forged for gaining control over the government. Indeed, the forging of coalitions is the quintessential political activity in which men engage, just as the making of decisions through conflict resolution is the primary function that political institutions serve.

It is by the quality of the decisions made that political institutions can be judged. These decisions may bear on how political decisions themselves are to be made, as for example when Constitutional questions arise. More typically, however, especially in a politically mature society, the decisions bear on some other dimension of society. The systems operating along two of those other dimensions, the economic and the anthropogenic, are to some extent self-regulating. Still, they are incapable of functioning entirely on their own, at least without giving rise to results that are unacceptable to the majority of persons living within the society. When the economy goes into a slump or cannot provide some essential item, when children are left without parents or the parents are unable to provide them with something essential to their development, the government as the formal part of the political system usually offers the only recourse. The political institutions, then, are society's standby steering device (Deutsch, 1966; Etzioni, 1968), responsible for filling the breach when other institutions fail and the only means in any case by which society as a whole can consciously influence the future. The mark of how well those institutions perform is the quality of the direction they give society.

Along the political dimension, too, the early Americans were particularly fortunate. The strong Federal union they were able to create in 1787, organized along embryonic democratic lines and consisting of smaller units similarly structured, gave the new nation a system of government that would be particularly responsive to the will of its citizenry. It also brought domestic peace, with one notable exception, to what would eventually become a nation of continental size. Together with the free-trade area which was thereby established and the rich natural endowment of the land, this was virtually all that was needed to launch the United States on the path of rapid economic growth that took place during the nineteenth century. The critical decisions made by the government, as in the areas of the tariff and transportation, were largely foreshadowed by the type of government created in 1787. Indeed, the establishment of the Federal union was the first major institutional innovation which helps to explain the subsequent rapid development of American society.

The third institutional dimension of society, the economic, also includes a portion of the society's value orientation. In this case, it is the portion consisting of economic beliefs—the importance placed on material goods, the desirability of cooperative forms of production, the necessity of a gold standard, etc. These beliefs define the parameters of economic activity. The economic system includes a portion of the political structure as well, this being the portion that makes economic decisions. Finally, the economic dimension includes the actual organizations through which, either directly or indirectly, physical commodities are "produced," that is, transformed from some previous state, and then distributed among the individual members of the society.

At the heart of this process is the allocation decision, the choice of using a particular resource among one of several competing ends. This decision can be made politically, that is, through the exercise of the government's command powers. In that case, there will be no separately distinguishable economic mode of allocation. Alternatively, the decision can be made through a market process by which one party gives up something in exchange for something else. Indeed, the effecting of an exchange is the quintessential economic activity, just as the supplying of the individual's material needs is the primary function served by economic institutions. Yet exchange by itself is seldom sufficient. Before there can be something to exchange, that something has to be produced; and this must generally be done in an organizational setting that involves little or no formal exchange. The economic institutions, then, combine exchange and command, the proper balance between them varying with the circumstances.

It is by the ability to meet the material needs of the individual members of the society, conventionally measured by per capita income, that the economic institutions are judged. The greater the quantity of physical commodities available to the individual—and to the institutions upon which the individual is dependent—the fewer will be the choices foreclosed to him for lack of material wherewithal. It is in this sense that the institutions that operate along the economic dimension can be said, insofar as they succeed in producing a higher per capita level of income, to increase the options available to the individual.

Along the economic dimension, too, the development of American society was speeded up by a major institutional innovation. That innovation was the modern corporation, or megacorp, initially resisted as a threat to the competitive order when it emerged in the form of a "trust" or "holding company" but today firmly established as the diversified, multinational enterprise. This point will be elaborated on in the second half of this essay.

The fourth institutional dimension of society is the human developmental, or anthropogenic, dimension. Its delineation is one important way in which the Ginzberg-Eichner conceptual framework differs from earlier analyses of societal development.[5] The anthropogenic dimension encompasses all the institutions that have emerged over time, beginning with the prehistoric family, for developing the competences of individual members of society. These competences include not only specific cognitive-motor skills but also the ability, through the internalization of certain values, to utilize those skills in a social setting. Competences, in other words, are various capacities to play selected social roles in life.

The anthropogenic dimension, like the political and the economic, includes part of the society's value orientation. In this case, it is that part of the value orientation that concerns the development of human beings, such as beliefs about the social malleability of individuals, homilies like "spare the rod and spoil the child," and the importance attached to human life itself. These values define the parameters of anthropogenic activity. The anthropogenic dimension also includes part of the political structure—the subcomponent that makes decisions affecting the development of the individuals—and part of the economic structure—the subcomponent that determines the allocation of human resources. Finally, the anthropogenic dimension includes the actual organizations that play a role in developing individual competences.

These anthropogenic institutions are of three types. There is first the family, into which the individual is initially born (or in which he is subsequently placed). The family is the primary developmental institution, and its function is to provide the emotional support, as well as the rudimentary competences, which every individual needs if his development is not to be retarded or thwarted. Then there is the school, in which the individual in more advanced societies is subsequently enrolled. The school is the secondary developmental institution, and its function is to supplement the efforts of the family, concentrating particularly on the development of cognitive skills. Finally, there is the employing organization, to which every individual eventually becomes attached. The employing organization is the tertiary developmental institution, and its function is to provide the real-life experience through which the competences partially acquired in the classroom become more refined.

The family and the school, if not the employing organization, have long been the subject of study by social scientists. The Ginzberg-Eichner model, however, considers these institutions not only as separate entities but also as part of a larger societal process by which individual competences are produced. What links these institutions is the developmental path which every individual follows during his lifetime. This developmental path involves the act of affiliating with successive and, in some cases, complementary developmental institutions, beginning with birth into a particular family and continuing sporadically thereafter as the individual moves through his life cycle. Indeed, affiliating with a developmental institution is the quintessential anthropogenic activity, just as the development of individual competences is the primary function that anthropogenic institutions serve.

The basis, then, for evaluating anthropogenic institutions is the extent to which they develop competences. The greater the number of those competences and/or the more advanced they are, the greater will be the options open to the individual. This is true for two reasons: first, because the individual himself will be capable of doing more, and thus of taking advantage of additional opportunities; and second, because the institutions that serve the individual will be able to draw from a richer talent pool in staffing their positions. It is thus by developing individual competences that the anthropogenic institutions contribute to the quality of life.

This anthropogenic dimension, too, has had its major American institutional innovation. This has been the democratization of education, beginning initially with the common school and now proceeding at the college level.

The four institutional dimensions of society which have just been delineated suggest a way of bringing some order to what often appears to be a confusing historical record. If the history of mankind is the account of how his social institutions have evolved, then it follows that there are four types of institutions—the normative, the political, the economic, and the anthropogenic—whose evolution can be traced. This taxonomy corresponds somewhat to the distinction which historians themselves customarily make between intellectual, political, economic, and social history.

Of course, no one institutional dimension is independent of the others. This important point has already been made, at least implicitly, in the discussion of the four separate dimensions where parts of each have been included as parts of others. Indeed, what has been described so far is the top half of a four-fold matrix as follows:

	Value orientation	Political system	Economic system	Anthropogenic system
Value orientation	VV	VP	VE	VA
Political system		PP	PE	PA
Economic system			EE	EA
Anthropogenic system				AA

Moving horizontally across the matrix, one can systematically consider the effect that one dimension of society has on another. On the other hand, moving vertically down the matrix as far as the main diagonal (indicated by the cell containing the same two letters) and then proceeding horizontally, one can trace out all the components of the dimension listed at the head of the column. As for the main diagonal itself, this simply delineates where the institutions of a particular type operate in their purest form, without having to take any other dimension of society into account.

All that remains, to complete the picture of interaction among the four dimensions, is to fill in the bottom half of the matrix as follows:

	Value orientation	Political system	Economic system	Anthropogenic system
Value orientation	VV	VP	VE	VA
Political system	PV	PP	PE	PA
Economic system	EV	EP	EE	EA
Anthropogenic system	AV	AP	AE	AA

It should be noted, however, that while this will bring out additional ways in which one dimension of society affects another, it will add no new components to any of the dimensions. As a case in point, while the decisions made by the political system are likely to influence society's value orientation (cell PV), that influence does not itself constitute a part of the value orientation as traced out in the top row. In other words, the bottom half of the matrix shows only the influences of one dimension on another, not the components of any particular dimension.

Thus the order in which the dimensions are listed in the matrix is not arbitrary. There is, in fact, a certain logical sequencing to the development of the four dimensions. The emergence of anthropogenic institutions, separate and distinct from the family, is predicated on the economic system's ability to generate the necessary social surplus, that is, margin above subsistence, to support a class of workers not engaged in the production of commodities. The development of the economy above the household subsistence level is, in turn, dependent on the existence of a government willing and able to carry out certain types of economic decisions. And finally, the existence of a government presupposes that a group of individuals occupying a certain geographical area share enough values in common so that they can agree on how the instruments of coercion should be used to enforce whatever collective decisions may be reached. In other words, development along any one dimension—except, of course, the normative—requires that development along the antecedent dimension has reached a certain critical, or minimal, level.

This view of the developmental process gives rise to both a static and dynamic model of society. In the static model, each set of social institutions has implicit within it an ultimate limit on the levels of development that can be reached. The value orientation may, for example, be compatible with the development of an effective political structure in the sense that the government is able to carry out the decisions essential for the survival of the society. The value orientation may even be compatible with the growth of an economy above the subsistence level as well as with the emergence of some anthropogenic institutions in addition to the family. But if the value orientation does not allow for the possibility of a change in the value orientation itself, the development will ultimately come to a halt as the full potential of the closed system of values is exhausted. Some might say that this is the model that best describes Chinese society from the time of Confucius until relatively recently.

But it is not just the value orientation that may set the ultimate limit on the development of a society. The political, economic, and anthropogenic institutions may each in their own way, by proving impervious to change, bring the evolution of the society to an end. Indeed, all four dimensions are so closely interrelated that it is usually only a matter of perspective as to which is seen as the source of rigidity. As long as all the institutions, taken together, can confine the deviations in the established patterns of behavior which inevitably and continuously occur, doing so within limits that preclude any significant qualitative change in those institutions, the society will remain a static one. This, of course, presumes the use of sanctions to suppress the deviant behavior of individuals and the existence of a mythology to explain away shortcomings in the institutions themselves.

How, then, do social institutions become transformed? In trying to answer this question, it is instructive to look at one of the institutional innovations already identified, the rise of the modern corporation, or megacorp. This is the subject matter of the section that follows.

* * *

The argument so far represents an attempt to apply systems theory, including cybernetics, to the study of social institutions through history. Indeed, the institutions that operate along three of the dimensions can be seen as cybernetic systems, using deviation-reducing, or "negative," feedback to alter their behavior and bring it more in line with the changing goals of those who comprise the society. In the case of the political system, at least when it is organized along democratic lines, the feedback consists of the voting behavior of the electorate. In the case of the economic system, the negative feedback consists of the time and energy commitments individuals are willing to make. Systems theory, however, includes the concept of positive feedback as well as that of negative feedback.[6]

Positive feedback is likely to be observed when a system can no longer survive simply by responding to the ongoing challenge of its environment in the usual way, that is, by altering its behavior in light of the new informational imputs but without changing the mode of response itself. When exogenous shocks threaten to overwhelm the system's capacity to deal with any feedback effects, only a fundamental reorganization of the system's internal structure, resulting in a new mode of response, will suffice to assure the continued survival of the system. When a system responds to some external threat in that manner, it can be decribed as exhibiting "positive" feedback. Indeed a positive feedback response of this sort at the institutional level is what is meant by institutional innovation.

The emergence of the megacorp can be understood precisely in these terms. The pre-existing system of economic organization, based on small, owner-managed proprietorships linked together by competitive markets, was faced with a challenge which it could meet only by radically restructuring itself. As a result, small, owner-managed proprietorships were transformed into megacorps, with control depending on executive position within a corporate hierarchy rather than on equity holdings, and the competitive markets were transformed into oligopolistic ones. Viewing the emergence of the megacorp in these terms suggests four major types of questions: 1) What was the nature of the challenge that the pre-existing system of economic organization proved unable to cope with? 2) What were the antecedent and/or parallel developments that made the restructuring of the economic system possible—that is, what were the elements out of which the new structure was created? 3) What were the sources of resistance that the new structure, like every social innovation, faced, and how was this resistance finally overcome? 4) What appear to be the limits within which the new mode of economic organization is able to continue coping with the challenges from its environment? Each of these questions will be taken up in turn.

The challenge to the old order

The inability of the pre-existing system of economic organization to survive can be understood at two levels. At the more superficial level, one can observe the effects of what was contemporaneously referred to as "ruinous competition." Playing by the rules of the game, which meant cutting prices whenever demand fell, businessmen found themselves with no choice but to continue supplying the market at prices that failed to cover their long-run average total costs. What confronted them, therefore, was the prospect of their capital eventually being expropriated by the forces of competition just as Marx had prophesied. Many individual industry studies, building on earlier, more general work, have confirmed the prevalence of this situation toward the end of the nineteenth century (e.g., Maybee, 1940; Hidy and Hidy, 1955; Williamson and Daum,1959; Jones, 1914; Graebner, 1974). One must ask, however, what lay behind the crisis, so unexpected in light of economic theory.

Here one comes up against the fundamental force of the evolving technology from the late eighteenth century on, particularly the part that was economically significant. There were two main thrusts of that technology. One was to reduce real space distances limiting human communication and interchange; the other was to make possible the production of standardized commodities on a continuous basis with little restriction on accelerated output. The first, constituting a transportation revolution, served to create new national markets, initially based on canals and later on railroads. The second, constituting an industrial revolution, made it possible to supply the expanding markets with a long-run falling cost curve.[7]

As long as the new markets being opened up enabled demand to keep ahead of the supply capacities of the new industries that were simultaneously being created, the twin-headed thrust of the evolving technology posed no threat to the existing system of economic organization. Indeed, it led to a "Golden Age" of competition, with the number of separately competing units rapidly swelling. But once the full potential of the new technology to expand output with ever declining costs began to be realized, the situation changed drastically (Eichner, 1969, chs. 1, 5, 10; Porter, 1973, ch. 2; Chandler, 1977, parts 3 and 4). With demand no longer able to keep pace with the growing supply capability, prices started to slip below long-run average costs, at least for those firms with older plant and equipment. Here businessmen ran up against the irreversibility of social processes. The heavy fixed, or "sunk," costs to which they had been forced to commit themselves by the capital-intensive nature of the new production techniques made it impossible to respond as merchants had traditionally done to falling prices, by withdrawing from the market. With a high ratio of fixed to total costs, it was best to continue producing even at prices that failed to cover all expenses. The industrialists who had succeeded the older commodity merchants found themselves caught in the grip of forces beyond their control. Whatever tendency there was for such a decentralized system of economic organization to generate cyclical fluctuations in demand only added to the woes of the industrialists.

Not only were these industrialists unable to respond as merchants traditionally had done by withdrawing from the market in times of depressed prices, they also found it all but impossible to respond in another traditional way, that is, by coming together and agreeing either to restrict output or maintain prices. The need for volume production to reduce the burden of the fixed costs forced every firm to grant special price concessions in order to attract additional business. As a result, agreements to restrict output or maintain prices usually collapsed as quickly as they were worked out. Since the agreements were unenforceable under the common law, businessmen could expect no help from the courts. They were caught in a classic "prisoners' dilemma" as the common interest in having the price level shored up was inexorably undermined by a situation that compelled each individual firm to pursue its own narrow self-interest to the detriment of all (Cyert and DeGroot, 1971; Day and Tinney, 1968; Luce and Raiffa, 1957, pp. 95-96; Rapoport and Chammah, 1965).

What the new development was able to build on

The modern corporation, or megacorp, which emerged after the turn of the century out of the ruins of the older competitive order was not created entirely out of new elements already at hand or clearly within reach. At least three of these critical building blocks, in addition to the evolving technology already noted, can be identified. They are 1) changes in corporate law, both statutory and case law; 2) the development of sophisticated financial markets; and 3) progress in management techniques, especially in the area of accounting. While there are some who have mistakenly seen one or more of these developments as a sufficient explanation for the Corporate Revolution, there is perhaps some justification for a more modest claim that each was, in its own way, only a necessary precondition. It is perhaps no accident that these three important antecedent developments involved all of the four societal dimensions earlier delineated except one—the normative.

It is well known that general incorporation laws were adopted by

most of the states as part of the Jacksonian movement of the 1830s; that
a similar change in the British law was delayed, as a reaction to the
debacle over the South Seas Company early in the eighteenth century,
until much later; and that first New Jersey and then other states changed
their general incorporation laws so as to permit holding companies.
What is not so well known is that incorporated enterprises were the
exception rather than the rule in manufacturing before the Corporate
Revolution; that British firms seem not to have been as hampered by
the lack of general incorporation laws as has generally been presumed;
and that the provision enabling one corporation to own stock in another
was not what was unique about the 1888 change in the New Jersey law
(Stoke, 1930, p. 571; Miller, 1940; Kessler, 1948). Indeed, the critical
role played by the law—and by lawyers—in facilitating the Corporate Revolution has yet to be recognized. With the exception of the
Sherman Act and the subsequent antitrust litigation (Thorelli, 1955;
Letwin, 1965; Dewey, 1959, chs. 9-11), this has been a much neglected
field of historical inquiry, perhaps because it falls in the crack between
legal and business history (but see Commons, 1957). That the evolution
of corporate law played a key role in the response to the crisis of the old
economic order can hardly be doubted, however.

What has just been said about the changes in corporate law would
apply, with only slight modification, to the development of financial
markets and the progress in management techniques. With respect to
the former, the little that is known is far outweighed by what still
remains to be brought out by further research. We know, for example,
as a result of Navin and Sears' (1955) work, that a market for industrial
securities did not emerge until the first trust certificates began to
circulate widely in the late 1880s. But how was the investment in
manufacturing financed before then? Indeed, how important has external financing been throughout the history of manufacturing in the
United States? If it has been as important as the fragmentary evidence
would suggest, then in what way was the development of a sophisticated securities market essential for the emergence of the megacorp?

Insofar as management techniques are concerned, we know a great
deal more, thanks to the work that has been done by Chandler and his
colleagues (Chandler, 1962, 1965, 1971, 1977; Chandler and Salsbury,
1965). We know, from them, how the railroads provided an early model
for decentralized management and how the modern executive group,
freed from day-to-day operating responsibilities, evolved. Moreover,
we know from Lee (1982, ch. 2) some of the important accounting

innovations which have led, among other things, to mark-up pricing practices. (On the role played by accounting techniques, see also Garner, 1968; Johnson, 1972.) Still, there is a great deal more to be learned in this area.

The pioneering role of the textile industry should also not be overlooked—although this was an industry which, until very recently, entirely escaped from the Corporate Revolution. Indeed, the reason why it did so, as well as why the railroads subsequently lost their position as the cutting edge of the new institutional developments, is itself a question that needs to be explored.[8] It may well be that one can learn more from the situations in which megacorps failed to develop or their growth was stunted than from successful cases. This point should be kept especially in mind if one wants to learn about the sources of resistance to innovation.

The sources of resistance

An institutional innovation, by its very nature, can be expected to encounter resistance. As a new way of doing things, and thus as a challenge to prevailing preconceptions, the innovation is likely to evoke the same sort of response that a foreign substance does when it enters an individual's bloodstream. That is, it will be regarded as a threat which must be mobilized against. In taking up the specific example of the megacorp, it is useful to examine the sources of resistance through the prism of the four-fold institutional matrix developed in the first part of this essay.

As already noted, it was only along the normative dimension that the megacorp failed to build on earlier developments. It is hardly surprising therefore that it was along this dimension that the resistance to the megacorp was sharpest and most unyielding. Nothing in the field then known as political economy, not even in the writings of the most vociferous critics, prepared the public for the notion that scrapping the existing competitive order would prove less than disastrous. Indeed, even now, nearly a century later, the situation is little changed. Despite the doubts which both Schumpeter and Galbraith have tried to implant in the minds of their colleagues, economists—whatever their other differences—are still inclined to view the megacorp and its accompanying oligopolistic market structure as a departure from the ideal of multitudinous enterprises competing in atomistic markets. The megacorp remains the bastard child of economic theory, its very existence—

let alone its continued success—a source of embarrassment. If one accepts the truth of Keynes' observation (1936, p. 375) that "practical men, who believe themselves to be quite exempt from any intellectual influences, are usually the slaves of some defunct economist," then one can begin to appreciate the hostile environment, insofar as the norms of society are concerned, in which the megacorp has been forced to operate. Indeed, it becomes all the more remarkable that the initial political response to the emergence of the megacorp did not snuff out the innovation.

That initial response, which comprised one facet of what historians have termed the Populist-Progressive movement, did not gain any significant momentum at the national level until Theodore Roosevelt by chance succeeded McKinley as president. The subsequent history has been variously interpreted (Hofstadter, 1955; Wiebe, 1967; Kolko, 1963). Suffice it to say that there emerged out of the political debate a major division between those who saw the megacorp primarily as a threat to the country's democratic institutions of government and those who saw it as a threat to the economic order as well; between those who viewed only some of the consolidations as culpable and those who viewed every departure from competitive conditions as a situation requiring vigorous corrective action; between those who regarded some form of regulation as the most appropriate remedy and those who regarded the break-up and dissolution of all combinations as the minimal solution.

The outcome of this debate was shaped by two factors. The first was the growing accommodation by the megacorps themselves to the sensitivities of the general public. It was not just that they became more "public relations conscious"—though that was certainly part of it. What really counted was that, in industries where strong rivals had not already arisen, market shares were allowed to decline to the point where no one firm had more than half the business. Oligopoly, it was discovered, served almost as well as monopoly to give the megacorp control over prices. In addition, megacorps learned to do without some of the more notorious means of limiting outside competition, such as rebates from the railroads.

The other factor shaping the outcome of the debate over the megacorp was the gradual realization by political leaders that the older competitive order, once destroyed in a particular industry, was virtually impossible to restore. The experience following the break up of the Standard Oil, American Tobacco, and DuPont companies clearly demonstrated this point. On top of this came the realization, as a result of the nation's efforts to mobilize against the Central Powers during World War I, that the megacorp was a much more efficient social institution for organizing production and distribution than what it had replaced. It was against this rock of the megacorp's greater capacity to supply goods at lower cost that the "bust-'em-up" approach eventually foundered. While the country has, from time to time, returned hesitatingly to that approach as the alternative of regulation has proven no more successful, the fact was that by 1920, with the Supreme Court's decision in the steel case, the megacorp had largely surmounted the political threat to its continued existence (Eichner, 1969, ch. ll; Dewey, 1959, ch. 16; Cuff and Urofsky, 1970).

The economic threat was of a different order. For a long time it was believed that combinations in restraint of trade, no matter how successful in the short run, would eventually be undone by the new suppliers attracted to the market as a result of the artificially raised prices. This was the reason it was considered sufficient for the common law merely to refuse to enforce any restrictive agreements, without have to prohibit them outright. Indeed, it was on this basis that the Supreme Court in the 1895 *E. C. Knight* case refused to apply the Sherman Act to holding companies. The economic threat which the megacorp faced, then, was from new firms entering the industries which had been consolidated and undermining the price structure. That not all the consolidations were successful in meeting this challenge can be seen from the companies, such as National Cordage and the original Corn Product Company, which were subsequently forced into receivership (Dewing, 1913, 1914; Livermore, 1935). Still, the majority of newly created megacorps did find ways to deal with the problem. While some of these techniques for restricting entry were later to be proscribed as being beyond the bounds of acceptable business behavior, others—such as acquiring control over all known deposits of some essential raw materials, building up consumer loyalty through advertising, creating a technological enclave through patents, or establishing an exclusive dealer network—were soon devised to take their place. Reinforcing the market position of every megacorp is at least some factor precluding easy entry by potential rivals.

The anthropogenic threat was also of a different order from the political one. Here the problem was how to recruit and train a new class of men, different from those who customarily went into business and indeed different even from those founding the megacorp. Previously, going into business meant being able to supply a certain amount of initial capital, together with the ability to engage in the give-and-take of haggling in the market place. Generally, the training came from relatives who were in business themselves and were thus willing to suffer the cost of a neophyte's on-the-job learning. For the new class of managers that the megacorp requires, the prerequisite background is instead some sort of technical skill, such as a knowledge of accounting, engineering, law or the like, together with the ability to work together as part of an executive team. The megacorp already has capital enough, while the ability to haggle in the marketplace is seldom called upon when price competition is being suppressed. The problem of how to recruit such a class of managers has, of course, been solved by the development of the business school as a part of the American university system. Executive training programs, developed in most cases by the megacorps themselves, supplement the work of the business schools. In some ways, this has been the easiest challenge for the megacorp to meet.

Each of the four types of challenges that the megacorp has faced—and so far, successfully met—involves a border area between business and some other branch of history. This means that in order to carry through on the story of the megacorp as a social innovation it is necessary either to broaden the usual parameters of business history or to combine business history with other fields of historical inquiry.

Limits on the development of the megacorp

It is probably too soon to say what will be the limits on the ultimate development of the megacorp. What is impressive are the limits the megacorp has already been able to transcend. The potential check on its growth from membership in a particular industry, one subject to eventual decline in the face of changing technology, has been avoided by the megacorp's shift into diversified, conglomerate activities (Chandler, 1962, 1965, 1977; Didrichsen, 1972). Similarly, the check on its growth from placement within a particular national economy has been avoided by the shift into multi-national activities (Wilkens, 1974; Vernon, 1971). At present, there is little reason to doubt that the megacorp will remain the dominant economic institution throughout the world for decades to come—even though specific firms may rise and fall as fortune dictates. What will be the new challenges along the normative, political, and anthropogenic dimensions which the mega-corp in its most recent incarnation as a diversified, multi-national enterprise has yet to overcome is still not clear, however. One can see the same clash between prevailing beliefs, existing political structures and ongoing patterns of recruitment and training on the one hand and the needs of the megacorp on the other which earlier marked American history now being played out on a global stage. Since history does not always repeat itself, and certainly not in the same way, it would be foolish to venture a prediction as to what the eventual outcome will be.

Afterword

This essay originally appeared, in slightly altered form, in *Business and Economic History*, 2nd Series, iv, and was addressed to business historians. As a general framework for the social sciences, it can be compared, on the one hand, with the work of Talcott Parsons (1951, 1956) and, on the other hand, with the work of certain Marxists (see, for example, Wallerstein, 1976; Harris, 1979). The framework itself is described in somewhat greater detail in *Controlling Social Expenditures* (Eichner and Brecher, 1979) as well as in essay four below. As a historical interpretation of what Gardiner Means (1962) termed the "corporate revolution," the essay should be supplemented by a reading of the author's *The Emergence of Oligopoly* (Eichner, 1969) and Alfred Chandler's *The Visible Hand* (1977).

Notes

1. For the main body of his work, see Parsons, 1951, 1954. But see also Parsons and Smelser, 1956. For interpretative commentaries on this not always lucid body of theory, see Black, 1961; Mitchell, 1967; Bershady, 1973. Also helpful is Parson's own intellectual biography (Parsons, 1970).
2. See Ginzberg, 1976. On the earlier work, see Ginzberg, 1966, 1971; Eichner 1973b, 1973c.
3. These categories can be compared with the Parsonian ones of pattern maintenance, goal attainment, adaptation, and integration.
4. In Easton's terms (1964), decisions are the output of the political system.
5. See the sources cited in note 2.
6. On systems theory, see Laszlo, 1972; Klir and Valach, 1967; Ackoff and Emery, 1972. On the concept of "positive" feedback, see Maruyama, 1963.
7. Although Taylor (1951) and Chandler (1977) deal adequately with the first of these technological thrusts, the second has been touched on in the literature only in passing. But see Chapman, 1974; Rosenberg, 1972.
8. In the case of the railroads' decline Martin (1971) has emphasized the effect of regulation.

3

Micro Foundations of the Corporate Economy

Economists have long been aware that the orthodox microeconomic theory has little relevance to the contemporary situation. What they generally do not realize is that there now exists an alternative body of theory—one which, though no less comprehensive and no less coherent, corresponds far more closely to what can be observed in the real world of corporate enterprise. This alternative body of theory, which represents a synthesis of certain ideas to be found within the managerial,[1] behavioralist,[2] institutionalist,[3] and post-Keynesian literature,[4] can be termed the "new microeconomics." The purpose of this review is to explain what is encompassed by that term.

The new microeconomics is intended, first and foremost, to provide a more useful model of firm and industry behavior. Instead of viewing the firm as merely the cat's paw of an impersonal market, it regards the business enterprise, especially when it takes the form of a modern corporation, or megacorp, as an important source of independent decision-making within the economy. The relevant set of decisions includes not just how much to produce and what price to charge, as the orthodox theory would have it. It also includes how much to invest and how to finance that investment. Indeed, the decision of how much to invest is far more important to the firm's continued success than the decision of how much to produce, with the decision of what price to charge being more closely tied to the former than the latter. The new microeconomics, however, is also intended to provide a more appropriate foundation for macroeconomic analysis. The output, price, investment, and finance decisions made at the firm level are critical in determining the macrodynamic behavior of the system as a whole, and if that macrodynamic behavior, as represented by the growth of output and employment as well as by the rise in the average price level, is to be adequately explained, it is necessary that the macro model rest on a solid micro foundation.

In the following sections, the essential features of what can be termed the ''corporate economy'' will first be described, along with those of its representative firm, the megacorp. This is an economy consisting of industries predominantly oligopolistic in structure, with a resulting ability to maintain over time a certain margin, or mark-up, above costs. After the essential features of this corporate economy have been specified, a model of mutually determined investment, prices, external finance, and output will be presented as the distinguishing centerpiece of the new microeconomics. This micro foundation of the corporate economy will then be compared with the orthodox theory of the firm. Next, the model of the corporate economy is examined at the macro level to see what light can be shed on the secular inflation which has bedeviled advanced market economies like that of the United States throughout the post-World War II period. The exercise is carried out first with an assumed absence of uncertainty and thus with an undisturbed secular rate of expansion and then, in a more realistic version of the same model, with allowance for the three types of unforeseeable events—major product innovations, interfirm competition, and a change in government policies—which might cause the economic system to deviate from that secular growth path.

The corporate economy and the megacorp

The corporate economy consists of k industries, as a subset of the n industries which comprise the enterprise sector, or production system, as a whole. These k industries sell their output either to each other or to a group of proprietary firms which are engaged in retail distribution; and they buy their inputs either from each other or from a second group of proprietary firms engaged in agriculture and other types of primary production. The k industries thus constitute a submatrix within the larger input-output system, with the industries represented by primary producers, retail distributors, and other noncorporate enterprises (e.g., residential construction firms) completing the system (Eichner, 1983b, reprinted below as essay seven; Pasinetti, 1981).

Not all of the k industries produce goods and services for final consumption. Some, in fact, specialize in the production of the capital goods used by the other industries to replace and expand their capacity over time. Indeed, it can be assumed that for each industry producing a good or service for final consumption (either by households or by the government) there are one or more other industries supplying that industry, in turn, with capital goods. (An industry may, of course, supply capital goods to more than one other industry.) Other industries specialize in producing material inputs, such as refined metals and chemicals. The industries producing this intermediate output, capital goods as well as direct material inputs, represent the difference between the k industries which comprise the corporate economy and the h industries which produce items for final consumption.

Whatever the type of good it produces, each of the k industries is oligopolistic in structure, with the four leading firms supplying 75 percent or more of the industry's output and with any new firms that might wish to enter the industry facing significant cost and other barriers. One of the four leading firms has a larger share of the market than the others. It is the dominant firm and the industry price leader (Shepherd, 1970; Blair, 1972). Like at least one of the other leading firms, the price leader is a large corporation, or megacorp (Eichner, 1976), with the following characteristics.

(1) The megacorp is an organization rather than an individual. This affects both the megacorp's goals and the way it makes decisions.

As an organization, the megacorp's goal is to expand at the highest rate possible, measured by the growth of cash flow or some correlate. It is expansion at the highest rate possible that creates the maximum opportunities for advancement within the organization, and thus the greatest personal rewards for those who are part of the firm's decision-making structure. To expand at the highest rate possible, the megacorp follows two rules: (a) it attempts to retain its present share of the market in the industries to which it already belongs—as long as those industries are expanding at the same rate as the economy or better, and (b) it periodically expands into newer, more rapidly growing industries while withdrawing from those in which the growth of sales is insufficient and/or the profit margin has been squeezed below the firm's target rate of return.

The megacorp, as an organization, makes decisions through a managerial hierarchy. At the top of this decision-making, or internal political, structure is the executive group, which consists of the chief executive officer and a number of senior vice-presidents (Gordon, 1945). It is the executive group that makes the key decisions. These include: (a) the target rate of return on investment; (b) the investment projects to be included in the annual capital budget; (c) the required mark-up; (d) the annual increment in wages, salaries, and dividends; and (e) any change in the amount of external debt. The executive group also determines which, if any, new industries or markets the megacorp will attempt to enter and who, from among the middle management, will succeed the present members of the group. In making these decisions, the executive group is constrained only by the laws of the countries in which it operates and by the possible loss of control to some outside group if the growth of dividends should fall below a certain rate or if other financial performance criteria (such as repaying loans as they come due) are not met (Wood, 1975).

(2) The megacorp operates not one but several plants in each of the industries to which it belongs, with each plant embodying in the form of a fixed set of technical coefficients the least-cost technology available at the time the plant was constructed (or last modernized). The multiple plants it operates have a significant bearing on the megacorp's costs, both as it varies output over the cycle and as it expands capacity over the longer period.

In varying its output over the cycle, the megacorp will either start up or shut down an entire production line, and in this way produce only at the least-cost point which has been incorporated into each plant's design. A production line consists of all the equipment needed, along with workers, to produce a particular good or service. The amount of labor hours, together with the quantities of raw materials, needed to keep that production line going is, in turn, what the associated set of technical coefficients represents. Usually, to reduce the overhead expense, a plant will consist of more than one production line. Still, with each of those production lines being a duplicate of the others, the same set of technical coefficients applies to the plant as a whole.

By either starting up or shutting down an entire production line (or plant segment) at a time, the megacorp is able to vary its output over the cycle without incurring any significant increase in its average variable, and hence marginal costs. Thus it can be assumed that the firm is subject to constant returns over the short period represented by the typical business cycle. The constant returns are predicated, however, on (a) the megacorp having a certain amount of reserve capacity, consisting of plants with vintage equipment and hence somewhat higher operating costs,[5] and (b) the megacorp using its finished goods inventory to bridge the gap between current sales and current output. The megacorp's reserve capacity, which is likely to be about 25 percent of total capacity in the case of a durable goods industry and about 20 percent of capacity in the case of any other type of industry, is what enables the megacorp to vary its output over the cycle by either starting up or shutting down an entire plant or plant segment. This reserve capacity enables the megacorp to handle any likely fluctuation in industry sales; thus it eliminates the opportunity for new firms to enter the industry because of unsatisfied demand. Changes in the megacorp's finished goods inventory, meanwhile, enable it to avoid any problem because of the discrepancy between current sales and current output. The amount of finished goods inventory is simply allowed to increase when sales are below the output of the production lines currently in operation, and it is allowed to fall when sales exceed that quantity of output (prior to an additional plant segment being activated).

Over the longer run, extending beyond any one cycle, the megacorp can be expected to add to its capacity so as to keep pace with the secular growth of industry sales. This is essential if the megacorp is not to lose market share over time. The new plants being added will, to the extent product innovation is occurring simultaneously in the capital goods sector, enable the firm to gradually reduce its labor-output ratio within that industry (as measured by its labor technical coefficients). This will certainly be the case if, as can be assumed, the cost of labor (measured by the money wage rate) has been rising relative to the cost of other inputs and the new plants therefore embody the latest labor-saving technology. Whether the firm's actual costs of production will also be declining will depend on which is rising more rapidly—money wages or output per worker (the latter measured by the rate of decline of the labor technical coefficients and hence, the firm's labor-output ratio). All that can be said with certainty is that, with new plants being added that embody the latest technology, the firm's costs will be less than they would otherwise be—and less when production is concentrated in the newer plants than when, because of an unusually high level of demand, the firm's reserve capacity has to be utilized. Thus it can be assumed that the expansion of capacity over time will be accompanied by a fall in the firm's labor-output ratio and, to the extent this is true of all firms within the k industries which comprise the corporate economy, by a secular rise in output per worker. The effect on the firm's unit costs of production will depend on the growth of money wages relative to output per worker.

(3) The megacorp is a price setter (or price matcher) rather than a price taker. This means that the prices in each of the k industries are seller- rather than market-determined, with those prices established by adding a certain mark-up, or margin, to the unit costs of production.

The set of list prices announced in advance of any sales by the dominant firm, or price leader, and then adopted as their own by the other leading firms will remain unchanged until the end of the current pricing period (typically a year in the case of durable goods industries, and six months in the case of other industries).[6] Those list prices will then be adjusted, depending on what has happened in the interim to the unit costs of production as a result of the growth of money wages relative to output per worker. Thus, in the short period, the mark-up, if not the price level itself, can be viewed as being fixed. While prices may change, depending on what is happening to the unit costs of production, the same mark-up will be applied to those changing unit costs in order to arrive at the new price list. What this means is that, in the short period, the mark-up (and hence the set of list prices, to the extent those list prices are based on the mark-up) is indeterminant. Within that time frame, the mark-up is simply as given.

Over the longer period, however, the mark-up is variable and indeed can be explained by the dominant firm's need for additional investment funds relative to the implicit cost of obtaining those additional funds by increasing the mark-up. The dominant firm can be expected to seek a higher mark-up when (a) the need for investment funds to expand capacity within the industry in line with the growth of sales (or to purchase new plant and equipment for some similarly essential purpose) exceeds the amount of cash flow being generated at the existing mark-up, and (b) the cost of increasing the mark-up is not excessive in terms of the long-term loss of industry sales due to the substitution effect, the greater likelihood of attracting new firms into the industry based on the entry factor, and the risk of retaliatory action by the government. Indeed, the cost of the additional internally generated funds, taking into account these last three factors, must be less than the cost of obtaining the same funds through an increase in the firm's external debt. Otherwise, the megacorp will find it more advantageous to tap the capital funds market. The mark-up established within the industry in the long period will be the one which balances off the expected returns from investment against the cost of obtaining the needed funds either internally from a change in the mark-up or externally by selling new securities (see below).

(4) The megacorp competes against other firms through the various types of investment it undertakes rather than on the basis of price. This makes the capital budget, followed by the advertising and research and development (R&D) budgets, the critical means by which the megacorp improves its long-term position, both within individual industries and throughout the economy as a whole.

Investment projects are routinely screened for inclusion within the capital budget by comparing the prospective rate of return with the megacorp's target rate of return. The target rate of return will depend on the rate at which the megacorp hopes to grow over time. Indeed, the firm's desired growth rate, adjusted to take into account any corporate profits tax, is the target rate of return. Thus, if the megacorp has the goal of expanding by 15 percent each year and the corporate profits tax rate is 50 percent, the target rate of return will necessarily have to be 30 percent. Any project with a prospective rate of return less than that figure will, even if all expectations are subsequently realized, preclude the megacorp from achieving its growth objectives. Because it is more easily calculated, the inverse of the payback period is likely to be used to approximate the prospective rate of return from a given project. Thus the prospective rate of return from a project that will enable the megacorp to recover any and all outlays within three years is approximately 33 percent. While, in choosing among projects, it might seem necessary to take into account what returns are likely to be realized beyond the payback period, those returns can be largely discounted because, being so distant, they are so uncertain. Restricting the projects to be included within the capital budget to those with a certain minimum payback period means that the megacorp is less vulnerable to an unforeseeable, and thus uncertain, future (see Blatt, 1983, Ch. 12).

There are two types of exceptions to the general rule that projects will be included within the capital budget only if their prospective rate of return, as approximated by the inverse of the payback period, equals or exceeds the megacorp's target rate of return. One type of exception is a project which, unless included, will jeopardize the megacorp's market position within an industry. The expansion of capacity in line with the growth of industry sales falls within this category. Since retention of its market share in the industries in which it expects to remain over time is a necessary condition for maximizing the growth of the firm, this type of project is likely to be given the highest priority within the capital budget. Indeed, it makes little sense even to attempt to calculate the prospective rate of return on such a project. Instead, the governing consideration is likely to be whether the firm wishes to continue including that industry among those to which it allocates its investment funds. The second type of exception to the general rule that projects will be included in the capital budget only if their prospective rate of return exceeds the target rate of return is a project that involves expansion into an entirely new industry or line of business. Although in this case an attempt will be made to calculate the payback period, strategic considerations may be sufficiently important that they will, in fact, dictate the decision. These strategic considerations include the need to neutralize a similar move by a rival firm, the desire to tie up certain sources of supply or avenues of distribution, and the importance of becoming familiar with a new technology.

(5) The megacorp's investment, pricing, compensation, and finance decisions are part of an integrated, sequential decision-making process which the executive group routinely carries out each year (Vickers, 1968). This means that no one of these decisions can be understood in isolation from the others. Each is complementary to the other, the entire set of decisions being the means by which the megacorp is able to maximize its growth over time.

The most important of these decisions, the one that shapes the rest of the decision-making process, is what investment projects are to be included within the capital budget. Still, before a capital budget can be developed, a financial analysis will have to be carried out, with an estimate made of the cash flow likely to be generated, under current sales projections, throughout the period covered by the capital budget. It is this cash flow estimate that provides a first indication of what is likely to be the increase, if any, in the capital budget. If, as may well be the case, the number of projects originating from within the organization that can meet the target rate of return and/or other criteria exceeds the cash flow likely to be generated during the year, the executive group will need to decide how to bring the two into balance by taking one or more of the following steps: (a) increasing the average mark-up within one or more industries, (b) arranging for external financing, or (c) eliminating or stretching out certain projects. The first option to be weighed will be an increase in the average mark-up within one or more industries. However, any decision to try to increase the mark-up will have to be part of a more comprehensive review of pricing policy.

A model for the "new microeconomics"

The situation in which the megacorp's executive group is likely to find itself upon reviewing the current set of list prices within a given industry can be represented by a group of diagrams (Figs. 1–9) (Eichner, 1976, Ch. 3).

Its cost curves will be those shown in Fig. 1. Because of the multiple

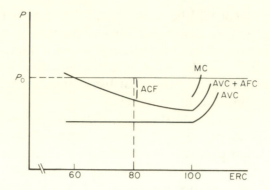

Figure 1

plants it operates, the megacorp is able to vary output with average variable, and hence marginal, costs remaining nearly constant up to 100 percent of engineer-rated capacity (ERC). Given its deliberately maintained reserve capacity, the megacorp will seldom operate in excess of 90 to 95 percent of capacity, so that only the interval between 65 and 95 percent of engineer-rated capacity represents the relevant range of these cost curves. The megacorp's total costs, which include average fixed or overhead expenses as well as the direct cost of labor and materials, will meanwhile decline steadily as output increases, this because of the greater volume over which they can be spread.

The list prices for the various goods, or product line, supplied by the industry can be expected to have been set, during the previous price review, so that on the average they cover the industry's total costs at the standard, or expected, rate of output plus a certain rate of average cash flow (ACF) or profit, π. This is shown in Fig. 1 by the price line, P_0. (The standard rate of output is the level of output that would be needed to supply the market in the absence of any cyclical fluctuations in sales. It is assumed, in Fig. 1, to be 80 percent of engineer-rated capacity, thus implying 25 percent reserve capacity as in the case of a durable goods industry.) The question facing the executive group, as it reviews the current set of list prices, is whether to try to effect a shift in this price line. While the megacorp will be in a better position to effect such a shift if it is the industry price leader, it can still expect to have some influence even if it is only one of the firms that matches the set of list prices announced by the price leader. Through public statements and similar means, it can at least make its preferences known to the price leader; and the price leader, to the extent it cannot act unilaterally, will have to take those preferences into account.

The first consideration in trying to decide whether there should be a shift in the price line, P_0, is whether there has been an increase in the cost of production since the last price review. It can be assumed that, at the very least, the firms in the industry will attempt to offset any rise in costs by an upward shift in the price line, in order to preserve the existing mark-ups. Whether the costs of production have been rising will, in turn, depend on what has been happening to (a) unit labor costs and (b) unit raw material costs. Any rise in unit labor costs will reflect the growth in money wages relative to the growth in output per worker while any rise in unit raw material costs will reflect the industry's position within the input-output matrix and/or supply-and-demand conditions within world commodity markets. The factors determining the past rise in unit labor costs and unit raw material costs will then be projected into the future to provide an estimate of what increase in the average list price will be necessary to offset the expected increase in the costs of production over the period until the next price review.

Once the expected increase in the unit costs of production has been estimated, the next consideration is what change, if any, in the average mark-up, m, would be optimal. (The mark-up, m, is simply the amount by which the price exceeds the average costs of production viewed as a proportion of those costs. It is therefore equal to the average cash flow, ACF, divided by the average costs of production, AVC + AFC, or just simply C.) The optimal change in the mark-up will depend on the demand for additional investment funds (so as to be able to finance a capital budget in excess of the cash flow being generated at the existing margin) relative to the supply cost of those funds, whether the funds are obtained internally or externally. That is, $\Delta m = f(D_I, S_I)$ where Δm is the optimal change in the mark-up; D_I is a demand curve for additional investment funds, based on the inverse relationship between the expected rate of return, r, and the amount of additional investment funds employed, ΔF; and S_I is the supply curve for additional investment funds, based on the opposite, or, direct relationship between the implicit cost of any additional funds, R, and the amount of those funds to be obtained, ΔF.

The implicit cost of any additional funds that might be generated internally through an increase in the mark-up will depend on three sets of factors: (1) what has already been termed the substitution effect, that is, the reduction in the growth of industry sales over time as determined by the price elasticity of demand, e; (2) the entry factor, that is, the

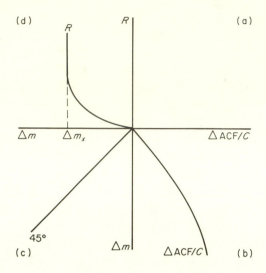

Figure 2

possible loss of market share to new firms attracted into the industry, as determined both by the minimal size firm likely to enter the industry, $\hat{q}$, and the probability of new entry, γ, associated with a given increase in the mark-up; and (3) the possible untoward consequences of retaliatory action by the government as the mark-up is increased, as determined by the probability of government intervention, ϱ. These three types of costs incurred by the megacorp, should it decide to increase the size of the average mark-up, can be converted into the equivalent of an implicit interest rate, R, by first applying the appropriate discount formulas (Eichner, 1976, Ch. 3) and then comparing the subsequent decline in cash flow with the more immediate gain in cash flow, the latter being the equivalent of an externally borrowed principal sum for each year there is a net gain.

An increase in the mark-up, Δm, is likely to lead to an increase in the average amount of cash flow generated per unit of output sold, $\Delta ACF/C$. This relationship is depicted in quadrant (b) of Fig. 2. The average cash flow being generated increases but at a decreasing rate, as the mark-up is increased because both the substitution effect and the entry factor can be expected to be greater the larger the increase in the size of the mark-up. Meanwhile, the implicit interest rate on these internally generated funds, R, will also increase as the mark-up rises. This relationship is depicted in quadrant (d) of Fig. 2. In the latter case the substitution effect and the entry factor cause the implicit interest rate to

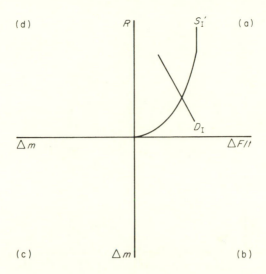

Figure 3

increase at an increasing rate. Indeed, beyond a certain point, say m_x, the probability of new entry into the industry or of retaliatory government action may be greater than the firm is willing to risk, establishing an upward limit on the possible increase in the mark-up. The two separate relationships depicted in quadrants (b) and (d) of Fig. 2 together determine the shape of the firm's supply curve for internally generated investment funds, S_I', as shown in quadrant (a) of Fig. 3. This supply curve is derived by first taking the values for $\Delta ACF/t$ and R associated with each change in the size of the mark-up, Δm, and then scaling up this locus of all common points, as could be shown in quadrant (a) of Fig. 2, by a factor equal to the firm's expected level of sales (its total engineer-rated capacity, ERC, multiplied by its standard operating rate, SOR). In this way the average cash flow generated shown on the right-hand axis of Fig. 2 becomes the total cash flow, or additional investment funds, $\Delta F/t$, shown on the right-hand axis of Fig. 3.

The supply curve for internally generated funds, derived in this manner, can then be compared with the demand curve for investment funds, based on the expected rate of return on the various projects considered for inclusion in the capital budget. The portion of the demand curve shown in Fig. 3 is, in fact, the portion represented by the projects which cannot be financed from the cash flow likely to be generated at the present mark-up. While an increase in the mark-up

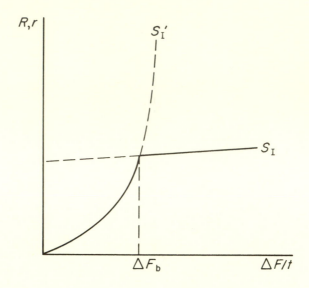

Figure 4

would, in this case, seem to make sense, the executive group would first need to take into account the firm's cost of external finance before making a decision.

The firm's cost of external finance, i, is a weighted average (based on the firm's optimal debt-equity ratio) of the interest it would have to pay on any new fixed-interest securities (bonds) and the inverse of the estimated price-dividend ratio at the time it would be likely to sell additional common shares. Both estimates would have to be adjusted to take into account (a) brokerage and other placement costs, and (b) the increased threat to the executive group's control from issuing new securities. This cost of external finance will then determine the shape of the firm's total supply curve for investment funds—those obtained from the sale of new securities as well as those generated internally by an increase in the mark-up. Such a curve, S_I, is shown in Fig. 4, with the portion extending from the origin to ΔF_b coinciding with the firm's supply curve for internally generated funds and the remaining portion coinciding with the supply curve for external finance. The latter is assumed, in Fig. 4, to have a positive slope, but if the firm is a relatively small factor in the capital funds market and the sums involved are not very large, the curve could be horizontal.

In deciding whether to increase the size of its average mark-up, the firm is likely to find itself in one of the three situations shown in Figs.

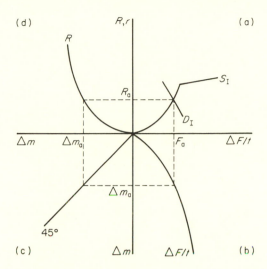

Figure 5

5, 6, or 7. In the first case, the firm's demand curve for investment funds, D_I, intersects the total supply curve for investment funds, S_I, to the right of the origin but below the point where it is less costly to borrow funds externally rather than generate additional cash flow by increasing the mark-up. In that situation, the firm can be expected to increase its mark-up by Δm_a and in this way finance, at an implicit interest rate equal to R_a, a capital budget which exceeds its current rate of cash flow by an amount equal to ΔF_a.

In the case shown in Fig. 6, the demand curve for investment funds, D_I, has shifted sufficiently to the left so that it now intersects the supply curve, S_I, to the left of the origin. While in this situation it might seem that the firm should be intent on lowering rather than increasing its mark-up—especially if, as the result of rising costs, it must still adjust its prices upward—this need not be the decision that the executive group will make under the circumstances. The long-term gains to the firm from lowering the mark-up and/or prices are not merely the opposite of the long-term losses, or implicit costs, of raising the mark-up and/or prices; and it may be best for the firm simply to maintain the same mark-up and/or price level, even if this means that it will be generating more cash flow than it needs to finance its capital spending. The additional funds can always be placed in short-term government securities or in CD's until they are needed. Moreover, a reduction in the mark-up and/or prices may upset the collective basis for price

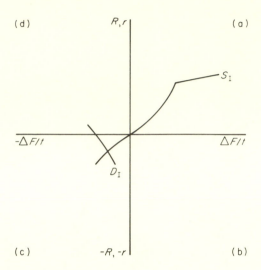

Figure 6

setting within the industry.

In the case shown in Fig. 7, the demand curve for investment funds, D_I, not only intersects the total supply curve, S_I, to the right of the origin; it also intersects it above the point where it is less costly to obtain additional funds from external sources. In this situation, the firm can be expected to increase the mark-up by Δm_b and in this way finance, at an implicit interest rate equal to R_b, a capital budget which exceeds the current rate of cash flow by an amount equal to ΔF_b. It will then consider whether to finance an even larger capital spending program by obtaining the necessary funds from external sources. While it might seem that additional investment outlays equal to $\Delta F_c - \Delta F_b$ would be warranted by the prospective rate of return relative to the cost of external finance, this move will place the firm in a somewhat different position vis-à-vis the capital funds markets, and so it will need to be considered separately as part of a subsequent external financing decision to be made only after consulting outside advisors. Without analyzing this subsequent decision in any depth (cf., Wood, 1975), it can nonetheless be seen how the investment, pricing, and finance decisions are all interrelated within the model of a corporate economy that has been developed so far, with the megacorp as the representative firm.

Once it has been decided what change, if any, in the size of the mark-up would be optimal, this change, together with the expected change in costs, will determine what change, if any, in the average list price will

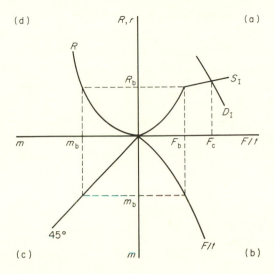

Figure 7

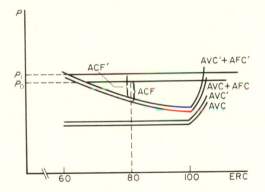

Figure 8

then be announced by the industry price leader and matched by the other firms in the industry. This new list price, as shown in Fig. 8, will then determine the vertical position of the industry's perfectly elastic supply-offer curve, P_1. The supply-offer curve is perfectly elastic because, at the average list price P_1, each firm within the industry is prepared to supply any quantity demanded. Indeed, it is the quantity then demanded at that price from each firm that will determine the sales volume for the industry as a whole until the next price review, and it is this sales volume to which each firm's output decision will be geared. Since the latter involves only the question of which plants or plant segments to operate while using the firm's finished goods inventory to make up the difference, it is a decision likely to be made at a level below that of the executive group. Still, it completes the process by which the level of investment as represented by the size of the capital budget, the rates of compensation and hence unit costs, the average mark-up and thus a set of list prices, and the amount of external borrowing are mutually and sequentially determined over the course of a year. These decisions made at the micro level by the megacorp are then the basis for the behavior of the corporate economy which can be observed at the macro level.

The model of the corporate economy compared with the orthodox theory of the firm

Before developing this model of a corporate economy more fully, it may be useful to contrast its micro foundations with the orthodox theory of the firm. The first important difference is that the orthodox theory is not set within an input–output framework. The significance of this difference can be fully appreciated only when, as in the section that follows next, the behavior of the economy as a whole is analyzed macrodynamically. Suffice it for now to point out that the absence of an input–output framework forces the microeconomic analysis into one or the other of the two modes that characterize the orthodox approach: either a general model involving all n industries but with no clearly defined technology and indeed with no real production system; or, alternatively, a partial model with each industry analyzed independently of every other industry. The first approach is, of course, the one favored by neo-Walrasians and the second, the one favored by latter-day Marshallians.[7] In this section it is the latter body of theory that will serve as the basis for a comparison with the model of a corporate economy outlined so far since it is this approach that not only dominates the intermediate level microeconomic theory textbooks but also is said to be of greater relevance in analyzing the actual behavior of business firms in the short run. The neo-Walrasian model will be taken up later when the question of longer-run tendencies is addressed.

The first thing that needs to be said about the Marshallian model is that, not being set within a general framework, the results established at the firm or industry level cannot be extrapolated to the system of production as a whole. Indeed, its conclusions may not hold for more than a single industry in isolation from the rest of the economy. The greater realism of the Marshallian approach (compared to the neo-Walrasian model, not the model of the corporate economy) is therefore at the expense of its generality and indeed its possible validity at the macro level. The next most important difference between the Marshallian model which dominates the orthodox microeconomic textbooks and the model of the corporate economy outlined above is the nature of the representative firm. Instead of a megacorp, the Marshallian model assumes a family-controlled proprietorship to be the typical form of business enterprise. This difference in the nature of the representative firm then leads to the following differences in the model itself.

(1) The goal of the firm is short-run profit maximization rather than the highest possible rate of expansion by the firm itself. In seeking to achieve this goal, the key decisions are made by the individual who, as paterfamilias, is the firm's owner–entrepreneur. There is no executive group sharing the decision-making power (although there may be one or two partners), and there is no lower-level group of managers to help in running the firm. The emphasis on short-run profits reflects both the uncertain future of the firm and the direct personal interest the owner–entrepreneur has in the amount of net revenue being earned. Without a protected market position, the firm cannot be sure of surviving far into the future, and the owner–entrepreneur therefore prefers to maximize the more immediate returns which, unlike any corporate cash flow in the case of the executive group, accrue to him directly.

(2) The proprietary firm, since its management is limited to one or two owner–entrepreneurs, is capable of operating only a single plant, which means that it is subject to decreasing returns when it expands output beyond a certain point. This gives rise to the familiar set of U-shaped cost curves found in intermediate level textbooks, with marginal, average variable, and average total costs all rising within the relevant range. The technical coefficients, rather than being fixed, are sufficiently flexible to accommodate varying combinations of labor and material inputs so that, even with but a single plant, output can be varied in the short run. Indeed, it is the need to offset the fixity of the capital inputs in the short run by relying on greater quantities of the variable inputs that accounts for the decreasing returns as output increases beyond a certain point. In the longer run, expansion takes place, not by the addition of new plants to existing firms but rather by the entry of entirely new firms, each with a single plant.

(3) The proprietary firm may be a price taker as well as a price

setter, with the former the more likely case. If the firm is a price taker, implying that it supplies an insignificant portion of the total market, it will have no real control over prices, which are determined by supply and demand factors at the industry level. The firm's owner–entrepreneur can only decide how much to produce, throwing that output on the market for whatever price it will bring. But even if the firm is a price setter, announcing in advance the set of list prices at which it is prepared to sell its output, the competition from other firms, both existing and potential, will be sufficient to prevent that set of list prices from exceeding the costs of production. It can therefore be assumed that the mark-up will be reduced to zero in the long run.

(4) Shaving the price is the only form that competition among existing firms takes. There is no advertising or R&D budget. While the firm may, from time to time, purchase new equipment financed through bank loans, there is no regular capital budget either. Investment is episodic, with the critical decisions being the one to enter the industry in the first place and then, when the firm can no longer compete effectively with the vintage capital stock it owns, the decision to retire from the industry.

(5) The proprietary firm therefore makes only one type of decision continuously over time. This is the decision of how much to produce, and it is a decision the owner–entrepreneur himself will make by comparing the marginal cost of the additional output with the marginal revenue that can thereby be earned. The owner–entrepreneur, by not allowing the marginal cost to exceed the marginal revenue, can be assured of maximizing his short-run profits through the one means he has of realizing that goal, to wit, by varying the firm's output. The pricing decision is largely in the hands of an impersonal market, even when the firm is nominally able to set prices in advance. Investment occurs too infrequently even to be analyzed as part of the normal decision-making process, and when it does occur, the firm can be expected to rely on bank financing because the firm's inability to maintain a mark-up in excess of costs prevents it from generating the funds internally—except as a windfall from unexpectedly high levels of demand.

The contrast between this Marshallian model and the model of a corporate economy presented earlier is clear, and there seems little point in asking which corresponds more closely to what can be observed in the real world. The one thing that can be said for the Marshallian model is that it can easily be grafted onto the other model by identifying the primary producers in the latter with the proprietary firms that are price takers and the retail distributors with the proprietary firms that are price setters. In this way, the model of the corporate economy can be further elaborated to include a description of its primary and retail distribution sectors, while the Marshallian model is limited to what it correctly describes—the peripheral sectors of the corporate economy.

The corporate economy at the macro level

One test of how useful this model of the corporate economy might be is how well it can serve as the microeconomic foundation for macrodynamic analysis. Can it account for some of the stylized historical facts of recent years—in particular, the secular rise in prices, together with the uneven expansion of the national economy? This is the exercise that will be carried out in the remaining sections of the essay.

It is necessary to distinguish, at the outset, the types of unforeseeable events, and hence the sources of uncertainty and instability, which originate within the corporate economy as just described and the types of unforeseeable events which originate from without. The former fall into two subcategories: 1) major product innovations (those that lead to a change in the number of industries), and 2) a change in the market position of the firms within any of those industries as a result of nonprice competition. The second type of unforeseeable event includes a change in either the rate of growth or in the composition of demand for the goods and services purchased by the government (or, for that matter, insofar as the model is an open one of a less than global system, in the rate of growth and composition of net exports). It also includes any other changes in the government's economic policies, such as a less accommodating stance by the central bank or a revision of tax schedules. (Unforeseeable changes in household spending patterns can be assumed not to occur, those patterns being determined entirely by the relevant set of income and price elasticities of demand as real wages and other forms of household income increase over time.) The absence of uncertainty in the model implies that none of the above unforeseeable events occurs, neither those that might have their origins within the corporate economy nor those that might have their origins without. At the outset, primarily for heuristic purposes, the analysis will be carried out on the presumption that uncertainty in this sense does not exist. Later this restriction will be relaxed to show what happens when major

product innovations, inter-firm competition, and changes in government policy are introduced into the model.

In the absence of any disturbance to the system from one of the three
types of unforeseeable events just identified, the corporate economy
can be expected to expand along a secular growth path that depends on
the per capita growth of real income within the household sector, as
determined by the secular growth of output per worker, $\dot{Z}_s$ (Pasinetti,
1981).[8] It is the secular growth of real income within the household
sector which, because of the effect on aggregate demand, will provide
the main impetus for the secular expansion of each of the n industries
which comprise the enterprise sector—both the h industries producing
items for final consumption and the $n - h$ industries producing capital
goods and material inputs—and it is the secular growth rates for each of
these n industries which, when properly weighted[9] and averaged, will
give the secular growth of aggregate output, G_s.

It will, of course, make a difference how the growth of real per
capita income made possible by the growth of output per worker is
distributed, first, between the other sectors and the household sector
and then, within the household sector, between workers and nonworkers if the two groups have different marginal propensities to consume. (The nonworkers include those receiving dividends and other
property income as well as those receiving transfer payments from the
government.) However, this complication will be avoided by assuming,
at least for the moment, that 1) the secular growth of output per worker
will, through one mechanism or another, be translated into higher real
income for the household sector, and 2) whatever the relative distribution of income within the household sector between workers and nonworkers, that pattern will be maintained over time. On these two
assumptions (both of which will later be relaxed), the corporate economy's secular growth rate will depend on the secular growth of output
per worker as the underlying determinant of the secular growth of
aggregate demand, with G_s closely approximating if not actually
equaling $\dot{Z}_s$.

How to explain the secular growth of output per worker in the
absence of major product innovations is somewhat of a problem, and
indeed the problem itself provides an important insight into the nature
of the corporate economy. For now it will suffice simply to say that, as
part of their nonprice competitive strategy, the firms in the capital
goods industries will continually expand their product lines to include
new types of equipment which, when purchased by other firms, enable

them to reduce their labor coefficients and hence their labor-output ratios. In this way, it is possible to postulate a certain rate of technical progress without introducing the further complication, at least at this point in the argument, of major product innovations. On this basis it can be assumed that the corporate economy, consisting of k oligopolistic industries and $n - k$ nonoligopolistic industries, is expanding along a secular growth path equal to, and determined by, the secular growth of output per worker, Z_s.

Not all n industries will be expanding at the same rate, however. The secular expansion of any one industry, $\dot{g}_j$, will depend on the income elasticity of demand for the goods and services it either produces directly (if it supplies items for final consumption) or indirectly (if, instead, it supplies capital goods and material inputs). To determine the growth rate for any particular industry, it is therefore necessary to take the growth rate for the system as a whole, $\dot{G}_s$, and adjust it either up or down by a factor equal to the income elasticity of demand, η_j, for the items of final consumption that each industry produces directly or indirectly. For industries producing final goods and services with an income elasticity greater than 1, the secular growth rate will be greater than $\dot{G}_s$, and for industries producing final goods and services with an income elasticity less than 1, the growth rate will be less than $\dot{G}_s$.

Thus a **G** vector, representing the secular growth rate, $\dot{g}_j$, for each of the n industries comprising the corporate economy can be derived by scaling an **R** vector, representing the income elasticity of demand, η_j, for each of the items entering into final consumption, by the aggregate growth rate, $\dot{G}_s$. This **G** vector, equal to $\dot{G}_s(\mathbf{R})$ or, with $\dot{Z}_s$ and $\dot{G}_s$ virtually interchangeable, equal to $\dot{Z}_s(\mathbf{R})$, will be identical to the secular growth rate of the final demand vector in a Leontief open model of production. It will indicate the rate at which the output supplied by each industry producing an item for final consumption will need to be increased over time in order to satisfy the growth of demand resulting from the growth of output per worker.

The secular growth rate for each industry, $\dot{g}_j$, as given by the **G** vector, is one of two factors that will then determine the mark-up, m_j, which will need to be established in each of the same n industries if the investment required for the secular expansion of the corporate economy is to be financed (Eichner, 1976; Eichner, Forman and Groves, 1982). The other factor determining the size of the required mark-up is the incremental capital-output ratio, v_j, for each of the same n industries (which, as a set, can be represented as a **B** vector). The incremental capital-output ratio is the value of all the capital inputs an industry must purchase to increase capacity by a given amount (that is, the quantity of each capital input, multiplied by its price and then summed up for all the different types of capital inputs that will be needed) divided by the value of the output that can be produced with that additional capacity. With each industry expanding at a rate equal to $\dot{g}_j$, plant capacity will need to increase by the same percentage if the growth of output is to keep pace with the growth of demand. With an incremental capital-output ratio equal to v_j, this means that the industry's outlays on new plant and equipment at any given point in time, proportional to output, must equal $\dot{g}_j v_j(p_j)$, or, dropping the subscripts and superscripts, $gv(p)$. If investment outlays equal to this amount are to be financed, either concurrently out of cash flow or with payment stretched out over time through an increase in debt service, then the price charged by the industry must exceed the average costs of production by an amount equal to $gv(p)$. In other words, the residual income of the industry, that is, the difference between the price and the average, or unit, costs of production, must be equal to $gv(p)$. This in turn means that the rate of profit, or margin, must be equal to gv, the reason being that the margin is simply the amount of residual income earned by the industry, π, viewed as a proportion of the price, p. With $\pi = gv(p)$, it then follows that $\pi/p = gv$. (As already noted, the margin, π/p or μ, can also be regarded as the average cash flow, ACF, being generated.) Since the mark-up is equal to the margin, μ, divided by $1 - \mu$, this means that the mark-up, m_j, in each of the n industries must be equal to $gv/(1 - gv)$ if that industry is going to be able to finance the investment that its expansion over time requires.

Note that it makes little difference to the argument whether the investment is financed internally or externally. While a resort to external financing will make it possible to step up investment outlays without immediately increasing the mark-up, the advantage is only a temporary one. If the external debt is to be serviced, the mark-up will in time need to be the same as it would if the investment were being financed concurrently out of cash flow. It is just that the industry will have gained some time before it need achieve that size mark-up. However, offsetting the time gained by relying on external financing is the fact that the industry will have to obtain the approval of one or more financial institutions for its investment plans, thus reducing the freedom of action by the firms in that industry.

The point is that, with the economy expanding at a certain secular rate, it is the growth rate for each of the individual industries, g, together with the incremental capital-output ratios for each of those same industries, v, that will determine the size of the required mark-up, m. This is true, irrespective of how the accompanying investment is to be financed, whether internally from cash flow or externally through an increase in debt. If competitive forces, such as those usually assumed in the orthodox theory, preclude an industry from achieving that size mark-up, then one of the necessary conditions for continuous expansion over time will not be met. This point goes far toward explaining why the type of economic system represented by the orthodox theory has evolved into the corporate economy (Eichner, 1969; Chandler, 1977). A mark-up equal to zero in any of the n industries is consistent only with a nonexpanding economy. While it is possible for some industries not to grow, and indeed even to go through a period of absolute decline, this cannot be true of most industries—not if the system as a whole is to continue expanding. In other words, the orthodox model is incompatible, at the microeconomic level, with a continuously expanding economy even if one assumes—however unrealistically—that all investment is being financed externally through the "savings" of the household sector. With a zero mark-up, an expanding industry will be incapable of reproducing itself and growing at the requisite rate in value terms. Expansion can occur, if at all, only through alternating periods of "boom" and "bust," the former assuring the necessary financing, as a result of the temporary increase in the mark-up, for the investment that must accompany the expansion and the latter serving to reduce the mark-up to the zero level required by the other long-run "equilibrium" condition of the model.

With the size of the mark-up, m, for each of the n industries explained, one need only add an explanation of what determines unit labor costs so as to be able to explain what determines the set of relative prices, or price vector, that will need to be established within the expanding system. Unit labor costs, together with the mark-up, will determine the value added per unit of output in each of the n industries, and this value added vector, multiplied by the Leontief inverse, $(\mathbf{I} - \mathbf{A})^{-1}$, will yield the required price vector. Unit labor costs will, in turn, depend on two factors: (1) the set of labor technical coefficients for each of the n industries, indicating the quantity of labor inputs (in hours) needed to produce a given amount of output, and (2) the money wage rate. Indeed, the unit labor costs for each of the n industries will simply be the product of these two factors, $w(l_j)$, where w is the money wage rate (assumed to be the same for all n industries, although this assumption can easily be relaxed) and l_j is the labor technical coefficient for each of the n industries. These unit labor costs, in conjunction with the mark-up, m_j, and the Leontief inverse, $(\mathbf{I} - \mathbf{A})^{-1}$, are then sufficient to determine the price vector, $\mathbf{P}$, for the corporate economy.

Based on the set of labor coefficients, l_j, it is possible to define a rate of growth of output per worker in each of the n industries, $\dot{z}_j$. The rate at which the labor coefficient becomes smaller over time, as the result of technical progress, can be represented by a negative growth rate, and the absolute value of this growth rate (that is, with the sign omitted) is the value of $\dot{z}_j$. This rate of growth of output per worker in each of the n industries can then be compared with the growth of output per worker, or the rate of technical progress, within the system as whole, Z_s, the latter being the weighted sum of the growth of output per worker in each of the n industries, $\dot{z}_j$.

The rate of technical progress is unlikely to be the same for all industries. This means that some industries will experience above-average rates of growth of output per worker. For these industries, $\dot{z}_j - Z_s$ will be positive and, with the money wage rate the same for all industries, their unit labor costs will be declining relative to the average for the system as a whole. Other industries will experience below-average rates of growth of output per worker. For them, $\dot{z}_j - Z_s$ will be negative and, as a result, their unit labor costs will be increasing relative to the average.

The extent to which each industry's unit labor cost, $w(l_j)$, is falling or rising relative to the average—depending on whether $\dot{z}_j - Z_s$ is positive or negative—will be the primary factor determining the change in the corporate economy's price vector over time. While a change in the growth rate for any of the n industries, $\dot{g}_j$, will also lead to a change in the price vector (due to its effect on the size of the required mark-up), this possibility can be excluded, at least for the moment, by the assumed absence of major product innovations. A change in the n industries' incremental capital-output ratio, v_j, although it would also affect the size of the required mark-up, is even less likely than a change in the industry growth rate; and this possibility can be excluded as well. On these grounds, the change in the corporate economy's price vector over time can be said to depend primarily on what is happening to each industry's unit labor costs, based on the growth of output per worker in that industry relative to the average, $\dot{z}_j - Z_s$.

Any such change in the corporate economy's price vector will be an additional factor, besides the growth of household income, in determining the rate of expansion for each of the n industries, $\dot{g}_j$. The growth rate for each industry given by $\eta_j(G)_s$ will be either boosted or reduced by a factor equal to $e_j(\dot{z}_j - Z_s)$, where e_j is the price elasticity of demand for each of the goods or services produced by the n industries. This is because $\dot{z}_j - \dot{Z}$ will correspond to the change in the industry's relative price over time, and this change in relative price, together with the price elasticity of demand, will determine the change in relative demand for that industry's output. With $\dot{z}_j - \dot{Z}_s$ taking a positive value, implying a relative decline over time in both unit labor costs and in the price that will need to be changed, the industry growth rate will be boosted beyond what it would be from the value of $\eta_j(\dot{G}_s)$ alone (or since G_s can be assumed to be equal to Z_s, from the value of $\eta_j(Z_s)$ alone). Conversely, with $\dot{z}_j - \dot{Z}_s$ taking a negative value, implying a relative increase in unit labor costs and the price that will need to be charged, the industry growth rate will be reduced below what it would otherwise be. How much the industry's growth rate will be either boosted or reduced will, of course, depend on the price elasticity of demand, e_j. What this means is that the growth rate for each of the n industries, $\dot{g}_j$, will depend on not just one but two sets of factors: the relative increase in output per worker, $\dot{z}_j - \dot{Z}_s$, multiplied by the price elasticity of demand, e_j, as well as the increase in output per worker for the economy as a whole, $\dot{Z}_s$, multiplied by the industry's income elasticity of demand, η_j. However, since η_j is generally greater than e_j, and $\dot{z}_j - \dot{Z}_s$ is unlikely to exceed $\dot{Z}_s$, it follows that the change in relative price—what can be termed the substitution effect—will only modify what is the principal determinant of the industry growth rate, namely, the growth in household income. It is for this reason that the possible substitution effect is introduced only now as a qualification to the earlier argument.

So far only the set of relative prices, or price vector, for the corporate economy has been explained. To derive the set of actual prices for each of the n industries, p_j, it is necessary to specify and account for the money wage rate, w, as well. That money wage rate serves as the numéraire for the system as a whole, and thus is the basis for converting the set of relative prices into a set of actual prices. Any money wage rate, w, together with a set of labor technical coefficients, l_j (which, as a group constitute the vector of labor coefficients, L), together with the residual income earned by each industry, π_j (which, again as a group, constitute the π vector) will be sufficient to produce the value added vector, V. That is, $V = wL + \pi$. This value added vector, in turn, when multiplied by the Leontief inverse, $(I-A)^{-1}$, will produce the vector of actual prices that will need to be established within the corporate economy. The weighted average of these actual prices constitutes the corporate economy's price level, P.

The link between the money wage rate and the price level can be seen more clearly by transforming the Leontief model of production which has been relied upon up to this point, based on other technical coefficients besides the labor ones, into a vertically integrated model of production in which all the other technical coefficients are replaced by a single labor coefficient for each of the h industries producing items for final consumption (Pasinetti, 1980, 1981). This single labor coefficient, l_j', represents not just each industry's direct labor requirements but its indirect labor requirements as well—the labor needed directly and indirectly to produce any material inputs. Since the Leontief inverse is the basis for deriving these vertically integrated labor coefficients, l_j' (which, as a group, constitute the L' vector), as well as the accompanying set of vertically integrated mark-ups, m_j' (which, as a group, constitute the M' vector), it need not otherwise be taken into account. The vector of actual prices that will need to be established within the corporate economy (for the h industries producing items for final consumption) is simply the product of the wage rate and the vector of vertically integrated labor coefficients multiplied by a factor equal to an identity matrix plus the vector of vertically integrated mark-ups. That is, $P = (I + M')(wL')$.

With the set of vertically integrated labor coefficients determined by the growth of output per worker in each of the n industries, it follows that any change in the price vector, P, must be due to a change in either the money wage rate or a change in the set of vertically integrated mark-ups. An increase in the money wage rate will mean an increase in the industry wage bill and thus an increase in the costs of production—unless, and to the extent, it is offset by the growth of output per worker. This leads to the conclusion that the secular growth of the aggregate price level—the weighted sum of all the individual industry prices which constitute the P vector—will depend on the growth of money wages, $\dot{w}$, relative to the secular growth of output per worker in the aggregate, Z_s. With money wages increasing more rapidly than the average growth of output per worker, the n industries will need to increase their prices, on the average, by the difference between the two growth rates if they are to cover the increase in their wage bill. That is, the aggregate price level will need to rise so as to satisfy the following condition: $\dot{P} = \dot{w} - \dot{Z}_s$.

It is, of course, possible that the price level within any one of the n industries will not rise sufficiently to cover the increase in the wage bill. In that case, the mark-up, m_j, will be reduced. Unless the mark-up was previously greater than necessary to cover the cost of financing the required rate of capacity expansion, this will, in turn, mean that either one or the other of two necessary conditions for maintaining the industry's growth rate will not be satisfied. One is the supply condition that the growth of capacity, and hence the growth of investment, be equal to the growth in the demand for each industry's output. The other is the value condition that the price be at least equal to the industry's wage bill plus any required mark-up, with the latter determined by the industry's growth rate and its incremental capital-output ratio. These two necessary conditions for the secular growth rate to be sustained at the industry level can be generalized for the economy as a whole. The supply condition would then be that the secular growth of investment in the aggregate, $\dot{I}_s$, be equal to the secular growth of aggregate output, $\dot{G}_s$, and the value condition would be that the price vector, $\mathbf{P}$, be such that it is at least equal to the wage bill in each of the n industries plus a sufficient amount of profit, or average cash flow, to finance the secular rate of expansion within each of those industries.

It is also possible, of course, that the growth of money wages will be less than the growth of output per worker in the aggregate. In that case, household income will not be increasing at a rate sufficient to sustain the growth in demand for the various items of final consumption—and thus the aggregate demand condition for maintaining the corporate economy on its secular growth path will not be satisfied. The aggregate demand condition, as distinct from the aggregate supply and value conditions, is that the growth of expenditures match the growth of real income and thus that there be no net savings within the corporate economy. (The stipulation that investment be equal to savings or, in a dynamic context, that the growth of investment be equal to the growth of savings is one of several ways the aggregate demand condition can be stated.)

Thus it can be said that, unless the aggregate price level rises at a rate equal to the difference between the growth of money wages and the growth of output per worker, at least one of the three conditions necessary to maintain the corporate economy's secular rate of expansion will not be satisfied. This indicates both the condition under which a secular rise in the price level can be expected—this being when the growth of money wages, $\dot{w}$, exceeds the average growth of output per worker, Z_s—and the three conditions which, by not being satisfied, can bring the corporate economy's secular expansion to a halt. The three conditions for maintaining the secular growth of output and employment are 1) the supply condition that the growth of investment in each of the n industries be equal to the growth in the demand for its product either directly or indirectly, and thus that the secular growth of investment in the aggregate, $\dot{I}_s$, be equal to the secular growth of aggregate output, $\dot{G}_s$; 2) the aggregate demand condition that the growth of aggregate income match the growth of potential output and thus that the growth of real wages and the other types of income used to purchase items for final consumption be equal to the secular growth of output per worker in the aggregate, $\dot{Z}_s$, with no net savings; and 3) the value condition that the price vector, **P**, be sufficient to cover the wage bill plus any required profit in each of the n industries.

Whether all three of these conditions, together with the condition necessary for price stability, are likely to be satisfied is a question that will be taken up later. At this point it need only be noted that the growth of the aggregate price level will depend on the growth of money wages relative to the growth of output per worker, and thus it is necessary to explain what determines the growth of money wages. The orthodox theory asserts that it depends on 1) the growth of the money supply, 2) the rate of unemployment or 3) both (as in the arguments made about the "natural rate" of unemployment within the context of a monetarist explanation of inflation). The alternative post-Keynesian explanation is that the growth of money wages depends on the wage norm adopted by trade unions in collective bargaining. The trade unions are assumed to have sufficient power so that whatever wage norm they adopt as their own will then determine the growth of money wages within the corporate economy. Indeed, the growth of money wages will be equal to this wage norm plus any "wage drift." Although the rate of unemployment (though not the growth of the money supply) may be one of the factors influencing the wage norm and thus the growth of money wages, the point is that the wage norm is not uniquely determined by any set of economic factors. It depends on a broader set of socio-political factors and thus can take a wide range of values independently of either the unemployment rate or the growth of output per worker.

This explanation of what determines the growth of money wages, when incorporated into the model of a corporate economy, suggests why such an economy may be susceptible to a secular rise in the price level. According to the model, it is necessary only that the growth of money wages, which are exogenously determined, exceed the growth of output per worker—the difference between the two being the rate of inflation (Weintraub, 1959, 1966). Indeed, the corporate economy would seem to be confronted by a second type of "knife-edge" problem besides the one first pointed out by Harrod (1939, 1948; see also Kregel, 1980). If wages increase by less than the growth of output per worker, Z_s, then the growth of aggregate demand will not be sufficient to sustain the secular growth rate. If, alternatively, wages increase more rapidly than Z_s, then the price level will rise at a rate equal to the difference.

The alternative models
of the long run compared

The model of the corporate economy developed so far can be compared with the neo-Walrasian general equilibrium model. Both are models of the long period (or long run), with uncertainty excluded by assumption. The important thing to note about the model of the corporate economy is that, even aside from its resting on a set of more realistic assumptions, it is able to explain the same two sets of variables as the neo-Walrasian model—those represented by the $\mathbf{Q}$ and $\mathbf{P}$ vectors—without having to posit separate supply and demand curves for each of the h industries producing items for final consumption.

In the model of the corporate economy, the quantity supplied by each of the h industries producing items for final consumption at time period 0, as given by the $\mathbf{Q}$ vector, will be equal to the product of the Leontief inverse, $(\mathbf{I} - \mathbf{A})^{-1}$, and the final demand vector, $\mathbf{D}$, at time period 0. That is

$$\mathbf{Q}_0 = (\mathbf{I} - \mathbf{A})^{-1} \mathbf{D} \qquad (1)$$

The final demand vector at time period 0 will be equal to the final demand vector at time period -1 plus the growth of that final demand vector, as given by the product of the growth vector, $\mathbf{G}$, and the final demand vector in time period -1. That is,

$$\mathbf{D}_0 = \mathbf{D}_{-1} + \hat{\mathbf{G}}(\mathbf{D}_0) \qquad (2)$$

with the circumflex over the $\mathbf{G}$ vector indicating that it has been transformed into a diagonal matrix. The growth vector, $\mathbf{G}$, will depend on the combined influence of two factors: 1) the income effect given by $\dot{Z}_s(\mathbf{R})$, and 2) the substitution effect given by $\mathbf{T}(\mathbf{S})$. That is,

$$\mathbf{G} = \dot{Z}_s(\mathbf{R}) + \mathbf{T}(\mathbf{S}) \tag{3}$$

where $\mathbf{R}$ is the vector of the income elasticity of demand, η_j, for the output of each of the h industries producing items for final consumption; $\dot{Z}_s$ is the secular growth of output per worker in the aggregate, a weighted average of the secular growth of output per worker, $\dot{z}_j$, in those same h industries, taking into account both their direct and indirect labor requirements (and therefore based on the secular decline in the $\mathbf{L}'$ vector); $\mathbf{S}$ is the vector of the (own) price elasticity of demand for each of the same h items of final consumption; and $\mathbf{T}$ is a vector representing the difference between the secular growth of output per worker in each of the h industries, $\dot{z}_j$, and the secular growth of output per worker in the aggregate, $\dot{Z}_s$. The growth of output per worker in each of the h industries, $\dot{z}_j$, it should be noted, can be represented by its own separate $\mathbf{Z}$ vector. With $\mathbf{A}$, $\mathbf{R}$, $\mathbf{S}$, and $\mathbf{Z}$ (or, alternatively, $\dot{Z}_s$ and $\mathbf{T}$) taken to be empirically estimable parameters and hence as givens, the $\mathbf{D}$ vector—and therefore the $\mathbf{Q}$ vector—must be considered fully determinate within the model.

Meanwhile, the price that will need to be charged by each of the n industries (both the h industries producing items for final consumption and the $n - h$ industries producing capital goods and material inputs) if they are to cover their costs of production plus finance the necessary expansion of capacity is given by a price vector, $\mathbf{P}$. This price vector is equal to the product of a value added vector, $\mathbf{V}$, and the same Leontief inverse. That is,

$$\mathbf{P} = \mathbf{V}(\mathbf{I} - \mathbf{A})^{-1} \tag{4}$$

where $\mathbf{P}$ is the set of prices that will need to prevail if the corporate economy is to satisfy the value conditions for maintaining the secular rate of expansion. This value added vector, $\mathbf{V}$, will, in turn, be equal to the sum of two vectors: 1) a scaled vector, $w\mathbf{L}$, representing the wage bill in each of the n industries which comprise the enterprise sector, and 2) a $\boldsymbol{\pi}$ vector representing the amount of residual income in each of those same n industries. That is,

$$\mathbf{V} = w\mathbf{L} + \boldsymbol{\pi} \tag{5}$$

Alternatively, based on the vertically integrated model of production, equations 4 and 5 can be replaced by the following equation:

$$P = wL' + \pi' \qquad (6)$$

where L' is a vector of the direct and indirect labor requirements for each of the h vertically integrated industries and π' is a vector of the direct and indirect residual income earned in those industries. It is possible to rewrite the price equation for the vertically integrated model, in terms of the required mark-up in each industry, as follows:

$$P = (I + M')wL' \qquad (7)$$

(A similar price equation for all n industries can be derived, but it is a somewhat more complicated equation since the mark-up on the material inputs purchased from other industries needs to be explicitly taken into account.) The M' vector will, in turn, depend on 1) a G' vector, representing the growth rate, $\dot{g}_j'$, for each of the h vertically integrated industries, and 2) a B' vector, representing the incremental capital-output ratio, v_j', for each of the same h industries. Specifically,

$$M' = \hat{G}'\hat{B}'(I - \hat{G}'\hat{B}')^{-1} \qquad (8)$$

The same equation, it should be noted, applies to all n industries, though with the G and B vectors replacing G' and B' in the equation. Substituting the right-hand side of equation 8 for M', one can rewrite equation 7 as follows:

$$P = [I - \hat{G}'\hat{B}']^{-1}wL' \qquad (9)$$

The B vector, and hence the B' vector, can be derived from a K vector the elements of which, k_{ij}, indicate how much of the capital goods produced by any other industry the j-th industry will need to purchase in order to expand capacity by a given quantum, $\hat{Q}_j$. Specifically, the elements of the B vector can be calculated as follows:

$$v_j = \frac{\sum_{i=1}^{n} p_i k_{ij}}{p_j \hat{Q}_j} \qquad (10)$$

However, it may be just as easy to estimate the B vector directly rather than attempt to derive it from a K matrix. In that case, equation 10 would be unnecessary. With the growth of money wages, w, exogenously determined (by noneconomic factors) and with L and B viewed as empirically estimable parameters and hence as givens, the M vector—and therefore the P vector—must also be considered to be fully determinate within the model.

However, the actual mark-ups that prevail need not be those given by equation 8. To satisfy the value condition for maintaining the secular rate of expansion, it is necessary only that the mark-ups not be any smaller. The M vector may, in fact, exceed the values given in equation 8 by a factor equal to $1/(1 - t)$ where t is the percentage of corporate profits that must go either for dividends and/or for taxes. [10] In that case, t becomes a second distributional variable, besides the money wage rate, which is exogenous to the model; and a constraint must then be imposed on the model if the demand condition necessary for maintaining the secular rate of expansion is to be satisfied simultaneously. The constraint is that, whatever the amount of dividend income received by rentiers or the amount of tax revenues obtained by the government, all of it must be used to purchase the final output of the corporate economy. It cannot add to net savings. In the case of any dividends that may be paid out, this means that what is not spent by rentiers on items of final consumption must be used to make up for any shortfall in the required mark-up in one or more industries; and in the case of any tax revenues, it means that the government cannot normally operate with a budget surplus.

So far, eight variables, or parameters of the model, remain unexplained and must therefore be taken as givens. They are A, B (or, alternatively, K), L, R, S, Z (or, alternatively, Z_s and T), w, and t. The first three of these parameters are the sets of technical coefficients that represent the current state of the technology. Once the initial values for these parameters have been given, they will depend on the rate of technical progress. This means that, if we ignore any product innovations, minor as well as major, and thus limit technical progress to process innovation, the A, B, and L vectors will be determinate within the model once their initial values have been given. They will depend on the Z vector, leaving only the two vectors representing the income and price elasticities, R and S, and the two distributional variables, w and t, along with the Z vector itself, still to be explained.

While the income and price elasticities cannot be determined within the framework of the model, and thus must be treated as givens, a constraint can be imposed, at least in the case of the income elasticities, if the demand condition for maintaining the secular rate of expansion is to be satisfied. The constraint is that the elements of the R vector, when properly weighted and averaged, must equal 1. Such a constraint is necessary to insure that there is no unspent income and thus no net savings. A similar constraint is necessary in the case of the two distri-

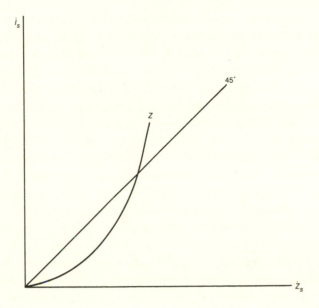

Figure 9

butional variables, w and t, to insure that the value condition for maintaining the secular rate of expansion will be satisified. This further constraint is that the growth of w and t together must not be less than the growth of output per worker. However, these two constraints are only that—constraints. They are not sufficient to determine the values of the model's **R**, **S**, w, and t parameters.

In contrast, the secular growth of output per worker—the weighted average of the separate elements comprising the **Z** vector—can be explained with only a slight elaboration of the model. Technical progress, it can be assumed, will be capital embodied, at least in part. This means that the rate of technical progress, as measured by Z_s, will depend on the rate of accumulation, that is, on the secular growth of investment, $\dot{I}_s$ (Kaldor and Mirrlees, 1962; Davenport, 1983). Specifically, the rate of technical progress can be said to be a decreasing power function of the rate of growth of investment, and thus can be represented by means of the Z function in Fig. 9, with a higher rate of investment, as measured along the horizontal axis, leading to the higher (but decreasing) rate of growth of output per worker shown along the vertical axis.

If one of the necessary conditions for sustaining the secular rate of expansion is to be satisfied, namely, the supply condition that the growth of final demand be matched by the growth of capacity, then the secular rate of investment, $\dot{I}_s$, will have to be equal to the secular growth of aggregate output, $\dot{G}_s$. At the same time, however, if another necessary condition is to be satisfied, namely, the aggregate demand condition that the growth of real income be sufficient to enable the final demand for goods and services to keep pace with the growth of supply capacity, then $\dot{G}_s$ will have to be equal to the secular growth of output per worker, $\dot{Z}_s$. Hence, if aggregate supply and aggregate demand are to be maintained in rough balance with one another, the secular growth of output per worker, $\dot{Z}_s$, must be equal to the secular growth of investment, $\dot{I}_s$. It is for this reason that the secular growth of output per worker, $\dot{Z}_s$, is determined in Fig. 9 by where the Z function intersects the 45° line, for it is only at that point that $\dot{G}_s$ will be equal to $\dot{I}_s$.

It should be noted that the rate of technical progress, especially when that term is broadened to include major product innovations, will depend far more critically on what is the nature of the social organization, both within the individual enterprise and throughout the larger society, than on $\dot{I}_s$. It is therefore the noneconomic parameters of the Z function which, by shifting over time, are likely to play the key role in determining the secular growth of output per worker. Still, once $\dot{Z}_s$ has been determined as in Fig. 9, it is only the **R**, **S**, w, and t variables that remain as unexplained parameters of the model. Given empirical estimates of those parameters (as well as the initial values for the **A**, **K**, and **L** vectors), one can then determine within the framework of the model the quantities that must be produced and hence supplied by each of the n industries which constitute the corporate economy, together with the set of prices that will need to be established in each of the same n industries if the system is to reproduce itself in value terms and expand at the secular growth rate given by the growth of output per worker. The quantities that must be supplied are given by the **Q** vector while the prices that will need to be established are given by the **P** vector. Thus the values for the **Q** and **P** vectors can be determined without having to specify, as in the alternative neo-Walrasian model, separate supply and demand curves for each of the n industries. In light of the difficulty economists have had finding empirical evidence for the existence of a separate supply curve for the types of industrial goods produced by the corporate economy, with variations in price as the principal determinant of the quantity supplied, this is no small consideration in weighing the relative merits of the two models.

The only offsetting advantage of the neo-Walrasian model would be if it could explain what remains undetermined within the model of the corporate economy which has now been fully specified. One could, in fact, claim that the neo-Walrasian model explains precisely the variables which, in the model of the corporate economy, must be taken as givens—namely, the R and S vectors, together with the money wage rate, w, and the dividend and/or tax rate, t. For this reason, one could even argue that the two models should be seen as being complementary rather than opposed to one another. Unfortunately, however, the utility functions and production possibility sets which are the basis for deriving the R and S vectors within a neo-Walrasian general equilibrium framework cannot be observed empirically. Moreover, while the dividend rate is said to be equal, within the neo-Walrasian model, to the interest rate and therefore to depend on the "marginal physical product of capital," the latter is again something that cannot be observed empirically. (The metaphysical nature of the utility functions, isoquants, and marginal physical product curves on which the neo-Walrasian model rests is stressed in the title essay of Eichner, 1983a, as well as in essay seven below). The corporate tax rate, meanwhile, is a parameter of the neo-Walrasian model no less than of the alternative model to which it is being compared. Finally, it is not clear that the growth of money wages depends on the growth of the money stock, as some would argue based on the neo-Walrasian model. Rather the evidence suggests a reverse line of causation, with the growth of money wages determining the growth of the money stock and hence with the growth of money wages still unaccounted for (Moore, 1979, 1983; Eichner, forthcoming, and essay five below). The factors that must be taken as exogenous in the model of the corporate economy are, then, no better explained by the neo-Walrasian model—or, indeed, by any other conventional model.

Thus there is little, if anything, to recommend the neo-Walrasian model of general equilibrium over the model of the corporate economy that has been presented in this essay. Indeed, it is the model of the corporate economy that would appear to be better able to meet the requirements of a "good" theory. Not only is it more parsimonious, requiring fewer unrealistic assumptions, it is also able to encompass a larger number of empirically observable phenomena—including the technical progress and accompanying economic expansion which are such a distinctive feature of the recent history of the United States and other advanced market economies. We shall now see what happens when the model of the corporate economy is further elaborated on to encompass the uncertainty created by the possibility of various unforeseeable events.

The corporate economy with uncertainty

In the model of a corporate economy developed so far, the secular growth rate, G_s, along with the rate of growth of prices, $\dot{P}$, is determined once the model's parameters, especially the $\mathbf{Z}$ vector, are given. That secular growth rate, however, will not necessarily be the balanced, steady-state one assumed in neoclassical growth models. Rather, it is almost certain to be an unbalanced one, with each industry's rate of expansion, $\dot{g}_j$, different. Some industries will be growing more rapidly than the average for all industries, and others will be growing more slowly—though, at least as assumed up to this point, with the rate of expansion for any given industry, whatever that rate may be, remaining the same. But it is not just that the growth path of the corporate economy will almost certainly be an unbalanced one. In addition, the corporate economy may well be subject to cyclical movements as it expands along that secular growth path. This next section will explore what might be the sources of those cyclical movements by introducing into the model three types of unforeseeable events. They are 1) major product innovations, 2) inter-firm competition, and 3) changes in government policy. Only after elaborating on the model in this way will it be possible to see what difference uncertainty makes, in the precisely defined sense of these three types of unforeseeable events, when it comes to explaining not just what determines the secular growth of aggregate output and employment but also what is responsible for any secular rise in the price level that may occur within the corporate economy.

Major product innovations will lead to the emergence of entirely new industries, and thus to a change in the number of industries that comprise the corporate economy. If the product innovations occur continuously, they will make each of the n industries subject to a "product life cycle" of youth, maturity, and decline (Ong, 1981; Shapiro, 1981). An industry, upon first emerging in the wake of a major product innovation (such as the development of railroad transportation, electrically powered motors, or computers), will experience a period of rapid expansion during which the industry's growth rate will exceed that of the economy as a whole as the product it supplies gradually succeeds in displacing an older group of products. The new product will displace the older group of products because of the entirely new uses to which it can be put and/or because of the lower cost at which it now enables an older set of needs to be met. This initial period of rapid growth will be followed by a period of maturity—the onset of which will be marked by the stabilization of market shares among a limited number of firms and during which the industry's growth rate will more closely approximate that of the economy as a whole. A final period of decline, during which the growth rate will fall significantly below that for the economy as a whole, perhaps even turning negative with the industry eventually disappearing, will complete the product life cycle and hence the life cycle of the industry itself.

The life cycle of individual industries that follows from recurrent product innovation will, when introduced into the model of a corporate economy, have two consequences of note. First, it means that the growth rate of individual industries—though not necessarily of the economy as a whole—can no longer be assumed to be constant over time. Indeed, that growth rate, $\dot{g}_j$, can be expected to accelerate initially, slow down subsequently, and then actually fall in a manner corresponding to each industry's period of youth, maturity, and decline. As already implied, this variation in the industry growth rate over time will affect the size of the required mark-up, m_j, and hence produce a slight change in the corporate economy's price vector. It will also, of course, require a change in the rate of investment within the same industries. Still, there would appear to be no reason why these adjustments in the other variables in the system which the variation in $\dot{g}_j$ over time will necessitate cannot be made without throwing the system as a whole off its secular growth path. The adjustments that will need to be made in both the size of the mark-up and the rate of investment will, after all, be slow and gradual. The only exception would be if the major product innovations occurred not continuously but rather, as in the Schumpeterian view, in concentrated spurts.[11] The second consequence of recurrent product innovation will be the effect it is likely to have on the nature of inter-firm competition. Indeed, this second consequence follows from the first.

With recurrent product innovation, the megacorp can no longer expect to continue expanding, or even to survive, simply by retaining its share of the market in the industries to which it already belongs. Eventually, unless it succeeds in entering other industries—those which, being relatively new, are growing more rapidly than the economy as a whole and which, moreover, have not yet settled down into a stable oligopolistic pattern with fixed market shares—the megacorp will decline along with the industries in which it remains rooted. The competition among firms which is crucial to the megacorp's long-term viability is therefore the competition to gain a foothold in the newer, more rapidly growing industries so that, despite the life cycle of individual industries, the megacorp can continue expanding at the same rate as the economy or better. This competition will add significantly to the climate of uncertainty in which the megacorp, at the micro level, is forced to operate.

The uncertainty for the individual firm within one of the k oligopolistic industries will already be greater than for the industry as a whole. This is because of the possibility that market shares may, in fact, change over time. Adding to the uncertainty faced by the individual firm is the possibly disappointing results from other types of investment besides any increase in capacity, both any effort that might be made to reduce costs by replacing obsolescent equipment and any effort that might be made to strengthen the firm's market position through advertising, R&D, and similar types of outlays. Not only are the returns from these types of investments difficult to estimate; so, too, are the implicit costs of obtaining additional investment funds by increasing the mark-up within the industry. The long-run price elasticity of industry demand, the probability of entry by other firms, and the likelihood of government intervention can only be guessed at. Still, as great as the uncertainty may be for the individual megacorp when it comes to committing itself in the way it must within one of the mature oligopolistic industries to which it already belongs, the uncertainty will be even greater when that firm must decide whether to expand into a newer, more rapidly growing industry. This is because a megacorp intent on diversification has no way of knowing how many other firms are planning a similar move. Indeed, it may well be that only some of the firms preparing to enter the industry will be able to obtain the minimal market share they need in order to reach an efficient scale of operation, and this means that the other firms planning to enter the industry will eventually be forced to write off the investment as a loss.

Thus the corporate economy appears quite different from the micro perspective of an individual megacorp faced with the unforeseeable outcome of inter-firm competition than it does from the macro perspective of someone viewing the system as a whole. Both the climate of uncertainty in which the individual megacorp finds itself and the greater stability of the system as a whole are, however, part of the same reality—the inter-firm competition (through investment, not price) being the source of the energy that drives the corporate economy forward along its secular growth path. It is just the difference in perspective that accounts for the two opposing views.

The result, so far, of introducing product innovation and inter-firm competition into the model of a corporate economy has been merely to approximate more closely the climate of uncertainty in which the megacorp, at the micro level, is forced to operate. The macro model itself remains largely the same. In particular, there appears to be no reason, as yet, why the corporate economy would not be able to continue expanding along its secular growth path. The greater uncertainty surrounding investment when product innovation and inter-firm competition are taken into account can be assumed to be insufficient by itself to produce any systematic cyclical movement in the economy. While investment in the newer industries that have not yet matured into stable oligopolies may be uneven, these industries are likely to account for too small a share of total investment to cause the economy as a whole to deviate significantly from its secular growth path. The failed expectations from other types of investment, meanwhile, are likely to largely offset one another—at least within the oligopolistic sector. To provide a credible explanation for the uneven rates of expansion actually experienced by the American and other advanced market economies, it is therefore necessary to introduce a third type of unforeseeable event—a change in government policy. First, however, it is necessary to introduce government itself into the model.

The government can be assumed to purchase a certain portion of the goods entering into final consumption, paying for these items out of its tax revenues plus whatever sums it, like the megacorp, chooses to borrow. There are thus three facets to the government's fiscal policy: 1) determining the level of expenditures; 2) establishing one or more tax rates, and 3) managing whatever debt has been accumulated. In addition, the government can be assumed to affect, through the open-market operations of the central bank, the growth in the amount of reserves held by the commercial banking system. The extent to which it is willing to accommodate the need of the banking system for additional reserves is, in fact, the nub of the government's monetary policy (Forman, Groves, and Eichner, 1984, as well as essay five below). Either or both of these two types of policy can be used by the government to slow down the economy's rate of economic expansion. The government can be expected to take this step if it has been persuaded by economists that the reason for whatever secular rise in the price level has been occurring is the "excess demand" generated either by too large a budget deficit and/or by too rapid a growth in the money supply. While the accompanying cyclical downturn will have little effect on the price level—the rate of inflation is determined, within the model, by the growth of money wages relative to the growth of output per worker and the cyclical downturn need have no effect on the growth of money wages—it will lead to a fall in real output and employment.

More important, insofar as the megacorp itself is concerned, the politically induced business cycle will add to the climate of uncertainty in which the firm must operate. Now, besides guessing correctly what are the newer, more rapidly growing industries into which it must eventually expand, the megacorp must gauge the impact of the government's policies. In particular, it must be careful not to confuse a cyclical movement around the trend line with a change in the trend itself. If, on the one hand, the megacorp views the slowdown in the economy as just another cyclical movement when in fact it portends a decline in the secular growth rate and, based on this false reading, it continues expanding capacity at the same rate, the megacorp will find itself with more capacity than it would like to have, even taking into account its need for a certain amount of reserve capacity. If, on the other hand, the slowdown is thought to represent a decline in the secular growth rate when in fact it is no more than just another cyclical movement, the megacorp may fail to expand its capacity as rapidly as the growth of industry sales requires. What makes it so difficult for the megacorp to correctly judge the situation is that whether the slowdown is just another cyclical movement or an actual change in trend will depend on what subsequent actions the government takes. If the government acts quickly and decisively to reverse its policies, the upshot will be little more than just another cyclical fluctuation in economic activity. However, if the government hesitates and then only languidly applies the necessary contra-cyclical antidote, the result will be a decline in the secular growth rate.

A similar type of confusion between a cyclical movement and a change in trend can touch off the wage-price inflationary spiral in the first place. As the economy recovers from a cyclical downturn, corporate cash flow can be expected to increase disproportionately. To the megacorp, this disproportionate rise in cash flow will merely offset the disproportionate decline in cash flow which, together with the cyclical downturn, preceded it. However, the trade unions, in coming to the bargaining table to negotiate a new labor contract, may view the disproportionate rise in cash flow as an increase in "capital's share" at the expense of labor and may insist on a more rapid rise in money wages. In other words, the trade unions may regard the disproportionate rise in cash flow as portending an increase in the secular growth rate, while to the megacorp the increased cash flow is simply part of the investment funds it must generate over the cycle to assure adequate financing of its capital budget. If the trade unions nonetheless succeed in obtaining their demands, the megacorp will feel that its unit labor costs have risen by the difference between the newly negotiated growth of money wages and the growth of output per worker, and it will insist on raising its prices accordingly. This rise in prices by megacorps in general will be viewed by the trade unions as reducing the real income of their members and, when the present contract expires, will be used by them as an argument for an even more rapid rise in money wages. In this way, a wage-price inflationary spiral can be touched off without any one party, either the megacorp or the trade unions with which it negotiates, being directly responsible. The underlying cause is a different judgment as to the secular or cyclical nature of the change in the rate of economic expansion.

It is, of course, the government that will have the final word in this matter. Depending on how soon it again changes its policies to slow down the economy, this in a vain effort to bring the inflationary spiral under control, it will produce either just another cyclical movement around the same trend or a change in the trend itself. Thus by introducing into the model of a corporate economy the third, and final, type of unforeseeable event—a change in government policy—not only is it possible to explain what causes the uneven expansion of advanced market economies over time, it is also possible to shed some further light on the nature of the wage-price inflationary spiral in which those economies find themselves trapped. When the government responds to the inflationary situation created by a rate of growth of money wages in excess of the growth of output per worker by deliberately slowing down the economy, one is likely to observe not just continued inflation but a decline in economic activity as well.

By introducing into the model still other types of unforeseeable events—such as an unusually poor harvest that drives up the price of food or a shift in the terms of trade that increases the cost of imported raw materials (through the emergence of OPEC or some similar cartel among primary producers)—one can expect additional ways in which a wage-price spiral can either be touched off or exacerbated. Whatever the origins or further stimulus to a wage-price spiral, however, the government's response of slowing down the rate of expansion by the corporate economy will only compound the problem of inflation by creating the problem of a cyclical downturn or, even worse, secular stagnation.

Only one last point, the stability of the corporate economy, needs to be taken up. If there should happen to be a significant departure from the corporate economy's secular growth path, whether because of an inappropriate response by the government to the problem of secular inflation or for some other reason, will the economy be able to return to that growth path—or will it, alternatively, be plunged into a deep depression either immediately or after a temporary but unsustainable boom? This is the question of the system's stability which will be taken up in the next and last section of this essay.

The stability of the corporate economy

The very features of the corporate economy that distinguish it from the type of economic system postulated by the orthodox theory are the features that, by insuring that aggregate output and employment will fluctuate only within certain limits, give the corporate economy whatever stability it has. These features are 1) the megacorp itself; 2) a system of credit money, reinforced by the willingness of the central bank to serve as a lender of last resort (if not to fully accommodate the demand for credit); 3) strong representation of workers' interests by trade unions and similar types of bodies; and 4) the government's commitment to reverse, through Keynesian macroeconomic policies, any cyclical decline in aggregate output and employment. Unfortunately, these same distinguishing features are also what make the corporate economy so susceptible to a secular rise in the price level. Moreover, the last three of these features can be significantly modified while leaving the corporate economy itself still largely intact. In that case, the corporate economy will no longer be so stable.

The megacorp as the representative firm within the corporate economy can be said to contribute to the stability of the corporate economy to the extent that the investment it carries out, based on the items included in its capital budget, is unaffected by the cyclical movements of the economy. Indeed, it is the competitive pressure on the megacorp to expand its capacity within any given industry in line with the growth of sales that insures that the supply condition necessary for maintaining the corporate economy's secular growth rate will be satisfied, at least within the k industries comprising the oligopolistic core. (The $n - k$ nonoligopolistic industries may therefore be more volatile. However, if those industries are only marginally important insofar as output and/or investment is concerned, the effect on the stability of the corporate economy as a whole can, for all practical purposes, be ignored.)

This is not to say that the megacorp's investment plans will remain unchanged in the face of a cyclical downturn in the level of economic activity. As already indicated, the megacorp is likely to cut back on its capital spending whenever it experiences a significant decline in sales, in part because its cash flow will be reduced and in part because it will now be forced to revise downward its estimates of the future secular growth of the industries in which it hopes to retain a share of the market. Still, it will not cut back altogether—especially on the longer term projects for which it has already made a substantial commitment of funds and/or which have long lead times. It will, in other words, gear its investment outlays to the longer term growth prospects of the industries to which it is committed, and this means that the cutback in capital spending will be less than the decline in the megacorp's realized cash flow. This lesser decline in capital outlays, relative to cash flow, will further contribute to the stability of the corporate economy in two ways.

First, it is the reason why the trend value for the growth of corporate investment is so high. This high trend value, together with the similarly high trend values for other types of durable goods purchases (particularly those by the household sector), establishes the secular growth rate around which total durable goods purchases will fluctuate over the cycle. Even in the face of a pronounced cyclical downturn in the level of economic activity, with the cyclical component of durable goods purchases exerting strong downward pressure on the economy, the secular growth of the same durable goods purchases will be the source of pressure in the opposite direction, cushioning the overall downward effect.

Second, to the extent that the megacorp's realized cash flow declines more rapidly than its capital outlays, it will be adding to the overall cash deficit for the corporate economy as a whole, with that deficit, because it means that funds are, on net balance, being added to the circular flow, serving to stimulate aggregate demand. Indeed, with a similar cash deficit by the government sector (occurring for similar reasons), the overall cash-flow feedback effect, together with the secular growth of durable goods purchases, will eventually be sufficient to reverse the cyclical downturn. A similar stabilizing mechanism operates on the ''up'' side of the cycle, with the overall cash surplus that will then be created, together with the same trend values for durable good purchases (which now moderate the overall growth of those types of expenditures), causing the cyclical boom to reverse itself.

This latter mechanism, however, will operate in the manner necessary to stabilize the corporate economy only if the monetary-financial system functions as it is meant to under a system of credit money. This means that the monetary-financial system must, at the very least, provide sufficient credit to fund any deficits, not just those by the government but also those by the corporate and other sectors as well, whenever the corporate economy's rate of expansion falls below the secular growth rate. Otherwise, the lack of credit will lead to an even further reduction in durable goods purchases so that, instead of helping to reverse the cyclical downturn, the actions of the banks and other financial institutions actually contribute to the cumulative decline in the level of economic activity. If the denial of credit is particularly severe, it may even precipitate a collapse of the monetary-financial system, making recovery all the more difficult (Minsky, 1982).

While the megacorp will thus contribute to the stability of the corporate economy by its greater willingness to carry through with any capital spending projects, even in the face of a cyclical downturn in economic activity, it will, on the other hand, through the system of price leadership that characterizes the corporate economy, make prices all but inflexible downward. The problem this creates is not, as is sometimes argued, that recovery from a cyclical downturn will be impeded. As can be seen from the set of equations used above to describe the corporate economy, the *level* of final demand, as distinct from the *composition* of final demand, does not depend on the price vector; and thus how flexible prices are will make little or no difference in how quickly the corporate economy can recover from a cyclical downturn. Moreover, the same system of price leadership that makes prices inflexible downward is what insures that both the supply and value conditions for the secular expansion of the corporate economy will be satisfied—with help, insofar as the supply condition is concerned, from the types of financial institutions that operate under a system of credit money. Rather the problem is that, with prices inflexible downward, the growth of output per worker cannot be translated into higher real income for the household sector through a secular decline in the price level. The same result must instead be achieved through a secular rise in money wages and the other forms of income received by the household sector—and in this way satisfy the aggregate demand condition for maintaining the corporate economy's secular growth rate. This is why trade unions or some other type of mechanism that functions to push up money wages and the other forms of household income is essential for the longer term, as distinct from the cyclical, stability of the corporate economy.

Moreover, not even the stabilizing influence of the megacorp's high secular growth of investment, along with the similarly stabilizing influence of the high secular growth of durable goods purchases by the household sector, can be counted on unless the government is prepared to act quickly and decisively to reverse, through Keynesian countercyclical policies, any downturn in the level of economic activity. Otherwise, the state of long-run expectations will not be such as to encourage both megacorps and households to take a longer run view insofar as durable goods purchases, or discretionary expenditures, are concerned. At the very least, the government must not take any actions—such as curtailing its own discretionary expenditures and/or raising tax rates when a cyclical downturn occurs (or, alternatively, stepping up its discretionary expenditures and/or lowering tax rates when the economy is already expanding at a more rapid rate than the growth of output per worker will permit)—that will exacerbate the situation and thereby overwhelm the corporate economy's built-in stabilizers. The problem is that the very features of the corporate economy that insure that aggregate output and employment will fluctuate only within certain limits are also the features that make the corporate economy so susceptible to an inflationary spiral as megacorps, trade unions, and the government exercise the power they have over prices, wages, and tax rates. This, however, is a point that will be more fully developed in the subsequent essays.

Afterword

This is a revised and expanded version of the article that appeared in *Managerial and Decision Economics*, November, 1983, under the same title. It carries forward the analysis of oligopolistic pricing first presented in ''The Determination of the Mark-up under Oligopoly''

(Eichner, 1973a) and in "A General Model of Investment and Pricing" (Eichner, 1980b), and then elaborated on more fully in *The Megacorp and Oligopoly* (Eichner, 1976). It does so by incorporating that analysis of pricing behavior within the model of an expanding production system that Luigi Pasinetti has outlined in *Structural Change and Economic Growth* (1981) as a synthesis of the work of Robinson (1956, 1962a), Leontief (1951, Leontief *et al.*, 1954), Sraffa (1960), and von Neumann (1945). In connection with that model of an expanding production system, see also Blatt (1983) and Lichtenstein (1983).

Notes

1. Marris, 1963; Marris and Wood, 1971; Baumol, 1967; Wood, 1975; J. Williamson, 1966.
2. Simon, 1955; Cyert and March, 1963; Monsen and Downs, 1965; O. Williamson, 1964. The work of the parallel British group includes Andrews, 1949, 1964; Andrews and Brunner, 1975; Wilson and Andrews, 1951; Downie, 1958; Wiles, 1956; Penrose, 1959; Loasby, 1976.
3. Means, 1962; Kaplan *et al.*, 1958; Clark, 1961.
4. Kalecki, 1954; Sraffa, 1960; Steindl, 1952; Robinson, 1962a; Sylos-Labini, 1962, 1974; Vickers, 1968; Eichner, 1973a, 1976; Pasinetti, 1981; Harris, 1974; Coutts, Godley, and Nordhaus, 1978.
5. Strictly speaking, the vintage equipment means that the firm's average variable costs will rise as its reserve capacity is tapped. However, the rise in average variable costs is likely to be slight and, in any case, will be outweighed by the fall in average fixed costs because of the greater volume.
6. The prices of certain items may have to be adjusted more frequently because of "competitive conditions." But the price list as a whole is likely to be retained even if the discounts off the list price become large and generally known.
7. The neo-Walrasian approach, first set out by Hicks (1939) and Samuelson (1948), reflects the work of Arrow, Debreu, and Hahn (Arrow and Debreu, 1954; Arrow and Hahn, 1971; Debreu, 1959). The latter-day Marshallians are those who, like Friedman (1976) and other prominent members of the Chicago school, prefer a partial to a general equilibrium framework.
8. The secular growth path referred to here is not necessarily a steady-state one, as will soon be made clear.
9. These weights, given the uneven rates of expansion by each of the n industries that the model incorporates, will themselves vary over time.
10. It is, of course, possible that both dividends and taxes must be allowed for in calculating the required mark-ups, in which case the $1/(1 - t)$ term would be compounded as follows: $1/(1 - t_2) \, 1/(1 - t_1)$ where t_1 is the proportion of after-tax income paid out in dividends and t_2 is the corporate income tax rate.
11. While it is clear that inventions occur in spurts, this does not mean, as Freeman (1982) has pointed out in discussing the Schumpeterian thesis, that the aggregate growth rate will thereby be affected. One would need to show that, after smoothing out the cyclical fluctuations in the growth rates of each of the n industries which comprise the enterprise sector, there still remained variations over time in the aggregate growth rate, that is, in the weighted average of the growth rates for each of the n industries (with n itself varying over time as new industries emerged and older industries disappeared).

4

An Anthropogenic Approach to Labor Economics

The usual approach, in economic modeling, is to treat something called "labor" as simply another commodity, subject like any commodity to the forces of supply and demand, with the balance between the two equilibrated through a market. The human capital concept which has come to dominate discussions of "labor" supply in recent years merely builds on this standard approach, the refinement being to take into account the time-related costs of and benefits from education and other forms of "investment" in human beings.[1] The purpose of this essay is to outline an alternative approach which, because it focuses on the cumulative acquisition of competences over time rather than on commodity-type transactions, can be termed the "human developmental" or "anthropogenic" model.[2]

The use of a somewhat different terminology is necessary and deliberate. The reason is that the usual commodity approach to the human factor in economic activity succeeds in explaining only certain facets of the role played by human beings in providing for their material needs. The commodity approach is not wrong in the sense of being unsupportable by empirical evidence. It is, however, limited in the types of problems on which it can throw light. To avoid the limitations of the language, and thus of the concepts employed in the conventional commodity approach, a somewhat different set of theoretical constructs, reflecting the broader perspective of the anthropogenic model, is required.

It should be pointed out that what is meant by the "conventional commodity approach" to labor economics is the implicit conceptualization that permeates economic theory in general and which then serves as the analytical skeleton around which more detailed discussions of labor economics, emphasizing institutional factors and other complications, are organized.[3] Thus, the fact that the commodity approach is seldom found in its purest form within the specialized literature is beside the point. It still dominates more general discussions bearing on labor matters, and even in the specialized literature it is this skeleton which shows through whenever the necessary qualifications must be omitted. As for the alternative anthropogenic model, it should be noted that, like much of the other work in the institutional tradition, it began simply as an effort to temper theory with a better understanding of how things actually work in practice.[4] The point has now been reached, however, where it constitutes more than just a gloss to the conventional commodity approach. Indeed, one can discern within this body of work the outline of a quite different conceptualization of the role played by human beings in economic activity.

In the several sections that follow, the anthropogenic approach will be contrasted with the conventional commodity model with respect to six different aspects. They are 1) the general framework of analysis, 2) the degree of ''activeness'' presumed on the part of the human resource factor, 3) the manner in which human resources are thought to become committed to alternative activities, 4) the role served by labor markets, 5) the factors determining the utilization—or employment—of human resources, and 6) the extent to which work represents disutility. For each of these six aspects the usual commodity approach will first be described, the alternative anthropogenic formulation will then be offered, and finally it will be shown how the first is but a special case of the second. The reader should be warned, however, that what follows is merely one individual's perception of the anthropogenic approach, and that others who have been active in developing the model might well offer a somewhat different formulation (cf. Ginzberg, 1976). Indeed, the main justification for ignoring these differences and focusing instead on the contrast with the dominant commodity model is that the anthropogenic approach is so little known to the economics profession in general, despite its potential for clarifying the role played by human beings in economic activity, that the first priority is simply to give it wider currency through a relatively brief, albeit idiosyncratic, synthesis of the work done to date within that conceptual framework.

The general framework of analysis

Economics as a discipline and labor economics as a subspecialty within it usually concern themselves with but a single type of process, that of exchange—typically through a market in which money is employed as a medium. The structuring of problems in this way permits economists to divide their analysis into two parts: a) an examination of the forces inducing some group or individual to give money in exchange for the item in question; and b) an examination of the forces inducing the group or individual on the other side of the transaction to surrender the item—perhaps after first having assured its availability—in exchange for money. Once the factors operating on the demand and supply sides of the equation have been delineated in this manner, economists are able to analyze how the opposing forces will balance out and thereby produce a flow of the item in one direction, a counterflow of money in the other direction, and a price ratio representing the mathematical relationship between the two. So rewarding has this mode of analysis been that economists have extended it, not only beyond the domain of internationally traded commodities to encompass the commitment of human beings to work activity, but also to areas seemingly distant from economic considerations, such as education, crime, and discrimination (e.g. Becker, 1957, 1964, 1968). Indeed, the economist, when turning his attention to matters outside the traditional boundaries of his discipline, is likely to view all social activity in terms of the exchange (or trading) process.[5]

The anthropogenic model does not deny the importance of exchange, especially with respect to supplying the material needs of the population under the economic systems that have evolved in all but the centrally planned socialist countries. However, it sees exchange as only one of four processes that may characterize any particular social activity. Exchange is, to be sure, the process quintessential to the economic dimension of society, but the economic dimension itself is but one of four such dimensions, each with its own characteristic process or dynamic. The other three dimensions besides the economic that need to be taken into account in any comprehensive analysis are 1) the normative; 2) the political; and 3) the human developmental, or anthropogenic. The normative dimension encompasses all the values, or beliefs, upon which individual activity is predicated. The dynamic process unique to this dimension is the dialectic by which various paradigms, or systems of belief, come into being, are then undermined by their inability to explain certain empirical phenomena, and eventually are supplanted by a newer, more general paradigm. The political system, meanwhile, encompasses all the mechanisms that exist for making conscious social choices among alternative courses of action. The dynamic process unique to this dimension is the formation of coalitions in order to gain control over decision-making bodies.

What is novel about the conceptual framework upon which the human resources approach is based is the delineation of the human developmental or anthropogenic dimension of society. This specification derives from the conviction that human competences, defined as the ability to utilize various skills in a social setting, are no less important than norms, societal decisions (including laws), and material goods in the functioning of societies; and that, furthermore, these competences evolve as a result of a process quite different from that which produces the other three building blocks of social organization—values, group decisions, and material resources. The anthropogenic process involves successive, or complementary, affiliation with developmental institutions, beginning with the family, continuing through the various levels of schooling, and then consolidating around the experience gained through employment, whether that effort is remunerated or not. Indeed, the three sets of institutions, the family, the schools, and employing organizations, are the separate components of a distinct anthropogenic system which are linked together by the career path each individual member of society pursues over his lifetime. Affiliation with one of these developmental institutions is the process quintessential to the anthropogenic dimension (Ginzberg, 1966, 1971, 1976; Eichner, 1973a, 1973b; Eichner and Brecher, 1979).

The human resources model, since it takes into account three other processes besides the one of exchange emphasized exclusively in the conventional economic analysis, is thus a more general approach to the study of social dynamics. However, more than just the question of generality is involved in dealing with the human factor in economic activity. The subject matter of labor economics reflects the congruence between the economic and anthropogenic dimensions (Eichner, 1973a; Lewin et al., 1974). On the one hand, it is the economy which, as a result of the level of activity generated, creates the employment opportunities whereby most competences are utilized and—even more important—further developed. Yet, it is the anthropogenic system that serves as the means by which those competences are acquired, in all their myriad forms. It is not just that the anthropogenic system must produce a range of competences beyond what is needed by the economy alone; that the functioning of the individual as savant, citizen, parent, and teacher is no less important than his functioning as worker. It is, *a fortiori*, that in dealing with the congruence between the economic and anthropogenic systems one must recognize that at least two quite separate processes, or dynamics, are at work: that of affiliation as well as that of exchange. Indeed, with the two simultaneously in operation, one should not be surprised to observe, given the additive rule that applies to dynamic processes, yet a third even more complex dynamic. In any case, the model of market exchange will be able to explain only limited aspects of what is the putative concern of the labor economist: the movement over time of individuals into employment status. This is due, not only to the complicating anthropogenic processes at work but also, even more fundamentally, to the radically different nature of the items "traded" in what are termed "labor markets."

The degree of "activeness"

The commodity trading model from which the conventional theory of labor markets has been derived implicitly assumes that it is inert physical goods that are being exchanged. The essential characteristic of such goods is that they are entirely passive, with zero degree of activeness. Lacking any independent will—not to mention the capacity to effectuate that will—they are merely acted upon; they do not themselves act. Indeed, they care not a whit what happens to them, either in the process of being traded or subsequently in the process of being utilized by a purchaser. It is a matter of indifference to the barrel of oil that is sold whether it is used to heat a house of God or a house of prostitution. Not caring how it is to be used and, even more important, not capable of acting on its own, an inert physical good is unable to foil the plans the purchaser may have for it. The purchaser, in turn, does not have to worry about devising a counter-strategy. There is no need, for example, to pay the barrel of oil a special premium or in some other way assuage its feelings so it will agree to heat the house of prostitution instead of the house of God (or vice versa).

The commodity trading model, then, ignores precisely what is more significant about human beings, namely, their ability to set and implement goals of their own.[6] While it might seem that the model would have to be significantly modified before it could be used to explain the willingness of human beings to accept employment, the conventional theory of labor markets makes no such concession. Instead the theory talks about labor services, divorced from the human beings who are to provide them. With the focus shifted from the concrete reality of individuals placing themselves under the control of others to the abstract notion of a labor service homomorphic with the physical inputs used in the production process, the commodity trading model can then be applied without any significant change in the mode of analysis. Labor services, just like commodities, are exchanged for money, the precise amount depending on the forces of supply and demand. It makes little difference, in this conceptual framework, that what is putatively being exchanged impinges on the personality of individual human beings.

The perception of what happens in the "labor market" is quite different when, as in the anthropogenic model, explicit account is taken of the fact that those subject to the process are active agents, with multifarious goals. Some, but by no means all, of these goals pertain to the satisfaction of material needs. Moreover, while human beings may be required to spend the better part of each week engaged in activities organized around the task of satisfying those material needs, even during the time they are so occupied they are not unmindful of their other goals in life. Finally, in attempting to achieve these goals, human beings do not merely follow simple and direct lines of action. They are, in fact, capable of executing quite complex strategies, sometimes by themselves and sometimes in conjunction with others. Both the multifarious goals human beings set for themselves and the complex strategies they follow in pursuit of those goals profoundly affect the nature of the employment relationship.[7]

The analysis of what happens on the job is complicated by more than just the fact that human beings, unlike inert physical goods, can be perverse. It is also that the use of human beings in the production process raises unavoidable teleological, and hence moral, issues. Take the case of the barrel of oil that is supplied through the market. Few would question that, once removed from the ground, it should eventually be used to serve some human end. But what about the individuals who must give of their time and energy if that barrel of oil is to be delivered as heating fuel at the point of consumption? Are they merely a means to the same end, that of providing the consumer with warmth? Or do they have interests, in terms of the conditions under which they must work and the compensation they will receive, that are no less deserving of protection than those of the consumer? The usual treatment of labor in economics, by viewing the human factor in the production process solely in instrumental terms, avoids these questions. That is why it can accept the notion of a trade-off between unemployment and inflation when, in fact, the consequences of the two are in no way commensurate with one another. But this sole concern with the consumer interest, to the virtual neglect of producer welfare, is arbitrary. By attaching significance to individual preferences only insofar as they influence what goods are produced, and not with respect to how they are produced, the conventional analysis predetermines the very conclusions it reaches; and thus it is something less than the value free scientific inquiry its proponents like to believe.

The anthropogenic model is more open on this point. Starting from the premise that the basis for judging social institutions is the extent to which they serve to increase the options open to individuals, it weighs the economic system's ability to deliver material goods against the number and types of employment opportunities that the same economic system is capable of providing. The latter consideration is no less crucial to individual well-being, and this is so for three reasons: 1) It is primarily through employment that, as long as the human input remains critical to the functioning of the economic system, individuals will continue to obtain the income necessary for purchasing goods and services. 2) Since individuals spend most of their waking hours on the job, the conditions of employment are critical to the quality of the everyday life experience. 3) It is largely through employment opportunities that, subsequent to their formal schooling, individuals continue to develop their capacities and acquire further competences. The emphasis, then, in the anthropogenic model is on the different ways in which individuals are able to increase their options in life, with the availability of physical goods being only one of them. It is for this reason that the anthropogenic model, unlike the more conventional treatment of the human factor in the production process, refrains from giving weight solely to the consumer interest (Ginzberg, 1976).

To focus merely on the increase in options, making this the principal result to be explained, is not enough, however. Without any basis for assigning a greater worth to any one individual over another, it must be assumed that all individuals are equally entitled to whatever options society has to offer. Yet the evidence is overwhelming that some individuals have more options than others. Why is this the case? To raise this question, as the anthropogenic model does, is to assert that the equity with which options are distributed is no less important a phenomenon to be explained than the aggregate increase in those options over time (Ginzberg, 1976, chs. 7, 14). The anthropogenic model goes further, however, than just to raise the issue. By pointing out the link between the employment opportunities a society is able to provide through its economic system and the resulting increase in individual options, even beyond any income earned, the model opens the way to a more complete understanding of the processes determining the differential development of individuals, and hence the relatively unequal distribution of options that is observable in contemporary society. However, to pursue this lead, one must first explore the nature of the employment affiliation, showing how it differs from the conventional notion of contracted labor services.

Contract vs. affiliation

In the conventional model of production, based on eighteenth-century theories of jurisprudence and social organization, the process by which individuals are integrated into the work force is viewed as though it were the result of contractual agreements similar to those that govern the movement of physical goods between producers and consumers around the world. It assumes that the terms and conditions of the contract, including the rate of compensation, are fully spelled out in advance, and that the two sides to the agreement voluntarily give their consent to those terms and conditions. Even more important, the conventional model assumes that there is a single moment in time, the "date" of the contract, when those terms and conditions are both fully understood and agreed to.[8]

It is on this last point that the anthropogenic model takes its departure from the conventional treatment of the human factor in economic activity. The integration of individuals into a work force is seen as occurring, not at any single moment in time but rather, in several stages over time (Freedman, 1969; Yavitz and Morse, 1973; Ginzberg, 1976). There are, in fact, six discrete steps: an extended period of recruitment (on the part of the employing organization) and search (on the part of the individual) followed by the relatively brief act of selection by the two parties sequentially but nonetheless independently of one another; a second extended period of orientation and indoctrination again followed by a relatively brief act, in this case, assignment of the individual to a particular job; and finally a third extended period of education and training ending with an evaluation that leads either to promotion, retention in the same position, or dismissal. It is, of course, possible for any one of these six discrete steps to be greatly compressed in time, especially if the position is a temporary one or requires little in the way of skill. It is also possible for the last two sets of steps to overlap somewhat. Still, the several stages involved point to the existence of a process—that of attachment to a particular employing organization—and not simply the working out at a particular point in time of a contractual arrangement that is henceforth binding on the two parties. For the important point is that the process may come to an end before it is fully completed, during any one of the successive stages. By so terminating the process, neither of the two parties can be said to have violated its obligations to the other.

Within the last few years a good deal of attention has been directed in conventional treatments of labor to the process of search (though not, interestingly enough, to the parallel process of recruitment) (e.g. Phelps, 1970; Whipple, 1973). The interest in search behavior has derived chiefly from the need to offer some plausible explanation of why wages have continued to rise, during recent recessions, even in the face of declining demand. However well this concession to realism may serve to salvage the larger body of standard economic theory, the fact remains that it still ignores two subsequent stages in the attachment process. It also continues the mistake of focusing on the rate of compensation as the sole determining factor in the attachment process. Both of these are oversights which the anthropogenic model seeks to avoid.

The anthropogenic model does not deny the importance of the size of money payment in determining whether individuals become attached to a particular employment organization (Freedman, 1969, pp. 117–19; Ginzberg, 1976, p. 80). What it rejects is an exclusive concern with that one factor alone. In an earlier era, when labor was performed primarily by farmers seeking to supplement the earnings from their own insufficient holdings, and even somewhat later, when a landless proletariat provided little more than "hands" for the new types of factory production, this emphasis on the "wage bargain" was perhaps not unwarranted. Human beings worked for others primarily because of the income it afforded them. But in a modern economy, when even those in the highest positions of authority in effect work for someone else and the types of jobs available are so diverse, requiring as they do such a variety of skills, other factors become important. Human beings become attached to a work force, even aside from the income it provides, because a) it offers a milieu for social interaction—a place to meet people and make friends; b) it provides a certain degree of autonomy—freedom from the arbitrary command of others; and c) it enables them to develop further as human beings—to increase their skills and competences. Employers, in turn, accept individuals as members of their permanent work force, despite the money outlays involved, because the individuals a) are able to take over a position within the organization and carry out some essential task without disrupting the flow of output, and b) have the potential for later assuming an even more demanding or responsible position within the organization (Ginzberg, 1976).

It is because neither employees nor employers can be fully assured at once on all these points that the attachment process takes a while to complete. Only time will tell what type of social milieu, how much autonomy, and what opportunities for personal growth a particular job offers. And only time will tell if the individual selected as a result of the recruitment effort will measure up to the standards of the job. It may, in fact, be necessary for either the individual or the organization to bring the process to a halt and start anew, not just once but several times. Once the process of attachment is completed, however, the result is an affiliation, at least for the individual, different only in kind from the affiliations by which he has gained his antecedent level of competence. This means a commitment by the organization to the individual and by the individual to the organization that cannot be terminated merely on whim. As in earlier affiliations, first with some family unit and then with various schools at successively higher levels of education, the individual is assured of the continuing benefits of that relationship, including the growth of competences, as long as he adheres to certain prescribed rules of behavior. Of course, attachment to an employing organization differs from the prior affiliations in various ways. The flow of money payment is reversed, the absorption of the individual into the organization is simply derivative of the organization's pursuit of more fundamental objectives, and the affiliation is more likely to be terminated in the face of economic adversity. Even the types of skills acquired are different. Nonetheless, this type of affiliation is no less critical to the individual's developmental process (Eichner, 1973a).

It is thus possible to trace out a succession of organizational affiliations by which each individual acquires the competences that are so essential for any constructive role he may play in society. This succession of affiliations marks the career path each individual follows, attachment to a particular employing organization simply marking the final steps along that route (Ginzberg, 1976; Eichner, 1973b). Once affiliation with an employing organization takes place, the career path may then lead to movement up some internal promotion ladder, to lateral shifts between organizations with or without advancement, or to a dead end until retirement from the work force occurs. For those who are part of the secondary, or peripheral, labor force,[9] the career path may even fall short of attachment to any particular employing organization, the work history including, at most, only a few briefly held intermittent jobs. The career paths that may be followed are therefore quite diverse. In each case, however, the transition from school to work—that is, from the secondary to the tertiary level of the anthropogenic system—is critical.[10] This leads to a somewhat different view of the labor "market" from that which prevails among most labor economists. Indeed, this is the fourth point on which to contrast the conventional approach to the human factor in economics and the anthropogenic model.

A true market or a mere linkage

Central to standard economic analysis is the notion that mechanisms described as markets serve as the primary allocative device, distributing resources among alternative, competing uses. These mechanisms are presumed to perform a "clearing" function, making sure not only that resources are put to the best possible use but also, just as important, that supply and demand remain in balance. The latter result is assured, so the theory goes, as long as the price variable is free to move up or down. Should the supply exceed the demand, a fall in price will lower the supply and increase demand, bringing the two back into balance. Similarly, should the demand exceed supply, a rise in price will lower demand and increase the supply. As already pointed out, the theory was first developed to explain the international trade of standardized commodities and then taken over, with little change in the argument, to deal with the human factor in economic activity. In the so-called labor "market," it is the wage rate as the price variable that supposedly moves up and down to perform the clearing function.

One need only consult Keynes' *General Theory* for a devastating attack on this view of how the labor "market" operates. *The General Theory*, in fact, offers two separate explanations of why labor markets are unlikely to clear, that is, assure "full employment"—neither of which depends on the power of trade unions to prevent wages from falling. The first argument is that it is difficult, if not impossible, to arrange matters so that wage reductions apply across the board to all workers simultaneously. This means that, at any one point in time, only some workers will be under pressure to accept lower wages, and with those lower wages a decline in their standard of living relative to other workers. As a result, the wage cuts are bitterly resisted—and not without justification. The fall in the wages of just some workers is unlikely to solve the general problem of unemployment. It should be noted that the argument implies either that there is no such thing as a single labor market or, alternatively, that there is no such thing as a single price—that is, wage rate—or structure of prices prevailing in that market. The second line of Keynes' attack is even more damaging to standard economic theory. Even if wage reductions could be negotiated across the board, full employment would still not be restored, for the very fact of the wage reductions would so discourage business investment that, operating through the multiplier process, the economy would wind up even further below the full employment level of income. In other words, the income effects arising from the wage reductions would far outweigh the substitution effects taking place within the firm (Keynes, 1936).

The anthropogenic model accepts these Keynesian arguments as valid, but points out an even more fundamental reason why the so-called labor market cannot effectively carry out its clearing function. It is because a key element in most commodity markets is missing. This is the presence of a "speculative interest"—or forward market—to prevent sellers from pushing prices up too high and to prevent buyers from forcing prices down too low. The speculative interest—brokers, other middlemen, even the buyers and sellers themselves—in effect acts as a secondary factor in the market, stepping in to purchase stocks that would otherwise go unsold and holding them for release until prices have again risen. Most markets clear only because the speculative interest sees to it that they do clear. In labor markets, however, there are no speculative interests because the input that human beings uniquely contribute to the production process cannot be stored. The time, together with the energy and competence, that individuals have to offer is lost forever once it is allowed to go unutilized. Not even those who provide the laboring time can store it; the most they can do is use it for their own private purposes (Eichner, 1973a; Friedlander, 1972).

For this reason, labor markets are more appropriately viewed as imperfect market-clearing mechanisms. When employing organizations have a need for additional workers to fill entry level positions and even when they have a need for experienced workers to fill higher level positions, it is true that the temporary gap between "supply" and "demand" is likely to be quickly closed by what appears to be the labor "market"—though not necessarily as a result of the wage rate rising. However, in the opposing situation, when both new workers and experienced personnel are seeking positions in greater numbers than are currently being opened up, the gap—in this case arising from excessive supply—will not be closed. The job seekers will find themselves queued up with no demand for their services, and thus the time, together with the energy and competence they are prepared to give to an employing organization, is irretrievably lost. Moreover, no lowering of the rate of compensation for their services is likely to remedy the situation—though this may not prevent the wage rate from falling. The explanation is the one implicit in Keynesian theory: the demand for labor is determined in the short run solely by the forces influencing the overall level of economic activity, of which the supply of manpower is not one.

There is thus an asymmetrical relationship between the economic and anthropogenic systems. The latter can be counted on to be quite responsive in supplying business organizations with whatever competent individuals those employing organizations require—with at most only a brief lag (Eichner, 1976). The economic system, however, cannot be counted on to assure places for all the graduates of the anthropogenic system. When one recognizes that the employing organizations are themselves a part of the anthropogenic system because of the on-the-job training they provide, it is possible to see the inherent nature of the difficulty. The more rapidly the economy expands, thereby providing additional employment opportunities, the more rapidly it will be producing experienced personnel ready and eager for more demanding assignments. The issue, then, is not whether competent individuals will be queued up waiting either for their first job or for advancement but rather, how rapidly the individuals will be able to move up along those queues until an opening occurs that places them a leg up on their career path. Since the queues include not only the younger generation emerging from the educational system but also the rural peasantry the world over hoping to find a place in an industrial, and even a postindustrial society, there is no reason to expect this asymmetrical relationship between the economic and anthropogenic systems to end in the near historical future.

Under these conditions, the labor market can only determine which individuals obtain the limited employment opportunities available.[11] It can do nothing to assure jobs for all who would like to work. Those who are unable to obtain employment represent an irretrievable loss for society, for it is impossible to stop the march of time that measures each individual's finite lifespan. Standard economic theory not only fails to properly specify the mechanism by which individuals are integrated into the production process; it also misunderstands how these same individuals are then used within the employing organization itself. This leads to the question of the factors internal to the firm which determine the utilization, or employment, of human resources.

The demand for human inputs

In conventional economic models, human inputs are seen as variable compared to the plant, capital equipment, and even the managerial capability of the owner-entrepreneurs. (The existence of large corporations, or megacorps, with management and ownership separated, is seldom recognized.) The firm is viewed as being able to alter production levels by using differing amounts of the variable input, that is, production workers, in combination with the fixed inputs. However, because of the law of variable proportions, the use of the additional workers to increase production leads, beyond a certain point, to diminishing marginal productivity. It is from this condition of diminishing marginal productivity that the firm's supposed demand curve for "labor" is derived. The curve is negatively sloped, implying that the demand for manpower inputs varies inversely with the rate of compensation. This relationship follows logically from the presumed technical conditions of production, in particular, from the diminishing returns that set in when, beyond a certain point, more variable inputs, like production workers, are used in combination with the same fixed amount of plant, capital equipment, and managerial personnel to expand output. The key assumption, of course, is that production is possible with flexible technical coefficients, that is, with differing amounts of the variable input relative to the fixed inputs (Eichner, 1976).

The anthropogenic model does not deny that the negatively sloped demand curve for "labor" may hold in certain cases—particularly in smaller enterprises using relatively unsophisticated technology. More generally, however, it holds that production is carried out as part of a complex social process, one in which the individual's unique contribution is necessarily submerged in the overall group effort. Each worker has a clearly delineated role to play—a job slot—in an organizational structure based on the following relationships: a) between workers and the capital equipment, b) between workers and the supervisory staff, and c) among different types of workers. For the most part, these relationships are fixed ones, arrived at as part of the organization's long-run search for optimal efficiency. The more sophisticated the skills or equipment required in the production process, the less flexible these relationships are likely to be (Eichner, 1976; Ginzberg, 1976). This has two implications. First, it means that adding more human inputs in the form of additional workers, rather than being the means of increasing output, simply imposes on the organization the burden of altering its internal structure. It is for this reason that new workers are seldom hired except to fill already existing slots in the organization, ones that have either been recently vacated or are about to be vacated by other workers. Second, it means that there is no way of determining the incremental contribution to the goals of the organization, whether those goals be profit-oriented or not, for any one worker alone or even for any one type of worker. The output depends on the functioning of the organization as a whole. Thus it is not possible to establish any direct relationship, negative or otherwise, between the number of workers employed by the organization on the one hand and either the productivity of the organization or the rate of compensation received by the workers on the other hand. That is, the negatively sloped demand curve for "labor" does not generally hold under modern conditions of production.

By carrying out the analysis as though the negatively sloped demand curve did apply, the conventional models miss what are the far more significant determinants both of productivity within the organization and the compensation received by workers. The productivity of the organization depends on the capacity of those in executive positions to deal with the most critical fact of organized work activity: that the goals of the individuals who comprise the organization, even in a managerial capacity, are not identical with those of the organization itself. Effective management requires both a positive and a negative response to this inherent conflict of interests. On the positive side, the individual's role within the organization needs to be structured so that, in meeting the imperatives of his work assignment, he is also moving closer to the realization of his own personal goals. In this way, the organization can harness, to the maximum extent possible, the individual's own drive and energies, the only source of dynamism for the organization itself. Still, since the goals of the individual and the organization can never be wholly reconciled, a negative response is required as well. This means placing as much pressure as possible on the individual members of the organization to avoid any behavior that is inimical to the short-run goal of optimal output and the long-run goal of survival and growth. The key to effective management—the source of what Leibenstein (1966) has termed "X-efficiency"—is thus the setting of a proper balance between positive inducements to better individual performance and negative strictures against subversive behavior. In large organizations, where relationships are more impersonal, the setting of this proper balance is, of course, more difficult—especially since the conflicts may be between different parts of the organization as well as between the organization and its individual members (Ginzberg, 1976).

Rates of compensation clearly play an important role in bringing the interests of the individual into line with those of the organization. Still, one should not place too much weight on that one factor. In the first place, the most deeply felt satisfactions that go with any job are those that are intrinsic to the work being performed. Money is generally a poor substitute for that type of reward. Secondly, the actual rates of compensation received by those who work for the organization usually depend on factors other than any differential contribution to the organization's goals. They depend, in part, on what has been termed the "internal wage structure" (Livernash, 1957)—the differentials in pay derived historically from balancing the organization's needs to maintain hierarchical relationships against the demands of the work force for equitable treatment. From the point of view of the organization, it is essential that those in supervisory positions receive a higher rate of compensation than those they oversee. Otherwise, the basis for internal discipline will be undermined. From the point of view of the individual members of the work force, however, it seems no less reasonable that those who perform equally difficult tasks or have been employed equally long by the organization should receive roughly the same rate of compensation. The internal wage structure represents the resolution of these conflicting pressures. In general, it permits the rate of compensation to be increased only because of a) time in grade, or seniority, and b) promotion to a more responsible and/or skilled position (Eichner, 1976; Ginzberg, 1976).

The entire set of differentials represented by the internal wage structure may itself be raised (or lowered) as a result of external factors. While in some cases this may reflect labor market pressure, more typically it is because the regional, industrial, or national norms of what constitutes a "fair" wage have been altered. Various sheltering mechanisms, such as an internal promotion system or credentialing requirements, usually help insulate the organization's wage structure from market forces (Freedman, 1976). With an established trade union movement, the norm is likely to be worked out in collective bargaining between representatives of the production workers and top management. Indeed, the collective bargaining agreement is likely to serve as a further sheltering mechanism. But even when formal collective bargaining does not take place, the organization is likely to take as the norm the rate of compensation paid by other organizations caught in a similar set of circumstances—with perhaps the one difference that the workers of the other organizations are represented by a trade union. It is for this reason that the agreement worked out in one of the "key" or "bellwether" industries with respect to wages and other forms of compensation is of such critical importance in determining the overall level of wages throughout the economy. The pattern established in one industry or sector is likely to be followed in others. The government itself, through Presidential intervention in the key industry's negotiations or through some form of "incomes" policy, may also have a hand in shaping the pattern (Eichner, 1976). Rates of compensation, then, depend on the internal wage structure as modified over time by the changing standard of what constitutes a fair wage in a particular region, industry, or the nation as a whole.

The supply of manpower

The conventional analysis, however, not only misperceives the nature of the firm's demand curve for "labor"; it also incorrectly specifies the supply curve. In the standard economic models, work is presumed to give rise to disutility. For this reason, in order to persuade individuals to make their services available, they must be paid a wage, the income compensating them for what they are giving up—their leisure—by working. The anthropogenic model recognizes that work is all too often distasteful to those who must perform it. Indeed, this has been true for the great majority of people throughout most of human history, and it is still true for too many people in the world today, even in developed and relatively affluent societies like that of the United States. Still, this is not an immutable condition. As the experience of at least some people demonstrates, and not just in advanced societies, work may also be a source of great satisfaction. And this is the case quite aside from any income work provides.

The limitation of the conventional economic analysis is that it recognizes only the need of society to have certain types of tasks carried out and the need of individuals to have access to income through employment. What it leaves out is the equally important need of individuals to have purposeful activity, a need attested to by the energy devoted to hobbies, sports, and other leisure-time pursuits. The purposeful activity is essential, not just for maintaining whatever level of physical and mental competence has previously been attained but also for enabling the individuals to continue developing as human beings. In responding to this need, individuals may even be led to perform socially useful tasks without insisting upon money compensation in return, their reward being enhanced abilities and self-esteem. In fact, were this not the case, the society would lack philosophers, artists, political activists, volunteer workers, and parents.

The need for purposeful activity, then, is a powerful force inducing individuals to make themselves available to organizations having a need for their services, regardless of the compensation to be received. When the need for on-the-job training as a follow-up to formal education is taken into account, the willingness of individuals to work, whatever the pay, emerges as even more significant a factor. Still, it is unlikely to be powerful enough to guarantee that all of society's necessary tasks will be carried out, and this is so for two reasons. On the one hand, individuals must first be assured that they will have sufficient income to satisfy the material needs not only of themselves but also of the other persons dependent on them. On the other hand, some of society's necessary tasks may yield so little intrinsic satisfaction—indeed, they may be so distasteful—that no one would voluntarily carry them out on his own if he could possibly avoid doing so. The strength of these two other factors depends, of course, on how equitably both income and work tasks are distributed.

In the conventional treatment of manpower, it is usually assumed that society's needs to have the less intrinsically satisfying tasks performed is met by playing on the desire of some individuals for differential income. Thus it is through the rate of compensation that the conflicting needs of the individual and of the society are supposedly reconciled. While this would lead one to expect the attractiveness of any job and the attendant salary or wage to be negatively correlated with one another, in fact no such relationship is observable in practice. Quite the contrary. The better paying jobs are often the more desirable ones in terms of fringe benefits, prestige, power, and feelings of accomplishment. The mistake of the conventional view here is in overlooking the mediating role of social institutions in determining the supply of human resource inputs.

It is naive to think of the individual as simply offering himself for one of the better jobs in society. Anyone who tries it on his own soon learns that the doors will simply not open for him. He must instead go through a series of preparatory steps that mark off the various career paths. In some cases, the preparatory steps involve attendance at certain types of schools and graduation with certain types of degrees. In other cases, they involve meeting the entry level requirements for employment with some bureaucratic organization or being accepted for membership in a trade union. In every case, however, there is more than one preparatory step, and the intervention of family, friends, schools, supervisors, and other influential persons is likely to prove crucial (Ginzberg, 1976).

The effect of this mediating role played by social institutions is to "wall off" the better jobs in society from all the others. Once an individual has made it to the shelter provided by professional training, internal promotion systems, seniority rules, and trade union agreements (Freedman, 1976) his further participation in the work force—indeed, his further advancement along a career path—depends primarily on noneconomic factors. While a change in employing organizations and even a change in careers may be made in order to take advantage of a better paying job, for the most part any move is likely to be dictated by career concerns such as the desire for more challenging work or by other considerations such as the desire to pursue a certain lifestyle. Even more typically, an individual is likely to find both his career and his income advancing in tandem as a result of the same institutional factors that shelter him from the competition of workers in general. Indeed, wages and salaries are usually set in such a way as to minimize their influence on career decisions. As long as the individual accepts the constraints imposed by the institutional arrangements that insulate his job from market forces, he can count on his income increasing steadily each year in line with the general rise in wages and salaries throughout the economy.

The situation is, of course, quite different outside the core of sheltered jobs. There individuals queued up in lines stretching back to rural hinterlands across the globe compete vigorously among themselves for the limited employment opportunities, hoping for access, even if it must await another generation, to one of the better jobs in society. It is there, among the peripheral workers, that the conventional view of labor markets comes closest to the mark (Morse, 1969; Friedlander,

1972). Even so, one should not exaggerate the importance of the size of the wage payment in determining labor force participation. On the one hand, the need for access to income leaves few with the choice of whether to work or not. While transfer payments provide something of an alternative, they are seldom available to males of prime working age. Illegal activities are another option, but like the resort to public assistance or some other form of transfer payment (Ostow and Dutka, 1975) pecuniary considerations are only one of the factors that influence the choice. For the majority, work is the only source of income. On the other hand, employing organizations can usually count on all the manpower they need of a relatively unskilled sort at the prevailing wage rate. The long lines of individuals in need of a job assure that. Thus it is not so much the size of the wage payment but rather the availability of employment opportunities, both in the sheltered core of the economy and on the periphery, that determines the supply of manpower (Eichner, 1973a, 1976).

In summary, then, the human developmental, or anthropogenic, approach involves a considerably broader view of the role played by the human factor in economic activity than is to be found in the conventional models upon which economists generally rely. This alternative conceptual framework encompasses not just the single dimension of an economic system producing goods and services, but three other dimensions as well, including a quite separate anthropogenic system that supplies the economic system with all its human resource inputs. Within this conceptual framework, human beings are viewed, not just as the means by which more goods and services are produced, but also as the ends that the entire set of social institutions, including the economic, is meant to serve by increasing individual options. Thus employment is important, not just because of the greater output it makes possible, but also, even more critically, because of the effect it has on the well-being of those who are thereby given a meaningful economic role to play. Moreover, the employment obtained represents not so much a contractual arrangement between equals as an affiliation by one party with another. This means that it occurs not at a single moment in time but, instead, as part of a process taking place over time.

Contrast this view of the human factor in economic activity with that reflected in the conventional economic analysis. Both are, to be sure, concerned with one of the two factors determining the total wage bill. But the conventional analysis, with its almost singular concern over the wage rate, seems, from a human developmental perspective, to place the emphasis on the wrong variable. First of all, the wage rate's supposed market-clearing role is greatly exaggerated, if it is of any relevance at all. How else can one explain the excess of workers seeking employment which exists as almost a permanent feature of modern life? Indeed, *The General Theory* should long ago have disposed of that argument. Moreover, because of the institutional manner in which it is determined for most workers, together with the fixed technical relationships which govern most of modern economic activity, the wage rate tells us hardly anything at all about labor's "productivity."[12] The significance of the wage rate lies entirely in the effect it has on the relative distribution of income among wage and salary recipients and in the role it plays in the wage-price inflationary process (Eichner, 1976).

In its preoccupation with questions of resource allocation under equilibrium conditions, the conventional analysis gives short shrift to the critical importance of employment in determining individual and family well-being. It is more than just a matter of being able to earn income—though, in a society in which earned income is the primary determinant of a family's standard of living, that factor is not unimportant. It is rather that an individual's entire sense of personal worth, especially during the adult years, depends on the ability to obtain a prideful place within the economic order. This is reflected in the high correlation between loss of job and various social pathologies such as crime, family breakdown, and mental illness (Brenner, 1973). From a human resources perspective, then, the most pertinent question to ask of any economic system is not whether resources are being optimally allocated—the primary concern of the conventional economic analysis—but rather 1) how much employment is being generated relative to the number of persons seeking it and 2) what determines the access of individuals to those jobs. Each issue has a special import, though for a different reason.

The amount of employment being generated is the single most significant factor in determining the rate at which new skills and competences are being added by the labor force, and thus the single most significant factor in determining the society's long-run potential growth rate. The rate at which employment opportunities are being generated is certainly more critical to the skill acquisition process than all the sums spent on education and other forms of training (Berg, 1970). This is because the supply of and the demand for manpower, rather than being independent of one another as assumed in the conventional analysis, are in fact highly interdependent, the proof of this being the greater growth of skills and competences from on-the-job training when the economy is expanding more rapidly. One essential research task still remaining is to measure more adequately this increase in skills and competences that occurs from economic expansion.

The access to jobs, on the other hand, is the single most significant determinant of what has been termed "social class," and it depends, in turn, on differential access to the intervening social institutions, including the school system, that mediate between employing organizations seeking additional manpower to fill job openings and the individuals seeking, not just temporary employment but rather, life-long careers (Ginzberg, 1976). Here the essential research task still remaining is to map out more completely how those intervening social institutions play their particular role in linking individuals to jobs, and how certain demographic groups are thereby disadvantaged in the process (Jencks, 1979; Canterbery, 1979b).

One can therefore state as follows what, from a human developmental perspective, ought to be the guiding principle of public policy. Employment should be expanded at a maximum rate, with access to jobs minimally dependent on the ascriptive characteristics of those seeking employment. In pursuing this policy, however, the government must be aware of two constraining considerations: 1) the need to avoid sacrificing social productivity for mere employment generation and 2) the need to avoid exacerbating the problem of inflation. The anthropogenic model throws important light even on these two subsidiary problems. In an economy in which human beings are increasingly employed in the manpower-intensive service sector, any effort to increase productivity cannot hope to succeed without the greater understanding of the human factor in economic activity already reflected in the human resources model (Ginzberg, 1976, ch. 16). Moreover, once it is recognized that labor "shortages" are seldom the problem, those seeking a solution to the inflation problem are unlikely to base their policies on the simplistic notion that the source of the difficulty is "excess demand." Indeed, they are unlikely to pursue policies that subvert the goal of generating maximum employment.

Afterword

This essay is reprinted, unchanged, from the *Eastern Economic Journal*, October, 1979. Eli Ginzberg's own view of the same body of material will be found in *The Human Economy* (1976). An effort to apply the anthropogenic approach to the problem of evaluating human resource programs is described in Eichner and Brecher (1979) where the theory itself is elaborated on somewhat more fully.

Notes

1. Although the emergence of the human capital approach is usually associated with Schultz (1961) and Becker (1964), it actually goes back at least to Marshall (1920, Bk. VI, chs. 4–5) and can even be traced to Petty. For the most recent critical survey of human capital theory, see Blaug (1976), while for the history of the concept, see Kiker (1968).

2. Though it is based primarily on the writings of Eli Ginzberg, director and founder of Columbia University's Conservation of Human Resources Project, other members of the Conservation's staff, both in their own writings and as contributors to the internal dialogue within the group, have played a key role in helping to shape this alternative approach.

3. Wachter (1974, pp. 641–42) seems to agree. At the heart of the "neoclassical theory" to which Wachter refers is the marginal productivity theory described by Thurow (1975). (See also Eichner, 1976, ch. 5, 1979c; Cain, 1976, especially p. 1216.)

4. Cf., Cain, 1976, pp. 1226–27. For a more complete discussion of the institutionalists, see Gruchy (1947) and Seligman (1962, ch. 3). It should be noted that Ginzberg was a student of both Wesley Mitchell and John M. Clark.

5. Thus even when economists as broad in their interests as Kenneth Boulding and Alfred Kuhn have attempted to provide an integrated model of the social sciences, they have tended to translate all social processes into exchange relationships. Boulding (1970); Kuhn (1963).

6. See the essay by Boulding in Berg, 1972.

7. This, of course, is the starting point for the fields of personnel management and industrial relations, both of which Ginzberg has contributed to. See Ginzberg and Reilley, 1957; Ginzberg and Berg, 1963; Ginzberg, 1976, Part 4.

8. Even as sophisticated an institutional economist as Commons did not seem to understand that a transaction involving the hiring of workers was a process taking place over time, and not just a single-moment-in-time bargain. Cf. Commons, 1934, pp. 52–93.

9. Morse, 1969; Freedman, 1976; Ginzberg, 1976, ch. 9. Thus the anthropogenic model developed by CHR encompasses as one of its elements the "dual" or segmented labor market thesis and indeed anticipated much of the current discussion of this thesis. (See Wachter, 1974; Cain, 1976; Gordon, 1972; Piore, 1979.)

10. Freedman, 1969; Reubens, 1977. This is why so much emphasis is placed on occupational choice. See Ginzberg et al., 1951; Ginzberg and Herma, 1964.

11. Thus the anthropogenic model encompasses, that is, is consistent with, the labor queue theory put forward by Thurow (1975), of which the screening hypothesis set forth by Blaug (1976) as the alternative to human capital theory stands as a variation.

12. It is this point which provides the linkage between the human resources approach and post-Keynesian theory. See Eichner and Kregel, 1975; Eichner 1976; Appelbaum, 1979.

5

The Demand Curve for Money Further Considered
(Written with, and based on the econometric work of, Leonard Forman and Miles Groves)

The convention in economics is to assume that what is termed the money stock—currency plus checkable deposits—is a variable that is exogenously controlled by the monetary authorities. This assumption makes it possible to assert that a change in one or more economic variables, including the short-term interest rate, influences the "demand" for money. It is on this basis that a demand curve for money is usually specified and, if the study is an empirical one, the parameters of that money demand equation estimated.

Cooley and LeRoy (1981), in a review of the econometric evidence from numerous studies, report they were unable to confirm that the demand for money depends "negatively on a short-term interest rate, representing a proxy for the opportunity cost of holding money. . . ." The parameter estimates vary so widely and depend so critically on what other variables are included as arguments within the function as to raise doubt that a stable demand curve for money actually exists. Indeed, Judd and Scadding (1982), acknowledging this point, have offered an explanation of why the demand curve for money must have shifted over time.

Cooley and LeRoy chose to focus on the econometric issues raised by the disparate results from empirical studies of the demand for money and did not pursue their observation that perhaps the theory itself ought to be reexamined. This essay picks up on the latter point, arguing that the specification of separate supply and demand curves for money is the wrong way to model the American or any other economy with a minimally advanced monetary and financial system. The argument can be summarized as follows:

98

1. The amount of bank reserves, and thus the monetary base, is not the exogenously determined variable assumed in both orthodox Keynesian and monetarist models but instead depends on the level of nominal income. This is because the central bank, in order to maintain the liquidity of the financial system, is forced to purchase government securities in the open market so as to accommodate, at least in part, the need for additional credit as the pace of economic activity quickens. With the amount of unborrowed bank reserves, and thus the monetary base, to a significant extent endogenously determined, it follows that the money supply is, to no less an extent, endogenously determined as well. It is therefore a misspecification to assume that the money stock, or any of its components, is entirely exogenous, subject to the control of the monetary authorities, and then to derive a demand curve for money based on that assumption. In reality, the demand for and supply of ''money'' are interdependent, with no possibility in practice of being able to distinguish between the two.

2. It is the demand for credit rather than the demand for money that is the necessary starting point for analyzing the role played by monetary factors in determining the level of real economic activity. This demand for credit consists of the demand for business loans and the demand for consumer loans; and it can be compared to the lending capacity of the commercial banking system, as measured by total bank deposits (demand and time deposits), to indicate the degree of liquidity pressure. The resulting ratio, L, can then be shown to be the most significant monetary determinant of durable goods purchases, and thus of the level of real economic activity itself—even more important than any long-term interest rate. It is therefore the ratio of bank loans to bank deposits as a measure of liquidity pressure, and thus of disequilibrium within the monetary-financial system, rather than just the amount of bank deposits (which, together with the amount of currency in circulation, is usually identified as the money stock) that influences the level of real economic activity.

These conclusions are based on the empirical evidence obtained in estimating the parameters of a post-Keynesian short-period model of the American economy as an alternative to more conventional Keynesian and monetarist models (Eichner, 1979; Forman and Eichner, 1981; Forman, Groves, and Eichner, 1984), and they are supported by that empirical evidence. Similar results, it should be noted, have been obtained for Great Britain by a second research group using a similar model (Arestis, Driver, and Jones, 1984. See also, theirs and the other contributions to Eichner, forthcoming). In the first section that follows, the evidence that the Federal Reserve Board's open-market operations are, to a significant extent, endogenously determined will be presented. In the second section, there will be an outline of the causal sequence by which a nonaccommodating monetary policy by the Federal Reserve System leads to a change in the level of real economic activity without the stock of money playing any direct role, and again some evidence presented. Finally, a brief comment will be made about the role of the money stock in determining the secular rise in the price level.

* * *

It is usually assumed that a change in the Fed's holdings of government securities will lead to a change, with the same sign attached, in the reserves of the commercial banking system. It was the failure to observe this relationship empirically[1] which led us, in constructing the monetary-financial block of our model, to try to find some other way of representing the effect of the Fed's open market operations on the banking system. The alternative approach finally adopted consists of viewing the Federal Reserve System as an integral part of the overall banking and financial system and only secondarily concerned with achieving certain macroeconomic targets, such as a high growth of real output and price stability.[2]

Within this framework, the relationship between the Fed's open market operations and the reserves of the commercial banking system can be brought out by means of the accounting identity which applies to the Federal Reserve System's sources and uses of funds. The accounting identity is as follows:

$$FGS + Res_B + \text{Other Sources (Assets)}$$
$$= Res_T + Cur$$
$$+ \text{Other Uses (Liabilities)} \tag{1}$$

where FGS is the Fed's holdings of government securities; Res_B is the commercial banking system's borrowed reserves (advances and discounts); Res_T is the commercial banking system's total reserves, and Cur is the amount of currency in circulation, that is, the amount of currency held by the public, Cur_P, plus the amount of currency held by banks as vault cash, Cur_B. The Federal Reserve System's other sources of funds, or assets, consist of 1) acceptances; 2) float; 3) gold stock; 4)

Treasury currency outstanding; and 5) other assets. The Federal Reserve System's other uses of funds, or liabilities, consist of 1) Treasury cash holdings; 2) deposits at the Fed by the Treasury, foreigners, and others; and 3) other liabilities.

Since the monetary base, M_B, is equal to total bank reserves, Res_T, plus currency in circulation, *Cur*, the above identity can be written as follows in first difference form with the change in the monetary base isolated on the left-hand side:

$$\Delta M_B = \Delta FGS + \Delta Res_B + \Delta \text{Other Sources} - \Delta \text{Other Uses} \quad (2)$$

or, with the components of the monetary base delineated,

$$\Delta Res_{NB} + \Delta Res_B + \Delta Cur_P$$
$$= \Delta FGS + \Delta Res_B + \Delta \text{Other}$$
$$\text{Sources} - \Delta \text{Other Uses} \quad (3)$$

where Res_{NB} is the commercial banking system's nonborrowed reserves which, since 1961, include the currency held by banks as vault cash. Subtracting ΔRes_B and ΔCur_P from both sides of equation 3 yields the following:

$$\Delta Res_{NB} = \Delta FGS - \Delta Cur_P + \Delta Fd_A \quad (4)$$

where ΔFd_A, or the net change in the Fed's assets, is the term (ΔOther Sources $- \Delta$Other Uses).

What equation 4 brings out is that a change in the amount of currency held by the public or any of the items included among the Fed's other assets represents a flow of funds either into or out of the Federal Reserve System, depending on the item and the sign attached to it, and that unless the Fed offsets this flow through the purchase or sale of government securities, the nonborrowed reserves of the commercial banking system will, as a result, change. Thus, in the face of a fluctuating public demand for currency, flows of gold into and out of the country (before 1971), variations in the amount of deposits held at the Fed by foreigners and others, changes in the amount of float and fluctuations in the Treasury's cash holdings, the Fed must engage in open market operations just to maintain bank reserves at a given level. This is the neutralizing component of a fully accommodating policy, and it is one reason why it is so difficult in practice to relate the change in bank reserves to open market operations. The other component of such a policy is the accommodating piece itself.

An increase in the demand for credit will, to the extent it is satisfied, lead to an increase in bank deposits (especially demand deposits). This is because banks make loans by simply crediting the borrower's account at the bank with the amount of funds being advanced. The increase in deposits will, however, require that banks maintain larger reserves at the Fed. Thus required reserves, Res_R, will increase and, unless the Fed acts through the purchase of government securities in the open market to provide banks with the necessary additional reserves, banks will find themselves with insufficient reserves to meet their legal requirements. While both the Fed's own discount window and the Federal funds market will provide some temporary relief (along with the system of delayed reserve accounting),[3] the fact is that, unless the Fed provides the additional reserves, the banking system can quickly become illiquid, with banks unable to convert the government securities they hold as secondary reserves into additional legal reserves (or cash) and indeed unable to make any further loans. If a significant portion of the nonfinancial institutions' outstanding debt needs to be rolled over, the inability of the banks to provide additional credit may lead to a rapid fall in the value of assets, as those turned down for loans seek to raise funds instead through the sale of their assets, and a serious financial crisis may then ensue (Minsky, 1982). It is to prevent this type of situation from occurring (or, if it should occur, as in 1969, to prevent it from worsening) that the Fed is forced to accommodate, at least in part, whatever demand for credit may manifest itself.

A fully accommodating change in the Fed's holdings of government securities, ΔFGS_A, can therefore be specified as follows:

$$\Delta FGS_A = \Delta Fd_A + \Delta Cur_P + \Delta Res_R \tag{5}$$

What equation 5 implies is that the Fed's open market operations, as measured by the change in its holdings of government securities, depend on a set of factors that reflect the changing level of economic activity and that the Fed's open market operations are, to this extent, endogenously determined. Empirical support for this proposition can be found by regressing the actual change in the Fed's holdings of government securities, using the quarterly data available for 1953 through 1978, against each of the right-hand-side variables in equation 5. The results are shown in Table 1. For the period as a whole, approxi-

Table 1

Variables Affecting the Federal Reserve Board's Open-Market Operations (as Measured by FGS)

Variables	Interval	1953-1978	1953-1961	1962-1978	1962-1972	1972-1978
FdA	coeff	−.76	−.66	−.77	−.64	−.81
	t ratio	14.84	6.70	12.10	6.35	8.39
Res_R	coeff	.75	.35	.81	.61	.92
	t ratio	6.89	2.79	5.58	4.15	3.88
Cur_P	coeff	1.10	1.42	1.04	.90	1.17
	t ratio	14.00	3.74	8.40	3.65	3.14
Const	coeff	25.37	−24.89	82.12	230.08	−169.91
	t ratio	.35*	.55*	.56*	1.42*	.28*
R^2		.80	.63	.74	.60	.76
D-W		2.95	2.22	3.12	2.22	3.57
Observations		104	36	68	44	28

*Not statistically significant at 5% level of probability.

mately four-fifths of the quarterly change in the Fed's holdings of government securities is accounted for by the three explanatory variables.[4] The evidence, then, is that the Fed's open market operations are, to a considerable extent, endogenously determined.

Thus, only a portion of the total change in the Fed's holdings of government securities—about a fifth— can be considered to be exogenous. This exogenous portion is the difference between the total change in the Fed's holdings of government securities and the change that would be required, based on equation 5, to fully accommodate the current demand for credit. That is,

$$\Delta FGS_D = \Delta FGS_T - (\Delta Fd_A - \Delta Cur_P + \Delta Res_R) \qquad (6)$$

where ΔFGS_D is that portion of the total, or actual, change in the Fed's holdings of government securities, ΔFGS_T, which is not endogenously

determined and which can thus be viewed as being exogenous. Moreover, only a portion of that exogenously determined change in the Fed's
holdings of government securities can be considered to be the result of
a deliberate policy decision. The rest will reflect the Fed's inability to
correctly anticipate the actual change in all the relevant variables, and
thus must be treated as an error factor. That is,

$$\Delta FGS_D = X_{M_1} + Err \tag{7}$$

where X_M is a policy variable reflecting a decision by the Fed either not
to fully accommodate the demand for credit (when its sign is negative)
or to accommodate the demand for credit more than is necessary (when
the sign is positive). Still, the important point is not how much of the
exogenously determined change in the Fed's holdings of government
securities reflects a deliberate policy decision and how much is inad-
vertent.[5] The effect, in either case, will be the same—a change in free
reserves, or the amount of nonborrowed reserves in excess of required
reserves, equal to ΔFGS_D.[6] The important point is rather that most of
the change in the Fed's holdings of government securities during any
given quarter will, as indicated by the regression results shown in
Table 1, be an endogenous response to the changing demand for credit.

If the change in the Fed's holdings of government securities
(through its open market operations) is, to a considerable extent, endogenously determined, it follows that bank reserves, too, are similarly
endogenous. This conclusion, if confirmed by other empirical studies,
has the following implications:

1. Models that assume bank reserves to be entirely exogenous are
misspecified, and any empirical results based on such models are
suspect. The same, of course, is true of models that assume that either
the monetary base or the money stock itself are exogenous since bank
reserves are the putatively exogenous component of those larger aggregates.

2. The demand for "money" (or some other monetary aggregate)
cannot be distinguished empirically from the supply by assuming that
economic factors impact only on the former, and not on the latter.
Again, any empirical results based on such a formulation are suspect.

These implications of the Fed's open market operations, and hence
bank reserves, being to a considerable extent endogenously determined
thus place in a somewhat different light Cooley and LeRoy's report that
they were unable to confirm, after examining the econometric evi-

dence, the existence of a demand curve for money as that function is usually specified. The theory cannot be confirmed because it is most likely incorrect.

The empirical work we have done in estimating the parameters of our model not only casts doubt on the existence of a separate demand curve for money; it also raises the question of whether the money stock—however that aggregate is defined—is the crucial variable linking the Fed's open market operations to a change in the level of real economic activity, such as the conventional LM-IS models would suggest.

* * *

Earlier work on the model had already suggested that the most important monetary-financial determinants of real economic activity, at least over the cycle, were twofold: 1) the degree of liquidity pressure, as measured by the ratio of bank loans to bank deposits; and 2) the cyclical movement of two long-term interest rates, the yield on high-grade corporate bonds, and the mortgage rate (Forman and Eichner, 1981). In constructing the monetary-financial block of our model, it was therefore necessary only to explain what was the process by which these two sets of variables were determined, and what role, if any, the various monetary aggregates, such as the monetary base or M1 and M2, played in the process.

The degree of liquidity pressure, L, is defined in the model as the ratio of bank loans—consumer as well as business loans—to bank deposits. The numerator thus reflects the demand for credit while the denominator measures the lending capacity of the commercial banking system as determined by its deposit inflows. When the former increase relative to the latter, the commercial banking system will become less liquid and thus less capable of providing credit.

The demand for credit over the cycle can, in turn, be explained largely by the cyclical movement in real economic activity, reflecting the working capital needs of business and the consumer durable financing needs of households. The demand for credit would appear to be insensitive to the cyclical movement in interest rates—although the amount of business loans will be affected, on the supply side, by the shift in the loan portfolios of financial institutions caused, among other factors, by a movement of the commercial paper rate relative to the prime rate (Forman, Groves, and Eichner, 1984).

Normally an increase in the demand for credit will lead to a corresponding increase in the deposits of the commercial banking system, leaving the ratio of loans to deposits for the most part unchanged. (Any cyclical movement in economic activity, because of its effect on the cash balances of different sectors, will alter this ratio slightly.) However, the rise in deposits will at the same time lead to an increase in the commercial banking system's required reserves. If the Fed responds by providing additional reserves (that is, if it pursues a fully accommodating policy with both X_{M_1} and Err equal to zero), no further effect will be felt. But if it acts otherwise, two consequences will follow.

The first is that the banks will be forced to sell off a portion of the government securities they hold as secondary reserves, so they can meet the loan commitments they have already made, while they simultaneously act to reduce their future loan commitments. But with the Fed no longer willing to purchase government securities, the banks will be forced to sell to other private parties, and this will have the effect of reducing the amount of deposits within the banking system as a whole. The banks will therefore find themselves under even greater pressure to curtail their lending activity, leaving them with no choice but to ration credit. Certain types of loans may, in fact, then become unobtainable, forcing nonfinancial institutions to cut back on their discretionary spending for lack of financing. This is why the liquidity pressure variable, L, helps explain the cyclical movement in business investment and other types of durable goods purchases independently of any change in interest rates.

The second consequence of the Fed's nonaccommodating policy is that the ratio of free to total reserves, Res_F/Res_T, will decline. The fall in this ratio, together with the simultaneous increase in the degree of liquidity pressure, will lead to a rise in the Federal funds rate as banks try to obtain from other sources the reserves which the Fed refuses to provide (except, grudgingly, through the discount window). The rise in the Federal funds rate will then be followed, with a lag, by an increase in the other short- and long-term interest rates—including, most importantly, the yield on high-grade corporate bonds and the mortgage rate. The cyclical rise in the two long-term interest rates will have a further dampening effect on the growth of certain types of durable goods purchases, especially plant and equipment expenditures by small business firms and residential construction.

The empirical evidence in support of the process, or causal sequence, just outlined whereby a nonaccommodating monetary policy leads to increased liquidity pressure, together with higher long-term interest rates and thence to a cyclical downturn in real economic activity, will be found in the equations that, as now estimated, constitute the monetary-financial block of the model we are constructing (Forman, Groves, and Eichner, 1984). (See also Arestis, Driver, and Jones 1984.) What is noteworthy about this causal sequence, assuming its existence is confirmed by other econometric studies, is that it makes no mention of the money stock, as conventionally defined—the principal determinant of the interest rate in a conventional Keynesian (though not monetarist) model.

The money stock as conventionally defined can nonetheless be derived within the model. With an additional equation to account for the amount of currency held by the public (i.e., nonbanks), the cyclical movements in M1 and M2 can both be determined since demand deposits and time deposits are otherwise explained within the model's monetary-financial block (as the denominator of the liquidity pressure variable). With this additional equation, it is then possible to show that the amount of currency held by the public plus the amount of demand and time deposits (that is, the money stock as conventionally defined) plays no role in determining either the degree of liquidity pressure or the cyclical movement in interest rates. This is because the money stock as conventionally defined is determined concurrently with and largely by the same factors as the degree of liquidity pressure—with the latter variable, and not the money stock, serving as the critical link in the causal sequence.

Some evidence in support of this last proposition will be found in the regression results reported in Table 2. While the degree of liquidity pressure, L, and the ratio of free to total bank reserves, Res_F/Res_T, are each significantly correlated with the cyclical movement in the Federal funds rate (equations 1 and 2), the same is not true for either the cyclical movement of total bank deposits, Dep, the cyclical movement of just demand deposits alone, DD, or the cyclical movement of the money stock as conventionally defined, M_1 (equations 3, 4, and 5).[7] It would therefore appear that while the short-term interest rate is affected by the degree of liquidity pressure, it does not depend on the variable which, in the conventional Keynesian models, is assumed to be its principal determinant; that is, it does not appear to depend on any measure of the "money stock." Moreover, while the degree of liquidity pressure and the ratio of free to total reserves together provide a fairly satisfactory explanation for the cyclical movement in the Federal

Table 2

Variables Affecting the Federal Funds Rate (1960-1978)

	Constant	L	F/T	DepΔ	DD	M_1	R^2
1	−.25 (1.41)	39.795 (5.30)					.265
2	−.51 (3.96)		−66.02 (11.38)				.63
3	.01 (.049)			−.07 (1.46)			.01
4	.04 (.21)				−.148 (2.17)		.047
5	.0059 (.029)					−.125 (1.65)	.022
6	−.63 (6.49)	31.16 (7.77)	−60.75 (13.89)				.7956
7	−.45 (4.35)		−72.54 (15.25)			−.249 (6.49)	.763
8	−.312 (1.677)	44.84 (5.069)				.0837 (1.075)	.2669
9	−.561 (6.037)	22.467 (4.835)	−65.69 (−14.94)			−.13 (3.209)	.8187

Data Source: DRI Macro Data Base.
Note: The numbers in parentheses are the *t* ratios.

funds rate (equation 6), replacing either of those two variables with the money stock, M1, or even including the latter as an additional argument does little to improve the equation's explanatory power (equations 7, 8, and 9).[8]

Thus it is possible to eliminate the money stock as conventionally defined from macroeconomic analysis altogether without any loss of explanatory power. The way in which monetary factors influence the level of real economic activity can still be explained in a way that is consistent with the empirical evidence. One need only take into account the demand for credit relative to the lending capacity of the commercial banking system. It is the demand for credit that, upon being satisfied by the joint action of the banks and the Fed—the former in actually making the loans and the latter in providing the banks with the required additional reserves—will lead to an increase in bank deposits (and thus to an increase in the money stock as conventionally defined while leaving the ratio of bank loans to bank deposits unchanged). And it is the demand for credit that, upon not being fully accommodated by the Fed (thus creating a disequilibrium condition within the monetary-financial system), will lead to an increase in the ratio of bank loans to bank deposits (while slowing the growth of the money stock as conventionally defined). The resulting rise in the liquidity pressure variable, L, will not only force banks to ration credit, but it will also, together with the parallel rise in the ratio of free to total reserves, lead to higher short- and long-term interest rates.

One can come closer to bringing out what it is that the focus on the money stock, as conventionally defined, is meant to illuminate—namely, the availability of the means of payment—by formulating the macroeconomic model within a flow of funds framework as we have done (see Eichner, 1979a). In this way it becomes clear that the availability of what serves as the means of payment by each type of nonfinancial institution—business firms, households, nonprofit organizations, governmental units, and the rest-of-the-world—depends first and foremost on its net cash inflow, that is, on its total revenue or income during the period less any cash outlays; and then secondarily on its access to credit, whether a loan has actually been obtained or whether the funds are simply available if needed through a line of bank credit. Within this framework, the focus is on the flow of funds throughout the economy as a whole without any effort to identify any particular stock of monetary assets as the effective constraint on the amount of those funds. The growth in the flow of funds depends solely on the rate at which the commercial banking system is willing to provide credit, or additional funds, supported by the willingness of the central bank to provide the necessary increase in bank reserves. The actual amount of bank deposits at any given point in time (along with the amount of currency, or Federal reserve notes, the public wishes to hold) is of little consequence. Thus the money stock, as conventionally defined, can for all practical purposes be ignored, greatly simplifying the task of constructing an empirically valid macroeconomic model.

It is not just that no reference need be made to the money stock or any of the other monetary aggregates in explaining the level of real economic activity. Omitting the money stock from the analysis avoids confusing a change in bank deposits alone (or bank deposits plus currency in circulation) with a change in bank deposits *relative* to bank loans as the variable through which the Fed's open market operations affect both the rest of the monetary-financial sector and the level of real economic activity. It is the latter variable, interpreted as measuring the degree of liquidity pressure, and not one of the monetary aggregates (incorporating bank deposits) that serves as the causal link.

Eliminating the money stock from the model has the further advantage that it avoids any need to distinguish the "demand" for money from its supply. It also renders moot the question of how the money stock is to be defined, thus avoiding another issue that has hampered empirical research. Indeed, the only disadvantage is that it would mean abandoning the LM-IS framework which has dominated macroeconomics ever since the Hicks-Hansen interpretation of *The General Theory* became the prevailing one. But then that might not be such a disadvantage (cf., Eichner, 1977).

* * *

Monetarists will, of course, object that eliminating the money stock from the macro model will leave the secular rise in the price level unexplained. While a more complete response to this objection must wait until we have finished estimating the pricing block in our model, still the evidence from other econometric studies (including the empirical work that has been carried out in connection with the best known Keynesian models) would suggest that the secular rate of inflation can be better explained by the growth of money wages in excess of labor productivity, together with other factors affecting the unit costs of production, than by the growth of the money stock. Indeed, the empirical work which has already been done in connection with our own model would suggest that, if an attempt is made to control the growth of the money stock in the mistaken view that it (or the monetary base) is an exogenously determined policy variable, the result will be not so much a slowdown in the rate of inflation (except to the extent the Phillips curve applies) as a decline in the level of real economic activity. From this perspective, the nonaccommodating policy on the part of the Fed which monetarists advocate is simply another means of trying to limit the growth of money wages, in this case through a higher unemployment rate and depressed commodity markets rather than some other, less self-destructive form of incomes policy.

Afterword

This essay has not previously been published. It is one of several papers to emerge from the econometric modeling project of the Center for Economic and Anthropogenic Research (CEAR), with Leonard Forman, assisted by Miles Groves, actually responsible for the empirical results on which the essay is based. Indeed, it is Forman who devised the way of measuring the degree of liquidity pressure which is used in the model. (See Eichner, 1979a; Forman and Eichner, 1981; Forman, Groves, and Eichner, 1983, 1984, as well as essay seven below for descriptions of the model.) The extent to which the money stock is an exogenously controlled policy variable is a question explored more fully in the essays by various authors, including Paul Davidson and Basil Moore, which have been brought together in Eichner, forthcoming. In this same connection, see also Davidson, 1972; Minksy, 1982; Kaldor, 1983; and Moore, 1979, 1983, forthcoming.

Notes

1. No matter what additional variables were included in the estimating equation, or how the equation was specified (e.g., first differences, growth rates, etc.), it proved impossible to obtain an R^2 greater than zero when regressing the change in the commercial banking system's nonborrowed reserves against the change in the Federal Reserve System's holdings of government securities, using the quarterly data available for the period between 1952 and 1978.

2. This alternative approach can be traced back to Guttentag, 1966; Hendershott, 1968; and Lombra and Torto, 1973. Indeed, it was the Lombra and Torto article that first enabled us to understand the lack of direct correlation between the Fed's open market operations and bank reserves (see fn. 1 above). See also Lombra (1981) and Lombra and Kaufman (1982), as well as Lombra's and Kaufman's contribution in Eichner, forthcoming, for the most recent work along these same lines.

3. Until recently, under the system of delayed reserve accounting, commercial banks had two weeks after the close of the period to obtain any additional reserves they needed to meet their legal requirements. Under the changes recently announced, they will need to maintain reserves equal to some average of their liabilities over a preceding two-week period.

4. Only certain of the items from the Fed's balance sheet were found to be correlated with the change in its holdings of government securities. These are 1) the amount of float, 2) the gold stock (in the earlier part of the period covered, before gold sales were terminated), 3) Treasury currency outstanding, and 4) Treasury deposits at the Fed. As for the other six items, see below, fn. 5.

5. An effort has been made to identify the size of the error factor by equating it with any change in the other six items from the Fed's balance sheet that were found not to be predictors of a change in the Fed's holdings of government securities (see above, fn. 4). This approach, however, understates the error factor since it makes no allowance for the possibility that the Fed incorrectly anticipated a change in the other variables included in equation 5. For a more complete discussion, see Forman, Groves, and Eichner, 1983 (reprinted in Eichner, forthcoming).

6. Again, this is explained more fully in Forman, Groves, and Eichner, 1983.

7. Except for the ratio of free to total reserves, the variables have all been detrended by calculating, for each quarterly observation, the deviation from some central tendency, whether it be the exponential growth rate as in the case of *Dep*, *DD*, and M_1, or the linear growth trend as in the case of *L* and the Federal funds rate itself. For a further discussion of this technique for minimizing the effect of any serial correlation, see Forman and Eichner, 1981.

8. While it might appear that the explanatory power of equation 6 could be in-

creased by adding M_1 as an additional independent variable (see equation 9), the slight increase in the value of the R^2 statistic from 0.80 to 0.82 is only because of the collinearity between M_1 and L and between M_1 and Res_F/Res_T. The collinearity is evident from the way the coefficients change when M_1 is added to equation 6 and by the correlation coefficient of 0.53 which has been calculated for L and M_1 (compared with a correlation coefficient of −0.16 for L and Res_F/Res_T and a correlation coefficient of −0.21 for Res_F/Res_T and M_1). M_1 would thus appear to have no independent explanatory power of its own (see equation 5). The statistically significant relationship which is often observed between M_1 and various short-term interest rates, such as the Federal funds rate, instead reflects the degree of liquidity pressure within the commercial banking system, L, and the ratio of free to total reserves, Res_F/Res_T, with which M_1 is correlated. L, $Res_{,F}/Res_T$ and M_1 all vary together over time because all three depend on how accommodating is the Fed's open-market operations. However, while the degree of liquidity pressure and the ratio of free to total reserves each exert an independent influence on the Federal funds rate, the same is not true of M_1. It appears to have explanatory power only because it is so highly collinear with L. What has just been said about replacing either L or Res_F/Res_T with M_1 or adding the latter explanatory variable to equation 6 applies, with only slight modification, if instead one replaces or supplements those variables with Dep or DD.

6
Stagflation:
Explaining the Inexplicable

Introduction

While most economists remain puzzled by the simultaneous occurrence
of unemployment and inflation, the phenomenon is readily explained,
and an appropriate policy response suggested, by a body of economic
theory which has only recently emerged to challenge the orthodox
Keynesian and monetarist models. The new analytical framework is
termed "post-Keynesian," both to differentiate it from the "neoclassical synthesis" which dominates the teaching of economics in the United States and to indicate that it represents a logical extension of Keynes'
own break with orthodox thinking. The new approach has its origins in
works published two decades ago, but it is only now coming to the
attention of American economists.

This essay consists of three parts. The first section describes the
salient features of a post-Keynesian approach, contrasting that approach with the orthodox neoclassical type of analysis. The second
section explains how the basic propositions of post-Keynesian theory
lead to a quite different understanding of stagflation and suggest a quite
different policy response from those to which the orthodox theory gives
rise. The third and final section discusses both the policy and intellectual implications of a post-Keynesian approach. While the principal
policy implication is that some form of incomes policy needs to be
added to the existing fiscal and monetary instruments for regulating the
pace of aggregate economic activity, it will be pointed out that such a
policy cannot be implemented in an institutional vacuum but must
instead follow from other changes to be made in the way economic
policy is determined. Among those changes are the following:

1. Better integration of the private interest groups that will be affected by any incomes policy into the process of economic decision making.

2. Better coordination of policy within government itself.

3. Better linking of policymaking bodies to technical secretariats with data collection and analytical capabilities.

The intellectual implication of the foregoing is that the post-Keynesian approach needs to be taken more seriously than it has to date by American economists, both within government and without. In this way, perhaps the country can recover from the present intellectual bankruptcy of economic policy.

I. The nature of post-Keynesian theory

Post-Keynesian theory has emerged as a synthesis of three unorthodox visions, each the contribution of a different individual. There is, first, John Maynard Keynes' view of the economy as a system with an integrity of its own, the behavior at the macro level being more than just an extrapolation of the behavior observed at the micro level.[1] There is, in addition, Roy Harrod's perception of the economy as a system in continuous motion, proceeding along an expansion path like a train hurtling between cities, and not simply coming to rest at some equilibrium stop.[2] Finally, there is Michal Kalecki's insight that the capital accumulation, or expansion, process is inextricably linked to how income is distributed and prices set.[3]

It was Joan Robinson in *The Accumulation of Capital* (1956) who first synthesized these three disparate visions in a single work of originality which marks the beginning of a distinctly separate post-Keynesian theory[4]—one that could effectively challenge the neoclassical synthesis being developed contemporaneously in Cambridge, Massachusetts.[5] If the neoclassical synthesis can be said to treat Keynes' arguments as a minor gloss on Walras and other neoclassical theorists, then post-Keynesian theory must be described as marrying Keynes with Harrod and Kalecki. The neoclassical synthesis and post-Keynesian theory represent the only comprehensive conceptual framework (aside from the Marxian one) for understanding how the American economy works. It is the neoclassical synthesis which has come to dominate in the post–World War II period not only the teaching of economics in the United States but also the formulation of public policy. To bring out the critical differences between these alternative paradigms, it is useful to explain why Keynes has been married to Harrod and Kalecki in the post-Keynesian approach rather than his arguments being treated as simply a minor gloss on Walras.

An understanding of the role played by effective demand, especially as influenced by any excess of public spending over tax revenues, has been the main intellectual factor in the ability of Western governments, including that of the United States, to avoid the massive and prolonged economic slumps that punctuated the pre–World War II period. This understanding derives primarily from Keynes' 1936 classic, *The General Theory of Employment, Interest and Money*. To the extent that large-scale unemployment has been prevented, Keynes' purpose in writing *The General Theory* has been largely achieved and the short-term but large-scale unemployment which haunted the 1930s generation of economists and public officials has been put to rest. Nonetheless, as the basis for formulating policy once the specter of large-scale unemployment was banished, the model developed by Keynes has a number of shortcomings. It was Harrod who first pointed out the most serious of these.

A. The shift to dynamic analysis

In *The General Theory* it is business investment that plays the critical role in determining the level of effective aggregate demand. (Ironically, in the work that has been used largely to argue the need for increased public spending, government expenditures figure hardly at all in the formal analysis.) What Harrod pointed out—along with American economist Evsey Domar—is that the influence of business investment is not limited just to increasing aggregate demand in the immediate run. Once the investment projects currently being funded have been carried through to completion, aggregate supply in the form of plant capacity will also be increased (Harrod, 1939, 1948; Domar, 1946, 1947, 1957). This latter effect is overlooked in the sort of static model on which Keynes based his arguments and which, even today, underlies most macroeconomic analysis.

Harrod's point was to show that increasing aggregate demand by stimulating business investment would not necessarily solve the problem of persistent unemployment. Although the problem might be temporarily ameliorated by the increase in aggregate demand, once the new capacity that the investment made possible were to come on line, it might well lead to a situation in which aggregate supply capacity exceeded aggregate demand, thereby discouraging further investment and producing a slump in business activity which would, in turn, cause unemployment to rise. Harrod, along with Domar, was able to indicate the conditions that would have to be met if the increase in aggregate supply from business investment was not either to overtake or, alternatively, fall short of the increase in aggregate demand produced by the same investment. These conditions for assuring that aggregate demand and aggregate supply grow apace are given by the well-known Harrod-Domar formula,[6] and they include, among others, that the propensity to save, the marginal social return on investment, and, most important of all, the rate of growth of investment all remain constant over time. For Harrod, the significance of the formula was in suggesting how unlikely it was that those conditions could actually be satisfied, and thus how unlikely it was that cycles in business activity could be avoided.

More important than the specific point Harrod tried to make, however, was the new mode of dynamic analysis he introduced. To take into account the more enduring impact of business investment on supply capacity, and not just the immediate effect on aggregate demand, it was necessary to show how the economy's expansion path over time was likely to be affected. This way of setting up the model was in sharp contrast not only to the traditional approach in economics but also to that followed by Keynes in *The General Theory*, where the focus is on the new equilibrium position at which the economy will come to rest. The difference between the two modes of analysis can best be brought out by indicating what happens when the respective models to which they give rise are left undisturbed. Whereas in the usual static model the economy settles down to a fixed level of activity, in the type of dynamic model upon which post-Keynesian theory is based the economy continues to expand indefinitely at a constant rate. This is the steady-state expansion rate given by the Harrod-Domar formula and which Harrod labeled the "warranted growth rate."

B. Long period and short period analysis

Robinson, in her writings, has made this dynamic mode of analysis more applicable to actual historical phenomena by distinguishing the short period from the long period (Robinson, 1956, Books 2 and 3; 1962b). It is only from the latter perspective, when all the factors that cause cyclical movements in the economy can be ignored through one device or another, that the Harrod-Domar formula applies. The warranted growth rate given by the Harrod-Domar formula is a theoretical construct useful only for interpreting long-term trends in the economy.

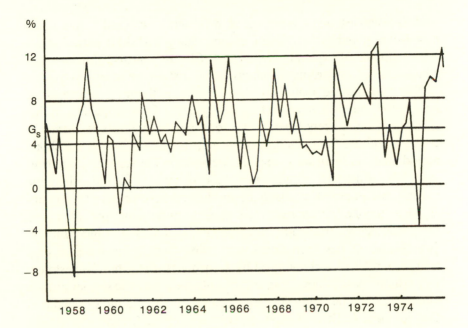

Exhibit 1

Annual growth rates for GMP, quarterly, 1955-78.

Note: GMP is the Gross Marketed Product. It is the GNP less the compensation of government employees and it is roughly equal to GPD, gross private product. G_s is the regular growth rate or trend line and for 1952–76 is roughly equal to 5.13%.

To understand the actual historical course the economy takes, a course marked by pronounced cyclical movements, it is necessary to complement the long-period analysis with a short-period analysis. The two need to be carried out conjointly—the short-period analysis because it allows for deviations from the warranted growth rate and the long-period analysis because those deviations can be explained only in reference to what they are deviations from.

Take the most recent performance of the American economy, as shown in Exhibit 1. Both the secular trend (the secular growth rate, $G_s = 5.11$ percent) and the fluctuations around that trend line can be clearly discerned. (The average deviation from the trend for the period covered by the chart was 3.03 percent, or three-fifths as great as the secular trend.) The same general pattern holds, whether one examines some earlier period in American history or the historical data from another advanced market economy. This record of continuous, though uneven, expansion is the most important economic fact of the past several centuries, and it is but one of the several "stylized" facts which post-Keynesian theory, with its combined long- and short-period analysis, is capable of explaining (Kaldor, 1961). In contrast, this fact runs counter to the underlying assumptions of a static neoclassical model.

The short-period analysis of post-Keynesian theory is linked to the long-period analysis in a number of ways. The most important is that both the secular trend, which the long-period analysis is meant to explain, and the fluctuations around that trend line, which the short-period analysis is meant to explain, depend on the same key determinant. This is the rate of investment. Indeed, investment plays the same critical role in post-Keynesian theory that relative prices play in neoclassical theory. An increase in business investment, provided it is accompanied by certain other adjustments, will lead to a higher secular growth rate. It has been found that, aside from some measure of a country's relative technological backwardness, the rate of investment is the single most important factor in explaining why the secular growth rate differs among the major Organization for Economic Cooperation Development (OECD) nations (Cornwall, 1977, Chapter 8). At the same time, the increase in investment, unless it can be maintained at a constant rate—along with the growth in the other components of "discretionary spending"—will set in motion the factors that produce cyclical movements in the economy. From a post-Keynesian perspective, then, both the secular trend and the fluctuations around the trend can be explained within the context of the same accumulation process. As long as the accumulation process proceeds at a steady pace, the expansion will be free of fluctuations—with the rate of expansion depending on the rate of investment. But once the growth rates start to vary, the economy can be expected to move off its steady-state expansion path, as given by the Harrod-Domar formula, and trace out the cyclical pattern which the historical data like those charted in Exhibit 1 reveal.

In simple models, the emphasis is usually on business investment as the key factor in explaining any cyclical movements; the implicit question is, how can a constant growth in investment be maintained. The changes that have occurred in advanced market economies like that of the United States during the twentieth century, however, require that other types of discretionary spending also be taken into account, with an understanding of the more limited role they play. On the one hand, consumer spending on durable goods, including housing, and the government's purchase of goods and services have the same multiplier effect as business investment, thereby serving to stimulate aggregate demand. On the other hand, they have no capacity-augmenting effect, thereby leaving aggregate supply unchanged. This suggests that maintaining the delicate balance whereby aggregate demand and aggregate supply grow apace is even more difficult than Harrod initially pointed out, and that an economic policy focused exclusively on manipulating aggregate demand through fiscal and monetary policies may itself exacerbate the problem of keeping the economy on a steady growth path.

C. The distributional issues

If it is necessary to combine Harrod's vision with Keynes' to develop a clear conception of an economic system expanding over time, it is necessary to add Kalecki's vision as well to see the interrelationship between the investment, or accumulation, which makes the expansion possible and the associated phenomena of distribution and pricing. Kalecki's point was that one needs to keep an eye on the division of the national income between wage and nonwage shares even as one carries through a Keynesian-type analysis with its division of the national product between consumption and investment goods. What can be shown, relying on the simplest of models, is that the higher the rate of investment, and thus the more rapid the rate of economic expansion, the lower will be the share of the national product, in the form of consumption goods, going to workers. This is because resources need to be diverted from the consumption stream and, with their purchase financed from the nonwage, or profits, share, used instead to expand productive capacity. The economy can be placed on a higher growth path only if the real wage is lowered; and there is thus an inverse relationship between the rate of expansion and the laboring force's share of the national income (Kalecki, 1939; Feiwel, 1975, Chapter 3).

The Polish émigré reached this conclusion on the simplifying assumptions that (a) there are no savings out of the wages paid to workers; and (b) all the profits received by other groups in society are used to purchase investment, and not consumption, goods. Other writers have shown that, although it needs to be elaborated on somewhat, Kalecki's basic point still holds even after his simplifying assumptions are relaxed.[7] Any use of nonwage income for purposes other than expanding productive capacity will, other things being equal, depress the real wage still further. As for any savings by workers, while these will certainly increase the workers' share of the national income—the profits, or interest, earned being added to their wage income—it will not alter the division of the national income between wage and non-wage shares. These further results have led post-Keynesian economists to identify the following variables (aside from the rate of technical progress) as the key factors determining the distribution of income: 1) the rate of investment; and 2) the marginal propensity to consume out of profits or, more precisely, the portion of nonwage income used for purposes other than to finance the expansion of productive capacity. The argument, it turns out, applies both to the long period and to the short.

The argument can also be further expanded to take into account not only the government's use of resources but also any shifts in the international trading relationships among countries, such as those produced by the hike in 1973 of Organization of Petroleum Exporting Countries (OPEC) oil prices. The government's purchase of goods and services for national defense and other noneconomic purposes is analogous to consumption out of nonwage income. These purchases lower the real wage without adding to the economy's productive capacity (and thereby without offering the hope of a higher real wage in the future). The same is true when, because of an increase in the price of oil and other natural resources imported from other countries, the physical quantity of goods exported, and thus the portion of the national product unavailable for domestic consumption, has to be increased. Government expenditures on infrastructure, e.g., transportation, and even on human resource development, fall in a somewhat different category, and their effect, as forms of social investment, on the real wage over time cannot be determined simply on the basis of an aggregate analysis.[8]

D. The role of money

What has been said so far about post-Keynesian theory would still hold even if, as is often argued, money were simply a veil behind which the allocation of real resources takes place. It is, of course, necessary to peer behind the veil and focus instead on the real resources which have been given a monetary value. And this is certainly what post-Keynesian theory attempts to do—though with an emphasis on how those real resources are expanded over time and not simply allocated. From a post-Keynesian perspective, however, money is more than just a veil. It is an important institutional feature of an advanced market economy like that of the United States, and it gives rise, not only to the important distinction between real and monetary flows but also to the possible divergence of investment and savings based on that distinction. Here, again, the original Keynesian vision needs an addendum.

Keynes, in his short-period analysis, was concerned only with the new equilibrium position that would be reached when investment and savings were again in balance. It was an equilibrium position determined by the multiplier effect of the new level of business investment and whatever other changes in discretionary spending had occurred. But in the short periods of actual historical experience, investment and savings never actually come into balance. This can be seen by examining the Federal Reserve Board's Flow of Funds Accounts and comparing the change over time in each nonfinancial sector's net cash inflow with its outlays on durable goods.[9] This relative balance between investment and savings—or between discretionary expenditures and discretionary funds—pushes the economy in two quite different directions.

On the one hand, to the extent that the outlays on durable goods in any one sector of the economy exceed that sector's cash inflow, additional purchasing power is injected into the income stream and the pace of economic activity will, as a result of that increase in purchasing power, be quickened. This can be termed the "cash-flow feedback effect," and it is the equivalent of what happens when, in a simple Keynesian model, investment is greater than savings. The cash-flow feedback effect also works in reverse so that when outlays on durable goods fall short of a sector's cash inflow, that is, when investment is less than savings, the rate of economic expansion is dampened.[10]

But any imbalance between a sector's outlays and its cash inflow will also have a second financial impact. This is the other side of the story. While it is usually assumed that any cash deficit in one sector will necessarily have to be offset by a surplus in other sectors so that, overall, the deficit is equal to zero, this need not be the case when an economy with a well-developed financial sector is in disequilibrium. With outlays exceeding cash inflow, the resulting deficit can be financed by loans of one sort or another.

Normally, the banking system steps in and, once assured as to the borrower's credit worthiness, provides the required additional liquidity with the result that, however defined, the stock of "money" in circulation shows an increase. Thus one finds a strong correlation between the size of the deficit in the various sectors of the economy—in the business and household sectors as well as in the government sector—and the money supply. The usual accommodating role of the banking system, however, can be reversed. Sometimes it is because of a combined weakness in the economy and in the banking system. Lending institutions may lack the reserves to provide additional loans when a general decline in sales and other revenues has forced business firms to seek credit, and the cutbacks in spending which must then be made, together with the failure to make payments on the existing debt, may well bring the entire financial structure tumbling down, as in the money panics of the past (Minsky, 1978). More typically, however, and this was especially the case after 1951, the accommodating policies of the banking system are likely to be reversed by the actions of the Federal Reserve Board. In that event, business firms, households, and even state and local governments may be forced to cut back on their spending, either because interest rates are deemed to be too high or those spending units simply cannot arrange the necessary financing. This serves to dampen the rate of economic expansion, just as a "looser" monetary policy, by encouraging greater reliance on credit, serves to stimulate the economy.

The likely divergence between "investment" and "savings" whenever the economy is in disequilibrium, together with the normal response of the financial sector, is not the only distinguishing feature of a monetarized economy. The existence of money prices, indicating the amount of purchasing power that must be surrendered in exchange for real resources, is another such feature. These "money" prices are different from the "shadow" prices of neoclassical theory which serve only as a measure of relative scarcity. Integral to Kalecki's vision is the recognition that money prices are linked to the process by which accumulation takes place and the resulting growth of real income is distributed between wage and nonwage recipients.

E. Business savings and profit margins

One of the underlying premises of neoclassical theory which Keynes chose not to jettison is that household savings are the primary source of the funds used to finance business investment. His argument did not hinge on that point, and in the case of the British economy in Keynes' time—with the family-controlled type of enterprise still dominant—it was not so easy to see how critical the distinction was between household savings and business savings. Kalecki, developing the same model from a different philosophical tradition and from a different national background, perceived the matter in a different light. He realized that business profits are the major source of the funds used to finance investment—an observation now confirmed by empirical evidence (Anderson, 1964; Bosworth, 1971; Eichner, 1976)—and, except for the costs of producing the goods being sold, nothing is more important in determining the level of those business profits than the prices business firms are able to charge. It is through changes in the price level that real wages can be held down and the amount of resources devoted to current consumption limited so that capital accumulation can take place according to business investment plans. Thus the prices established by business firms play a key role in the growth and distribution process. In particular, they are the means by which the nominal claims against total output, as represented by money income, are deflated to make them compatible with the available real resources (Kalecki, 1954; Feiwel, 1975).

Firms need not be monopolistic for the prices they set to play this key role. They need not even be price setters, although Kalecki, like post-Keynesian economists after him, recognized that firms in the economy's industrial sector are more likely to be price setters than the price takers postulated in neoclassical theory. All that is necessary is that, through some combination of market power and current levels of demand, firms be able to establish the margins above cost that will bring them sufficient net cash inflow, or savings, to finance their planned investment while at the same time pushing down real wages to the level needed to free the necessary real resources. Even if all the required funds cannot be generated internally, as long as the banking system is willing to extend credit the results will be the same: Business firms will be able to obtain the real resources they need to carry out their investment plans. And if, by some chance, there should be an insufficient amount of those resources to satisfy both consumption and investment demands, then the ability of business firms to raise their prices to keep pace with the rise in costs, including that of labor, will assure that it is not the investment demands that go unmet (Steindl, 1952; Eichner, 1976; Kenyon, 1978).

The margins that firms are able to establish are what determine the rate at which business savings will be generated relative to the growth of sales. How much net cash inflow will actually be realized once a particular margin has been established depends on the state of the economy, in particular, on the level of aggregate demand, which itself depends on the rate of business investment and other forms of discretionary spending. It is for this reason that post-Keynesian economists argue that it is not savings that limit or determine investment, as neoclassical theory suggests, but rather the reverse (Kregel, 1971). The margins above cost will, of course, vary from industry to industry, depending on what barriers to entry and other limitations on competition exist (Bain, 1956; Sylos-Labini, 1962; Eichner, 1976). But the relative size of the margins is less important than the fact that all firms depend on margins of some sort—to survive if not to flourish and expand. It is these margins that, if they can be maintained, provide the funds needed to finance capital expansion internally at the same time they establish the set of prices that will deflate the nominal claims against real output to bring them into line with the available real resources.

F. The microfoundations

Thus the microfoundations of post-Keynesian theory derive from Kalecki's vision. These microfoundations, unlike the core of neoclassical theory, do not have to exclude from the analysis by assumption the most important economic institution to emerge over the past century. This is the large corporation, or megacorp, that has grown to become the multi-product, transnational conglomerate that, along with the other giants in its class, dominates the world economy. It is the megacorp that, because of its strong market position, has been able to maintain the margins needed to assure high rates of business savings and thereby to generate the funds needed to finance high rates of investment. Indeed, over the past century, the megacorp has been the economy's primary instrument of capital accumulation (Eichner, 1976).

Nor does post-Keynesian theory need to exclude by assumption, or treat as an aberration, the industrial trade union which emerged in the megacorp's wake and which now serves as the laboring force's countervailing weight in the bargaining over relative income shares. Both the industrial trade union and the megacorp are easily encompassed within a post-Keynesian framework. If this is not apparent from what has already been said, it will become clear when, in the following section, the problem of stagflation is examined from a post-Keynesian perspective.

II. The interpretation of stagflation

To understand the forces that have led to the current problem of stagflation, it is necessary to begin with the technical progress which underlies the dramatic improvement in the standard of living over the past several centuries. This technical progress manifests itself economically in the secular or long-term rise in output per worker. Without this rise in output per worker, there would be no way to improve the standard of living for any group in society except at the expense of some other group. Economists still lack a firm grasp of the factors behind this phenomenon. While it is clear that the technical progress depends, ultimately, on the growth of technical knowledge, the process whereby the one is transformed into the other is only imperfectly understood. The one thing that can be said with some confidence is that, with an adequate stock of knowledge available to be exploited, the rate of technical progress, as measured by rising output per worker, depends on the rate of capital accumulation. With whatever new plant and equipment is being added to the existing stock embodying the latest technological advances, output per worker can be expected to increase as investment proceeds apace—provided the demand for the increased output exists (Robinson, 1956, 1962b; Eichner, 1976).

A. Distribution of the benefits from technical progress

While an essential part of the economic problem facing any society is how to organize production to maximize technical progress, a no less essential part of the problem is how to arrange the distribution of the benefits from that technical progress. The conventional solution has been to rely on market mechanisms, with falling prices the key to assuring the widest possible dissemination of any benefits from technical progress. The emergence of the megacorp, however, has effectively closed that option. Businessmen learned from their experiences during the depression decade of the 1870s that falling prices were likely to reduce their profit margins to the point where, because of the inability to replace worn out plant and equipment, whatever capital had been invested in their firms would eventually be expropriated. Rather than allow this to happen, businessmen took the series of steps that marked the merger and consolidation movement at the turn of the century. The result was to create the type of oligopolistic enterprise, the megacorp, which today dominates the industrial sector of the American economy and which, acting in concert with its major rivals, is able to maintain a significant margin above costs, even in the face of sharp contractions in demand (Eichner, 1969; Chandler, 1977).

The shift to an oligopolistic industrial structure, already apparent in the United States by the end of World War I, has largely achieved the purpose of protecting profit margins from falling prices. But, as the experience over the next decade demonstrated, merely preventing prices from falling was not sufficient to assure continuous economic expansion. With technical progress leading to a rapid increase in output per worker but with no mechanism available for assuring that real wages would rise to keep pace—through higher money wages if not through falling prices—the economy found itself on an unsustainable growth path. Without a secular rise in real wages, consumer purchasing power could not be maintained. The investment boom of the early 1920s ended, choked off by the failure of consumer purchasing power to expand broadly, while the high rates of cash inflow from the margins that megacorps were nonetheless able to maintain simply fueled the speculative excesses of the decade's second half (Soule, 1947; Galbraith, 1955).

This defect in the operative distributional mechanism of the American economy has now been partially remedied by the collective bargaining power of industrial trade unions. First nurtured during the 1930s but achieving social acceptability only in the crucible of war, like the megacorp itself, industrial trade unions today serve as the principal mechanism whereby real wages are able to keep pace, through higher money wages, with the growth in output per worker which technical progress makes possible. The trade union movement is able to play this role because of a negotiating stance which demands that the groups it represents receive their "historical share" of the benefits from technical progress. This negotiating stance, backed by their collective bargaining power, enables industrial trade unions to insure that one of the essential conditions for steady-state expansion in the long period is realized. The condition is that the growth of real wages over time be roughly equal to the growth of output per worker. With the market power of the megacorp preventing real wages from rising as a result of falling prices, the industrial trade union sees to it that real wages rise through higher money wages.

B. The role of trade unions

Still—and this is the important lesson to be learned from the post-World

War II experience—the power of the trade union movement is an imperfect mechanism for pushing up real wages to keep them in line with the growth of output per worker. Not surprisingly, in exercising their collective bargaining power, industrial trade unions tend to err in favor of the groups they represent, with the result that money wages are apt to rise more rapidly than output per worker. This, in turn, leads to an increase in the unit cost of production and, with megacorps acting to maintain their profit margins, to an increase in industrial prices. Just as money wages need to keep pace with the growth of output per worker, not falling short of that mark if the steady-state rate of expansion is to be maintained, so money wages must keep pace with the growth of output per worker, not exceeding that mark if the expansion path is to be an inflation-free one. Indeed, from the dynamic perspective of post-Keynesian theory, the growth of money wages in excess of the secular rise in output per worker provides the starting point for understanding the causes of inflation. It is because industrial trade unions have a tendency to push up money wages beyond that noninflationary limit that they provide only a partial remedy for the defect in the economy's operational distribution mechanisms which the market power of megacorps has created (Eichner, 1976).

The above argument should not be taken to suggest that the collective bargaining power of the trade union movement is the fundamental cause of the secular inflation which the United States has experienced since the end of World War II. This would be an unfair inference to draw for several reasons. The most important, of course, is that if it were not the collective bargaining power of the trade union movement that was being counted upon to make sure that money wages rose at the same rate as the secular growth in output per worker, some other mechanism would have to be found to bring about the same result. Industrial trade unions have not sought this role. They have simply come to fill it by default. Moreover, this role which industrial trade unions play has received the implicit endorsement of the government at the highest level. The endorsement takes the form of Presidential intervention in the contract settlement, or key bargain, reached in the bellwether industry that will set the pattern for the rest of the unionized work force, and this intervention is likely to be buttressed by guideposts, Pay Board rulings, or whatever other means the government uses to exert influence over the collective bargaining process. Indeed, it is by intervening in one or more of these ways that the government indicates what it believes to be a fair and reasonable increase in workers' wages. The role played by industrial trade unions is thus only the most conspicuous feature of a far more subtle socio-political process which actually determines the growth of money wages. Finally it should be pointed out that if, and when, some other mechanism is substituted for the pattern bargaining, buttressed by Presidential intervention in one form or another, which presently determines the growth of money wages, that mechanism will have to be able to cope with the same complicating factors that now make it so difficult for the trade union movement, in seeking to preserve labor's "historical share" of the benefits from technical progress, to hold the growth of money wages to a noninflationary rate.

C. A shift in the growth rate

The factors that invalidate the simple rule that money wages should rise in line with output per worker are twofold, each reflecting a different determinant of relative income identified earlier. The first of these complicating factors is the growth path that society, through its political system, has chosen. As pointed out above, the more rapid the rate of economic expansion, the lower the proportion of the economy's real output that will be available to workers and other household members for current consumption. This does not mean that the real wage must necessarily decline. With the economy continuing to expand, but with the rate of investment now boosted to put the economy on a more rapid sustainable growth path, the real wage might even increase, at least in absolute terms, even if it is not able to grow quite at the same rate as before. The point is that the relative share going to workers will necessarily have to decline so that a proportionately greater part of the increase in real output can be used to expand productive capacity.

Thus the simple rule, that real wages should rise in line with the secular growth of output per worker, no longer holds when the economy shifts from one sustainable growth path to another. The rule needs to be modified to take into account the change in the rate of investment, and thus the change in the share of income going to business enterprises in the form of profits that must occur if the shift to a different growth path is to be accomplished. If industrial trade unions or any other group with the power to make its views felt tries to apply the simple rule, insisting that the relative distribution of income between workers and other groups remain unchanged, then one of two results will follow: either the attempt to shift to a new growth path will be frustrated or, alternatively, the shift to a new growth path will be accompanied by an inflationary wage-price spiral as first the money costs of production are increased, threatening the margins needed to finance investment, and then business enterprises respond by increasing their prices, thereby preserving the margins.

One of the difficulties in avoiding the latter result is that it is by no means clear when a shift to a new growth path is occurring. The shift initially coincides with, and is indistinguishable from, the economy's more conspicuous cyclical movements (Eichner, 1976). Typically, it is only when a period of economic recovery and expansion continues for longer than anticipated without a cyclical downturn that a more rapid rate of secular expansion can be discerned. Similarly, it is only when the recovery from the downturn is delayed or less rigorous than expected that a less rapid rate of secular expansion becomes evident. Moreover, the same redistribution effects that occur with a change in the secular growth path are likely to be mimicked when there are cyclical movements of the economy. As pointed out above, a higher secular growth rate is likely to be accompanied by a decline, in relative terms, of the wage share of national income, and the same is true during the expansionary phase of the cycle. One can expect to observe a disproportionate increase in profits and other nonwage income. Conversely, one can expect to observe a disproportionate decline in profits when the economy slips into a recession (Eichner and Kregel, 1975; Eichner 1976).

If the disproportionate increase in profits which occurs when aggregate demand is high is interpreted differently by trade unions and megacorps—with trade unions regarding the higher profits as secular in nature and megacorps regarding the higher profits as only cyclical—then the likelihood of a shift to a more rapid growth path being accompanied by a wage-price inflationary spiral is considerably enhanced. Trade unions, acting to preserve their historical share of the benefits from technical progress, will insist that the rate at which money wages increase be raised. Megacorps, on the other hand, regarding the higher profits as being only cyclical, will react to any boost in the rate at which money wages increase as though it were a threat to the margins they need to finance investment. They will raise their prices. The tragedy in this oft-repeated scenario occurs when the government, alarmed by the rise in industrial prices, acts to constrain the growth of the economy, thereby confirming the megacorp's pessimistic view that the disproportionate increase in profits previously enjoyed was merely a cyclical phenomenon (Eichner, 1976).

D. Consumption out of nonwage income

The other factor, besides any shift to a different growth path, that makes the simple rule for apportioning the benefits from technical progress no longer applicable is a change in the portion of nonwage income devoted to noninvestment purposes. If the economy consisted only of business firms that supplied goods and services along with households that consumed those goods and services, then the nonwage income would be identical to the profits being earned by business firms and any use of those profits other than to finance investment would involve the purchase of consumption goods. Even without introducing any further complications, it is possible to envision a situation in which the proportion of profits devoted to consumption might increase. The megacorps could decide to boost the rate at which they increase their dividend payments, thereby enabling their stockholders to command a larger share of the consumption goods presently being produced. Or, rather than favoring their stockholders, the megacorps could increase the salaries and perquisites of their top executives while providing them with more sumptuous quarters in which to work. Still, what are likely to be far more important in determining the overall distribution of income are the other ways, in an economy that consists of more than just domestic producers and households, that the proportion of non-wage income devoted to noninvestment purposes can be increased.

One of these ways is through the instrument of government. The resources that government is able to command through taxes are analogous to business investment in that they reduce the amount of resources available for direct consumption by households. (Whether those resources are indirectly consumed by households through the public goods which government provides is another matter.) At the same time, the resources commanded by government are similar to consumption goods in that they do not serve to augment the economy's productive capacity. (The exception would be investment by the government in the economic infrastructure, e.g., transportation, energy.) Thus, any increase in the share of aggregate output going to government has the same effect as an increase in consumption out of profits. It will lower the real wage, at least relative both to profits and to government revenues. For this reason, a major shift of resources into the public sector—such as occurred in the mid-1960s with the creation of the antipoverty programs and, more recently, with the dramatic rise in publicly subsidized health care—can itself initiate a wage-price inflationary spiral. This will be the result if, despite the greater proportion of the benefits from technical progress which are now to accrue to the groups served by government programs, trade unions insist on the same growth of money wages—and the megacorps, to protect their profit margins, respond by raising prices.

A secular shift of resources into the public sector, of the sort just pointed out, should not be confused with deficit spending by the government. The latter is essentially a short-period device for enabling the political authorities to place the economy on a different growth path, much as the firing of inboard rockets enables space engineers to place a satellite in a different orbit (Eichner, 1976, 1977a). While the shift of resources into the public sector may initially be brought about through deficit spending and while both are likely to be accompanied by a decline in labor's relative share of national income, still the two are different. Any decline in labor's relative share which occurs as a result of the higher level of aggregate demand temporarily produced by deficit spending is simply a cyclical phenomenon, and its effect is not likely to be felt beyond the current oscillation around the trend line. For all practical purposes it can, and should be, ignored. The decline in labor's relative share produced by a secular shift of resources into the public sector, however, will be as long lasting as the shift itself and needs to be fully taken into account.

What has just been said is not necessarily an argument against resources being shifted into the public sector. That issue hinges on the indirect benefits from the increased public goods the government is able to provide relative to the direct benefits households can expect to derive from a more rapidly growing real wage (Eichner and Brecher, 1979). The point needs to be made simply as a warning that if a secular shift of resources into the public sector is decided upon, it is almost certain to be accompanied by a slower growth in real wages. And if, despite this fact, trade unions insist on maintaining the same growth of money wages, the basis for a wage-price inflationary spiral will have been laid.

What has just been said about the shift of real resources into the public sector applies with no less cogency to the use of transfer payments to increase disproportionately the income of nonworkers. Any increase in the rate at which the income of nonworkers is growing, either because transfer payments themselves are growing disproportionately or because the eligible population is expanding more rapidly than the work force, will lower the growth of workers' real wages. If technical progress—and thus the rate at which real income can be increased—is measured by the secular growth of output per worker, it then follows that, if others besides members of the work force are to share in the benefits of technical progress, the share available to workers will perforce be reduced. As long as the division of income between workers and nonworkers remains unchanged, the income of each group can increase at a rate equal to the secular growth of output per worker without creating a problem. But once the division of income, for one reason or another, becomes more favorable to nonworkers—as it has in recent years, in part because of the way the social security program is structured—the basis for a wage-price inflationary spiral will have been laid, just as it will be if there is a shift of real resources into the public sector. This argument can be extended to cover other nonworkers besides those who receive transfer payments. Indeed, it applies to the income received by the megacorps' stockholders and other rentiers. Any disproportionate increase in their income will also be at the expense of workers' real wages.

E. A shift in the international terms of trade

The other way in which the proportion of nonwage income devoted to noninvestment purposes can be increased, thereby lowering the growth of real wages, is through a shift in the international terms of trade so that the prices of imported raw materials rise. Eventually the higher prices for raw materials will have to be offset by an increase in the share of aggregate output that flows to other countries in the form of exports. The resources thereby diverted to the rest of the world are similar to the resources commanded by government. Since they add neither to the consumption of households nor to the productive capacity of business firms, they lower the real wage in the immediate run without creating the prerequisite conditions for real wages to grow more rapidly over the longer run. While attention has been largely drawn to the rise in oil prices by the OPEC nations following the Arab boycott in 1973, this is but one example of the higher prices for imported raw materials which have followed in the wake of the American government's decision two years earlier to scuttle the Bretton Woods agreement and allow the dollar to float downward. Indeed, a currency devaluation's primary effect on an industrialized country dependent on imported raw materials is to increase the cost of those raw materials.[11]

A shift in the international terms of trade, like a shift to a more rapid growth path or a shift of resources into the public sector, need not be inflationary. It becomes inflationary only if, despite the relative decline in real wages which must necessarily follow, money wages continue to grow at the same rate as before. With the rate at which money wages are growing threatening their profit margins, the megacorps and other business firms can be expected to raise their prices, thereby triggering a wage-price inflationary spiral.

There are thus a number of ways in which a wage-price inflationary spiral can be initiated: by a shift to a more rapid growth rate, by a shift of resources into the public sector, by a shift in the international terms of trade, or indeed by a shift of any sort that necessarily implies a decline in the growth of real wages. Whatever the means by which it is triggered, however, the wage-price inflationary spiral reflects essentially the same underlying imbalance: a growth of money wages that exceeds the growth of real wages as determined both by the rate of accumulation and by the proportion of nonwage income devoted to noninvestment purposes. If the rise in money wages exceeds this maximum rate of increase in real wages, thereby placing the economy on an inflationary growth path, the fault no more lies with the trade union movement for pushing up money wages as best it can to protect the group it represents than with the megacorps for pushing up prices to protect their profit margins. The fault lies instead with the absence of any overriding social mechanism for seeing to it that the growth of money wages is limited to the noninflationary maximum.

F. The influence of aggregate demand

So far no mention has been made of demand factors. This omission is deliberate. It is possible to provide a fairly complete explanation for the recent inflationary experience of the United States, based on post-Keynesian theory, without any particular emphasis on demand factors. This, in turn, hints at why the government's antiinflationary policies over the past several decades, designed primarily to act as a brake on aggregate demand, have been largely ineffective. Still, this does not mean that demand factors can or should be ignored. Indeed, they are important in two ways—though only as further qualifications to the main explanation already given as to the underlying causes of inflation.

First, the higher prices that need to be paid for raw materials may reflect more than just a shift in the international terms of trade. In the case of the United States and other countries with a significant primary products sector, there is also the possibility of a shift in the domestic terms of trade. That possibility is enhanced if, as in the case of American agriculture, the primary products sector consists of a large number of relatively small producers, with prices governed for the most part by impersonal market forces, much as the neoclassical theory assumes. In that event, the domestic terms of trade between the predominately competitive agricultural sector and the predominantly oligopolistic industrial sector will shift, depending on demand factors. When the level of aggregate demand is unusually high, with the rate of economic growth above the secular average, prices in the agricultural sector are likely to rise more rapidly than those in the industrial sector because the prices in the agricultural sector are governed largely by demand factors—unlike the prices in the industrial sector, which depend primarily on long-term supply considerations. But when the level of aggregate demand falls off, as it usually does at some point during the cycle, prices in the agricultural sector will not just rise less rapidly than those in the industrial sector, they may actually decline. Whichever the case, however, the terms of trade will shift against the agricultural sector.

That sector occupies a strategic place within the American economy. Since the United States is a major supplier of foodstuffs to other nations, agricultural prices depend on demand conditions in the world economy as well as in the domestic economy. The sector therefore serves as a link between the two spheres of economic activity, with any change in the international terms of trade affecting the domestic economy through its impact on food prices. This international connection is in addition to the influence exerted on food prices by domestic demand factors. Food prices are, in turn, a major determinant of real wages (along with the cost of shelter). When food prices rise, the real wages of workers are thereby reduced. This leads to the sort of discontent among rank-and-file trade union members that forces their leaders to respond by pushing for higher money wages. It represents yet another way in which a wage-price inflationary spiral can be triggered, in this case through the shifting terms of trade between an agricultural sector that is competitively structured and the household sector, as a result of changes in aggregate demand.

The second way in which the influence of demand factors needs to be taken into account as part of a comprehensive explanation for the recent inflationary experience of the United States is by looking at the role played by government itself. What the historical record shows is that the government, when confronted by a wage-price inflationary spiral triggered in one or more of the ways just described but with no other explanation available for the phenomenon except the "excess demand" thesis derived from neoclassical theory, has usually reacted by seeking to curtail the growth rate. The means employed, either fiscal or monetary policy, have been less important than the result achieved—for example, one of the government-engineered recessions which has marked the post–World War II period. Only gradually has it come to be recognized that this policy response, successful as it may be in reducing the growth rate, along with employment and real income, has little or no effect on price levels. Indeed, it simply produces "stagflation."

Government contracyclical policy has therefore become a major destabilizing factor in the American economy, confirming Kalecki's prophecy of a political trade cycle to replace the regular trade cycle of the pre-Keynesian era (Kalecki, 1943; Feiwel, 1975). However, it is not just that the government's contracyclical policy is likely to prove ineffective, at least in dealing with inflation. Even more a source for concern is the fact that a policy which seeks to control inflation by curtailing the growth rate only exacerbates the conflict over the distribution of income which lies at the core of the inflation problem. With the emphasis on limiting aggregate demand, business investment is likely to be discouraged as the megacorps and other firms adjust their capital expenditures to the new secular growth path which government policy has dictated. And with the rate of accumulation thereby lowered, technical progress—which is the source of the higher output per worker, and thus the source of any increased real income over time for all members of society—will be lowered as well. The conflict over how that income should be distributed can only be heightened by its decline.

III. The policy thrust of post-Keynesian theory

Post-Keynesian theory would be of little value to public officials if it were able to provide an explanation for stagflation but could suggest no cure. Indeed, the explanation would be questionable. That is why the discussion must now turn to the matter of public policy.

From what has already been said, it should be clear that "stagflation"—the simultaneous occurrence of rising prices and depressed business conditions—can easily be prevented. The government need only abandon its policy of trying to control inflation by reducing aggregate demand. While this remedy would leave the problem of inflation unattended to—a serious flaw, in view of how easily a wage-price spiral can be triggered and how unfair the resulting redistribution of purchasing power can be—it would at least not compound the problem by adding the woes of rising unemployment to the woes of rising prices. A theory, such as the post-Keynesian one, can be useful if it does no more than indicate how to avoid making a bad situation worse. Still, the problem of inflation would remain. The real question, then, is whether post-Keynesian theory can suggest an alternative public policy, one that will keep the economy on a noninflationary growth path without the country being forced to settle for too low a rate of economic expansion.

A. Incomes policy

In fact, such a policy is implicit in post-Keynesian theory—just as a policy for combating widespread unemployment could be deduced from *The General Theory*. The policy required to keep the economy on a noninflationary growth path is often referred to as an "incomes policy"—though it is not necessarily what some people have in mind when they use the term (Eichner, 1979). It does not, for example, simply mean a policy for holding down money wages. As already indicated, the rise in money wages is only one of the ways in which the claims against the growing social surplus that technical progress brings can exceed the increased real resources that are actually becoming available. No, an incomes policy must be seen as applying to all forms of household compensation—to dividends and rents as well as to money wages.[12] Unfortunately, this is not how economists have always viewed an incomes policy.

Moreover, an incomes policy cannot, in a democratic society, simply be imposed. It must instead gain acceptance among the different economic interest groups within the society as the fairest and most equitable basis for distributing the benefits of technical progress. This requires that a consensus first be reached, through the appropriate representative bodies, about the principles that will govern the apportionment of any increase in the social surplus. It also means facing up honestly to the distributional issues. Thus an incomes policy needs to be preceded, at the political level, by some minimal societal agreement as to how the benefits from technical progress are to be distributed. The fact that the market alone is incapable of rendering this judgment, in the face of the pricing power which the megacorps, trade unions, and foreign cartels are capable of exercising, is what makes an incomes policy an essential addition to fiscal and monetary policy.

It was because neither of these points was sufficiently appreciated that previous efforts to establish an incomes policy in the United States—and this includes both the guideposts under Presidents Kennedy and Johnson and the Pay Board rulings under President Nixon—eventually had to be abandoned. In both cases, the restrictions on the growth of money income applied primarily to wages.[13] Moreover, the policy itself was simply promulgated by the executive branch, with little or no discussion beforehand with the groups that would be affected by it. It is hardly surprising, therefore, that the efforts so far to establish an incomes policy have been frustrated by opposition from the groups, such as the trade unions, whose support is essential to the success of any such policy.

The point is that an incomes policy cannot be successfully implemented in an institutional vacuum, no more than a monetary policy can be successfully implemented without a central bank and fiscal policy without a legislative committee to review the government's budget as a whole. The new institution that needs to be created if there is to be a more effective incomes policy will be especially difficult to establish since the government, acting alone, cannot make the policy work . The various economic interest groups that will be affected—and here one needs to mention not just the trade union movement but also consumer, farm, and other groups as well—cannot be expected to give the new institution their necessary support unless they are assured a role in shaping its policies. This means that some way will have to be found to involve these various interest groups in the functioning of the new institution.

B. A social and economic council

What is being recommended here is the creation of a quasi-governmental body—a social and economic council is perhaps the best way to describe it—on which would sit representatives of the various economic interest groups that must give their support to an incomes policy, together with representatives of the governmental units that play a key role in setting the nation's economic policies. The council would serve as a forum for both the private and public interests represented on it, and its function would be to work toward a consensus on the fundamental question of economic policy that must be resolved before the outlines of a noninflationary incomes policy can even be discerned. For what will become clear, as the exercise of formulating an incomes policy is carried through to completion, is that an incomes policy is largely derivative from other, more fundamental social choices. The post-Keynesian theory described above, especially the explanation for inflation that has been offered, indicates what those fundamental choices are.

There is, first, the choice among alternative growth paths. The government, through its fiscal and monetary policies, can readily place the economy on any one of numerous growth paths, even if it cannot always insure that the growth path will be held to for long. Whatever the choice, it implies a certain rate of investment, or capital formation. And whatever the rate of investment, this will, in turn, limit the growth of the household sector's real income. The choice, therefore, is between a higher level of real consumption in the immediate run and a higher rate of growth of real consumption over time.

Then there is the choice among alternative consumption patterns. As pointed out above, any use of nonwage income for noninvestment purposes will have the effect of reducing real wages and other types of household income. The resources commanded by government, whether to provide additional public goods or simply to redistribute income among households, fall in this category. And thus the second fundamental choice is between the growth of private consumption financed out of private income and the growth of a public sector that involves a certain mix of programmatic activities and transfer payments.

These two choices will go a long way toward determining what the actual figures for a noninflationary incomes policy are likely to be. There are, however, other factors that need to be taken into account.

There are the disturbances which can occur in international commodity and other types of competitive markets, causing the price of raw materials to rise beyond the control of any national government. (There are also the planned currency devaluations and the actions by international cartels which lead to the same result. Indeed, the latter two types of deliberate acts are often the underlying cause of the disturbances that occur in international commodity markets.)

Then there are the supply bottlenecks which exist within certain sectors of the domestic economy, causing the prices of essential consumption items to rise disproportionately. (Housing and health care appear to be two most important items of household consumption the price of which has been affected by bottlenecks and other supply constraints.)

This is not to suggest that the loss of real income from these factors should simply be acquiesced to by government. In most cases, an appropriate policy response can be devised which, with sufficient time allowed for its effect to be felt, will at least ameliorate the underlying condition. For example, reform of the international monetary system could probably avoid the type of currency devaluation that arises from speculation and then leads to a rise in the cost of raw materials. At the same time, long-term agreements between producing and consuming nations could probably stabilize the price of key commodities. Similarly, the nation's housing and health care programs could be reformed to incorporate better cost-containment features. The common feature in each of these policy responses, if it is to counteract rising costs effectively, will have to be an emphasis on long-term supply capacity. Still, these policies cannot be expected to have much effect in the immediate run, and thus the disturbing factors they are intended to ameliorate must be taken into account by the social and economic council when considering what is likely to be a noninflationary rate of growth of wages and other forms of household income.

Not only in giving weight to these disturbing factors but also in making the more fundamental choices that underlie an incomes policy, the social and economic council will need the assistance of a technical staff trained in economics, statistics, and related disciplines. An intelligent choice among alternative growth paths, for example, cannot be made either by the private groups represented on the council or by any of the public members until the full implications of any option have been spelled out. The same is true of the choice among the alternative consumption patterns that are possible, through public policy, once a growth path has been chosen. What will be the implications, not just in terms of broad aggregates such as investment, real wages, and employment, but also in terms of the impact on particular sectors of the economy and even on particular industries and household groups? It would be the responsibility of the technical staff, or secretariat, attached to the social and economic council to provide the answers to these and any other questions that might arise in the course of the discussions within the council.

C. *The role of the secretariat*

What is envisioned is a process whereby the council would first be presented by the secretariat with the broad options that exist insofar as the fundamental choices that need to be made. As the council, through its deliberations, narrows these choices, the secretariat would then provide more detailed analyses, tracing in full the implications of the choices toward which the council was moving. In preparing background papers for the consideration of the council's members, the secretariat would work closely with the technical staffs of all the different groups, private and public, represented on the council. Indeed, a primary objective of the secretariat would be to reconcile, as much as possible, any discrepancies or conflicts in the position papers prepared by others. In thus building on the concurrent analytical efforts of the groups represented on the council, the secretariat would seek to develop as broad a consensus as possible as to the implications of the policies being recommended—this as a necessary basis for developing as broad a consensus as possible on the policies themselves.

Success in achieving such a consensus would be important since, to avoid overstepping constitutional boundaries, the social and economic council would necessarily be without the power to implement policies on its own. Its influence would instead depend on the actions taken by the private and public groups represented on it. Even if one or more of these groups was unwilling to act in accord with the consensus developed within the council, this fact would become known during the council's deliberations, and the policies to be recommended would be formulated with that likelihood in mind. At the same time, the consequences of any group, private or public, not acting in accord with the consensus developed within the council would be fully spelled out, and the other groups represented on the council could bring pressure to bear on the recalcitrant group. The inability of the council to take any action on its own would not preclude public officials, both within the executive branch and within Congress, from doing what they think necessary to support the consensus developed within the council.

Thus the logic of a post-Keynesian analysis, when applied to the problem of inflation, points to more than just the need for an incomes policy. It also points to the need for a new set of quasi-governmental institutions so that the noninflationary growth of household income can first be determined, this as the culmination to a series of more fundamental social choices, and then that figure used as the basis for an incomes policy. The required new institutions are 1) a social and economic council, on which would sit representatives of private interest groups as well as key public officials, and 2) a secretariat to provide the council with technical back-up support. The council, because of its broadly representative nature yet limited powers, might well be able to remove two of the major obstacles presently blocking the successful implementation of an incomes policy. These two obstacles are 1) the lack of support for an incomes policy among the private groups that are affected by it, particularly trade unions and 2) the lack of coordination among government bodies in setting overall economic policy.

D. Winning the support of trade unions

If inflation is due in part to money wages rising more rapidly than output per worker, then the support of the groups that negotiate money wages on behalf of workers—and this means primarily, though not exclusively, the trade union movement—is critical to the success of any incomes policy. Yet trade unions can hardly be expected to support a policy that offers little except the promise of holding down money wages and thereby forcing workers to surrender the one protection they have against inflation. The way an incomes policy would work, as outlined above, might have a better chance of winning the support of trade unions and other groups precisely because holding down money wages would be only part of a much larger agreement or "social contract" that would be worked out even before the social and economic council came into being.

In the first place, it would have to be agreed that whatever ceiling was suggested for the growth of money wages would apply to other types of household income as well, in particular, to dividends. In this way, the trade union movement could be reassured that its members would end up no worse from an incomes policy than households in general. More important, however, the trade unions, in return for surrendering some of their control over money wages, would be given a greater voice in the decisions that determine the growth of real wages. As already pointed out, the key to the growth of real wages is the rate of investment, or capital formation, and this depends to a large extent on the rate of economic expansion which the government's fiscal and monetary policies have dictated. The trade union movement, together with the other private interest groups whose support is essential to the success of an incomes policy, must therefore be assured of having a larger role in the formulation of overall government policy. This prior understanding, if there is to be a noninflationary incomes policy, is related to the need for greater coordination of policy within government itself.

A number of important steps have been taken in recent years to improve the coordination of economic policy within government, the most important being the new congressional budgeting procedures. Still, it continues to be the case that different parts of the government often find themselves working at cross purposes with one another in trying to influence economic events, and this occurs as much within the separate branches of government as among them. Moreover, given the different mandates that the different parts of government have and the determination with which they can be expected to protect their independence of action, the problem has no permanent solution. It can only be mitigated. In this respect, a social and economic council, on which would sit key officials from throughout the government, could be expected to have a salutory effect. In the course of going through the exercise required to produce an effective incomes policy—in particular, making the series of fundamental social choices that will determine what is the noninflationary growth of household income—the public officials on the council will have to indicate what actions the government can be expected to take. And if it becomes clear that those actions are somewhat in conflict with one another, especially after the secretariat has completed its task of reconciling the various projections, then the public officials on the council will come under the same pressure to shift their stances in support of the consensus being developed within the council as would any of the private interest groups that might be tempted to strike out on their own. Through the give-and-take that would characterize the social and economic council's deliberations, greater coordination of policy within the government would be likely to follow.

It is not enough, however, that the government act with greater unity. It is also important that the government, in deciding what actions to take, give weight to the policies that will assure support and cooperation from the private parties—particularly trade unions but also the megacorps and other business enterprises as well—whose support and cooperation are essential to the success of any incomes policy. For trade unions, and even for megacorps, these policies are preeminently the ones that will enable the economy to expand, at whatever rate is chosen, with the least possible deviation from the trend line. They are policies that will minimize any cyclical fluctuations. Indeed, it will no doubt be found that policies that minimize cyclical fluctuations are policies that go far toward maximizing the rate of expansion itself. These, of course, are the very same policies that lead to a rapid growth of real wages and profits while sparing workers and others the ill effects of unemployment and depressed business conditions.

If, in the past, the government was unwilling to pursue these types of policies, it was primarily because of the fear that by doing so it would add to the rate of inflation. However, with both industrial trade unions and the megacorps lending their support to a noninflationary incomes policy, this fear no longer need dictate government policy. A bargain could in effect be struck: nonrestrictive growth policies in return for trade unions agreeing to hold down the growth of money wages and the megacorps agreeing to limit profit margins. It is this bargain, or "social contract," that would provide the essential starting point for the social and economic council's deliberations so that, aided by its secretariat, the council could develop a consensus around the set of policies, private as well as public, that would place the economy on a steady, noninflationary growth path.

E. Getting the process going

Only two further problems need to be addressed. The first is how to get the whole process going—in particular, how to initiate the dialogue among the various parties, private and public, so that a "social contract" can be worked out and the institutions necessary for developing a noninflationary incomes policy put in place. Actually, this is the easier of the two problems. It requires only that some neutral body, say a private foundation or a public interest group not identified with either organized labor or industry or even with the government, act to convene the various parties so that the dialogue can begin. The body sponsoring this initial get-together must be one in which the various parties that are to participate can have trust, and indeed the success of the endeavor is likely to depend heavily on the individual chosen to preside over the plenary gathering. It should be someone with long experience in working with the leaders of organized labor, industry, government, and the other groups whose support is essential to the success of any incomes policy.

If the plenary gathering were to succeed in hammering out the necessary social contract, it could then be given quasi-official status, transforming itself into the social and economic council described above. Since the council, even after it received official recognition, would have no power of its own, there should be no objection to its coming into being in this manner. Indeed, the lack of statutory authorization at the outset would be a clear advantage since, if the conference were unable to accomplish its task of achieving agreement on a social contract, the effort could be abandoned and the parties participating in the endeavor would not find themselves trapped on a legally constituted body whose usefulness had already ended.

The success of the plenary gathering in working out the details of a social contract and transforming itself into a social and economic council would depend not only on the individual chosen to preside over the conference but also on the quality of the staff work carried out in preparation for the conference. This leads to the other problem that needs to be addressed before one can have confidence in the course of action being outlined.

F. The intellectual obstacle

This second problem concerns not the political implications of post-Keynesian theory but rather the intellectual implications. The plenary gathering to discuss a social contract, like any subsequent meetings of the social and economic council emerging from that group, cannot be expected to reach agreement unless there is confidence among the various parties participating that the options being presented to them have been correctly analyzed. Here the continued dominance of the neoclassical orthodoxy among American economists is likely to do great mischief. As long as economists continue to hold on to false hope that inflation can be brought under control through fiscal or even more simplistic monetary instruments, there will be reluctance to take the much more difficult step of putting into place a whole new set of institutions so that an incomes policy can be added to the stock of policy tools. And even if this reluctance can somehow be overcome because policymakers in their desperation are willing to turn to unorthodox solutions, economists operating from a neoclassical perspective are likely to continue to muddy the waters.

In truth, the options cannot even be clearly perceived, let alone correctly analyzed, from a neoclassical perspective. Thus the staff work that must be carried out in preparation for any plenary gathering must somehow transcend the current orthodoxy in economics. And this must continue to be the case even after agreement has been reached on the nature of the social contract and the technical staff has been transformed into a permanent secretariat attached to the social and economic council.

Fortunately, even here there are some grounds for optimism. The majority of economists have little faith in or commitment to neoclassical theory. They use it in their teaching and research only because they know of no better alternative. They might, in time, be persuaded that a post-Keynesian approach opens up the possibility of far more productive work. They would certainly find that any empirical research, which now simply leads to anomalous findings, would be given a boost rather than being held back by what the theory leads one to expect.

Still, as Keynes warned on an earlier occasion, one should not underestimate the power of vested ideas to lead men of practical affairs down false paths—at least in the short run. And this, in turn, suggests that perhaps the greater problem in trying to follow the course of action outlined above will be the intellectual deadweight of the neoclassical orthodoxy in economics. As the earlier sections of this essay indicated, economic theory can be changed to fit the reality through the adoption of a post-Keynesian perspective. But it is not clear how quickly economists can be won over to that more realistic, and therefore more useful, perspective. It is therefore not clear how quickly policymakers can be expected to choose with confidence a more effective strategy for dealing with stagflation.

Addendum

A government can no more manage the economy without an incomes policy than it can without a monetary policy. Just as the internal dynamics of the economic system put the monetary authorities in a position where they must either accommodate the need of the banking system for reserves or else restrict the availability of credit—which, in either case, is a policy that will affect the economy's performance—so the same internal dynamics create a situation in which what is a fair rate of increase in the money rate of compensation for wage earners and other household recipients of income must be determined. The government can, of course, allow the policy to be decided upon by some group which is relatively insulated from the electoral process—e.g., the Federal Reserve Board or the management and labor negotiators in some bellwether industry—but that will not shield the government from the political consequences of whatever policy is decided upon. The question, then, is not whether the government should have an incomes policy—in the post-Keynesian era it really has no choice in this matter—but rather what type of incomes policy it should have.

Insofar as the mechanics are concerned, as distinct from what numerical value should be attached to the income standard, five separate types of incomes policy can be distinguished. They are:

1. *Mandatory wage and other controls.* Under this type of incomes policy, the income standard established by some board or other governmental body is backed by the full coercive powers of the state.

2. *Voluntary wage and other income guidelines.* In this second case, the income standard is backed only by the suasive and/or extralegal powers of the state (e.g., the power to withhold government contracts).[1]

3. *A "free market" incomes policy.* Under this type of incomes policy, the government uses its other policy instruments to generate sufficient unemployment to moderate wage and other income demands. The other, more direct powers of the state need not be exercised, though the reduced reliance on coercion is at the expense of those left unemployed. It is in implementing this type of incomes policy that what is thought to be the relevant Phillips curve, assuming there is actually some relationship between unemployment and the inflation rate (Eichner, 1976; 1980a), serves as the basis for setting policy.

4. *A tax-based incomes policy (TIP).* Under this type of incomes policy, the taxing powers of the government are used to obtain compliance with the income standard. There are two main types of tax-based incomes policies, or TIPs—those that penalize noncompliers through higher taxes (the stick approach), and those that reward compliers with reduced tax liabilities (the carrot approach). There are also numerous variations on these two main types.

5. *A planning-subordinated incomes policy (PIP).* Under this type of incomes policy, the task of determining the appropriate income standard is subordinated to some planning process, governmental or otherwise, which is focused primarily on the long-term expansion and competitive position of the national economy. The income standard is but one of several required conditions if the broader planning objectives are to be met, and it is then agreed to by the relevant parties as part of some overall "social contract" covering the actions that need to be taken on all sides if the collaborative effort is to succeed. Again, there are two main types of planning-subordinated incomes policies (PIPs)—those in which the planning process is directed by government agencies, and those in which private groups, such as banks, take the leading role. Again, there are numerous variations on these two main types.

Exhibit A shows the major changes which have occurred in the type

Exhibit A

Types of Incomes Policies
1940-1982

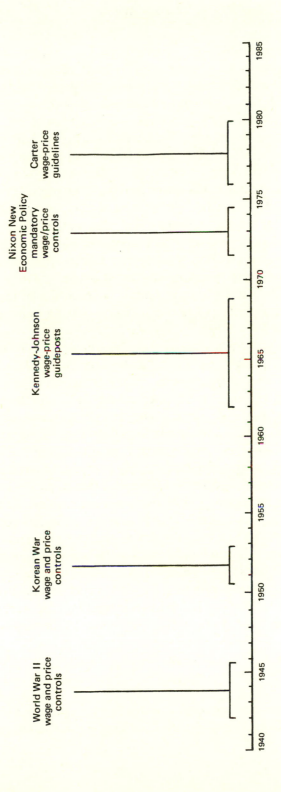

World War II wage and price controls

Korean War wage and price controls

Kennedy-Johnson wage-price guideposts

Nixon New Economic Policy mandatory wage/price controls

Carter wage-price guidelines

of incomes policy relied upon by the U.S. government since 1940. The types shown are only the first two listed: the mandatory controls and the voluntary guidelines. In addition, the period between the end of the Korean War's mandatory controls and the Kennedy-Johnson adminis- trations' voluntary guidelines, the period just before and the period just after the Nixon administration's mandatory controls, and the period from the end of the Carter administration down through the present have each involved the third of the three types of incomes policy identified above. Excluding the last, it can be said that twenty out of the last forty years have seen one type of incomes policy or another adopted by the government while, if the "free market" type of incomes policy is taken into account, the proportion is even higher (the exceptions being confined largely to the years before 1950).

Two observations are warranted by the above.

1. It is possible to recognize the need for an incomes policy, and indeed even to put one into effect, without being forced to opt for mandatory controls.

2. Two types of incomes policies have yet to be tried in the United States. In the case of other countries which have had more success with an incomes policy, it is the planning-subordinated type of policy they have adopted. The examples are the Scandinavian countries, France, West Germany, Austria, and Japan. A tax-based incomes policy, though increasingly advocated in the Anglo-Saxon countries, has yet to be adopted, and thereby tested, in any country.[2] Rakowski (1983) is correct in identifying as the key problem of any incomes policy the obtaining of agreement, among the affected parties, as to what is a fair rate of increase in money rates of compensation. This may be why the planning-subordinated type of incomes policy, since it provides both a broader context within which to consider this question and a mecha- nism for bringing together the parties who must come to agreement, is the one that has been adopted by countries that have so far had the most success with an incomes policy of any sort—although it should be noted that the guideposts under Kennedy and Johnson were, for a time, quite successful until they were undermined by the Vietnam War (Eichner, 1976, pp. 263–270).

Afterword

A slightly longer version of this essay was originally published by the Joint Economic Committee of Congress in 1980 as part of the volume on *Stagflation*, one of that committee's Special Studies on Economic Change (Eichner, 1980a). The overview of post-Keynesian theory presented in the first part of the essay can be supplemented by looking at Eichner and Kregel, 1975, and Eichner, 1979b. See also Kregel, 1973; Shapiro, 1977, and Davidson, 1980. The analysis of the inflationary process presented in the second part of the essay and the discussion of the required policy response found in the third and final section is drawn from Eichner, 1974, 1976. Insofar as the required policy response is concerned, see especially Eichner, 1976, ch. 8. The addendum on the various forms an incomes policy can take was originally published in the *Journal of Post Keynesian Econonomics* as a response to an article by Rakowski (1983) in which, after acknowledging that the problem of inflation derives from conflicts over the distribution of income, Rakowski equates an incomes policy with "controls" and then proceeds to argue that any such "controls" will not be successful in the absence of agreement as to what is a fair distribution of income.

Notes

1. Although this vision is perhaps more fully developed in *The General Theory* (Keynes, 1936), it is already discernible in the earlier *Treatise* (Keynes, 1930).

2. The vision is first found in Harrod's 1939 article but is better developed in his 1948 book. See Kregel, 1971, chapter 8.

3. For the most important of Kalecki's essays in English, see his 1971 volume. See also Kalecki, 1938, 1954; Feiwel, 1975.

4. Although *The Accumulation of Capital*, together with its companion volume, the *Essays in the Theory of Economic Growth* (1962), is the most important of the early major works in post-Keynesian theory, the contribution of Robinson's contemporaries at Cambridge University, England, should not be overlooked. Piero Sraffa's *The Production of Commodities by Means of Commodities* (1960) is in a class by itself, providing as it does the broadest possible foundation for revitalizing economic theory, but the work of Nicholas Kaldor as presented in a series of journal articles (Kaldor, 1955–56, 1960a, and 1960b) needs to be acknowledged as well. Moreover, there is the contribution of the American institutionalist economists, particularly Gardiner C. Means (1962) and John M. Clark (1961), in developing the micro foundations of post-Keynesian theory, along with the similar contribution of the Oxford pricing study group in England (Wilson and Andrews, 1951).

5. Although the neoclassical synthesis first appeared in Samuelson's dissertation (1948) as well as in the first edition of his well-known introductory textbook, the extension of that framework to a growing economy did not come until Solow's (and Swan's) separate 1956 articles.

6. $G = s/v$, or, in the version put forward by Harrod, $G = s/C$, where G is the growth of output, s is the marginal propensity to save, and v or C is the incremental capital/output ratio.

7. Robinson, 1956; Pasinetti, 1962, 1974, chapters 5–6. The basic formula for

understanding the distribution of income is

$$P/Y = [1/(S_p p - S_w) \cdot I/Y] - [S_w/(S_p - S_w)]$$

where P are profits, Y is the national income, S_p is the marginal propensity to save out of profits, S_w is the marginal propensity to save out of wages, and I is investment (Eichner and Kregel, 1975, pp. 1296–1300).

8. The issue here is whether the social rate of return on these types of expenditure is not just positive but indeed at least equal to the social rate of return on plant and equipment and other types of private investment. The issue needs to be approached, at the micro level, on a program-by-program basis. It is at this point that the recent literature on program budgeting, program evaluation, and similar types of analyses of the public sector spending become relevant. See Dorfman, 1965; Schultze, 1968; Rivlin, 1971; Eichner and Brecher, 1979.

9. The Flow of Funds Accounts typically refers to the net cash inflow as "Gross Savings," to the outlays on durable goods as "Tangible Investment," and to the difference between the two as the "Net Financial Investment."

10. This insight into the workings of a market economy derives not from Keynes (1936) and his short-period equilibrium model but rather from Myrdal (1939) and Metzler (1947) and their short-period disequilibrium models.

11. The devaluation will also have the effect of loosening the constraint on the price of domestically produced industrial goods that imported substitutes provide. This is because the devaluation raises the price of imported industrial goods as well as the price of imported raw materials (Eichner, 1976, p. 67; Eichner, 1977b).

12. While some would argue that all of the profits earned, and not just the portion paid out in dividends, should be limited, this differential treatment follows from the post-Keynesian distinction between consumption out of profits and any reinvestment of profits. The latter, it can be assumed, is governed by the rate of economic expansion and therefore does not need to be controlled directly. Of course, this argument ignores the possibility of capital asset appreciation, financed out of an expansionary monetary policy, and the resulting ability of capital asset-holding households to finance additional consumption out of capital gains (Eichner, 1976, pp. 280–283). It also ignores the possibility that the retained profits will be invested in ways that provide social returns far below the private returns (ibid., pp. 283–286).

13. An effort was made, as part of the wage and price controls established during the Nixon administration, to place a limit on dividends, and this limit was even lower than on wages.

Notes to the Addendum

1. Robert Guttman, in a private communication, has pointed out the recent tendency of governments to use the wage standard set for government employees as a device for influencing private wage settlements. This can be regarded as just a more sophisticated way of implementing a voluntary set of guidelines—or, as Guttman argues, as a separate form of incomes policy.

2. The British in 1976, by threatening to deny government contracts to firms violating its wage standard, have come the closest to adopting a tax-based incomes policy. Whether this can be considered a test of TIP, and even what the results of that experiment were, is unclear.

7
The New Paradigm
and Macrodynamic Modeling

Introduction

There seems to be some confusion as to what is meant by the term post-Keynesian. The fact that other terms, such as neo-Keynesian, neo-Ricardian, Cantabridgian, and post-classical, have been used to denote the same body of theory or important parts thereof has contributed to the confusion. Moreover, there are certain essential elements which have yet to be widely recognized as being a part of the same overarching paradigm. Samuelson, in the preface to the latest edition of his *Principles*, has further muddied the waters by turning on its head the distinction between orthodox Keynesian theory, based on the neoclassical synthesis, and an opposed post-Keynesian theory.

The purpose of this essay is to clarify what is meant by post-Keynesian theory. I hope to show that it constitutes an alternative to the prevailing theory in economics, an alternative which is both comprehensive, accounting for the widest possible range of economic phenomena, and coherent, able to meet any test for logical consistency. Even more important, I hope to show that it can serve as the basis for an empirically relevant model of advanced market economies like those of the United States and Great Britain, a model that can show the way out of the stagflation trap in which the more orthodox models, Keynesian as well as monetarist, have placed those economies.

It is less controversial to say what post-Keynesian theory is not than to say what it is.

Post-Keynesian theory is not neoclassical theory. This means it is not based on any of the four theoretical constructs which, as I have indicated on other occasions, constitute the core of neoclassical theory (Eichner, 1981, 1983a). These four theoretical constructs are:

1. A set of indifference curves—or any other putative mapping of

individual utility functions—which, when aggregated for all households, are thought to represent the relative preferences for any two or more goods by the society as a whole.

2. A set of continuous, or smooth, isoquants for each and every good produced which, when taken together, represent all the combinations of labor and other inputs that can be used to produce those goods.

3. A set of positively sloped supply curves for all the different firms and industries that comprise the enterprise sector of the economy, based on the assumption that firms are both short-run profit maximizers and price takers.

4. A set of marginal physical product curves for all the inputs used in the production process, not just the labor inputs but also, even more critical, the "capital" inputs.

Moreover, post-Keynesian theory is not even the neoclassical synthesis. This means that, in addition to the four theoretical constructs just identified, it is not based on the presumed existence of either a set of LM-IS curves or a Phillips curve.

Post-Keynesian theory avoids the use of all six of these theoretical constructs because they lack any basis in empirically observable reality. Their use would defeat the purpose of post-Keynesian theory, which is to explain the macrodynamic behavior of actual economic systems.

This does not mean that, in any particular analytical exercise, every one of the neoclassical constructs must be scrupulously avoided. For heuristic or other reasons it may, in fact, be better not to challenge the orthodox theory, directly on one or more of the above points. What it means rather is that, to fall under the post-Keynesian rubric, the argument must not depend in any critical way on the six theoretical constructs that constitute the core of the neoclassical synthesis.

While it may be less controversial to say what post-Keynesian theory is not, this is not very helpful to those who, being no less critical of neoclassical theory, are looking for something positive to put in its place. For this reason I will say no more here about what post-Keynesian theory is not and instead will concentrate on explaining what post-Keynesian theory is.

Post-Keynesian theory can be said to consist of a theory of production; a theory of household demand; a theory of growth and distribution; a theory of prices and pricing, a theory of money, credit, and finance; and a theory of wage determination and inflation. These six elements of post-Keynesian theory, which I would argue form a coherent whole, can be compared with the six elements that lie at the heart of the neoclassical synthesis, both in terms of what they take for granted about the real world and in terms of what they are able to explain about that world. I shall say a bit more about these six elements shortly. First, however, a brief word about the analytical framework of post-Keynesian theory.

Post-Keynesian theory is concerned about historical time as distinct from logical time. This means it is concerned with processes that can proceed in one direction only—forward. The most important of these processes is the one that produces the uneven expansion of economic systems over time which is so clearly discernible from the historical record. It is this primary focus of the theory that gives rise to the fundamental distinction within post-Keynesian theory between a long-period analysis, representing an effort to explain the observable secular trends, and a short-period analysis, representing an effort to explain the cyclical fluctuations, or deviations, around those trend lines. While some post-Keynesians may disagree, I would argue that both types of analysis, short-period as well as long-period, are essential—and indeed complementary to one another. This is the basic methodological position underlying the econometric model of the American economy which my colleague, Leonard Forman, and I are constructing in an attempt to demonstrate the empirical validity of post-Keynesian theory (Eichner, 1979a; Forman and Eichner, 1981). To be sure, the long-period analysis is frequently based on models of steady-state expansion which, since they apply only in logical time, would seem to run counter to the emphasis in post-Keynesian theory on actual historical processes. Still, to the extent that these models merely give rise to a series of testable hypotheses about the relationships which must hold in the long period, they do not subvert the purpose of post-Keynesian theory, and in fact are indispensable for shedding light on the observable secular trends. It is the empirical testability of the propositions, and not the manner in which they are arrived at, which is critical.

Let us now turn to the six elements which constitute the larger body of post-Keynesian theory.

The post-Keynesian theory of production

The post-Keynesian theory of production is based, in the simplest case, on an open Leontief model, such as the one shown in Exhibit 1. This model consists of an enterprise sector, or production system, disaggregated into n industries, each producing a different good. With n taking

Exhibit 1

The Leontief Production Model

The Leontief production model consists of n sectors, or industries, each producing intermediate and/or final output as follows:

	Value of Intermediate Output $\hat{P}A\hat{Q}$				Value of Final Output $\hat{P}X$	Value of Total Output $\hat{P}Q$
Value of Intermediate Output $\hat{P}A\hat{Q}$	$p_1 a_{1\cdot1} Q_1 +$	$p_1 a_{1\cdot2} Q_2 +$	$p_1 a_{1\cdot3} Q_3 + \cdots +$	$p_1 a_{1\cdot n} Q_n$	$+ \; p_1 X_1$	$= \; p_1 Q_1$
	$+$	$+$	$+$	$+$	$+$	$+$
	$p_2 a_{2\cdot1} Q_1 +$	$p_2 a_{2\cdot2} Q_2 +$	$p_2 a_{2\cdot3} Q_3 + \cdots +$	$p_2 a_{2\cdot n} Q_n$	$+ \; p_2 X_2$	$= \; p_2 Q_2$
	$+$	$+$	$+$	$+$	$+$	$+$
	$p_3 a_{3\cdot1} Q_1 +$	$p_3 a_{3\cdot2} Q_2 +$	$p_3 a_{3\cdot3} Q_3 + \cdots +$	$p_3 a_{3\cdot n} Q_n$	$+ \; p_3 X_3$	$= \; p_3 Q_3$
	$+$	$\cdot$	$\cdot$	$\cdot$	$\cdots$	$\cdots$
	$+$	$+$	$+$	$+$	$+$	$+$
	$p_n a_{n\cdot1} Q_1 +$	$p_n a_{n\cdot2} Q_2 +$	$p_n a_{n\cdot3} Q_3 + \cdots +$	$p_n a_{n\cdot n} Q_n$	$+ \; p_n X_n$	$= \; p_n Q_n$
	$+$	$+$	$+$	$+$	$=$	$=$
Value Added $\hat{V}Q$	$wl_1 Q_1 +$	$wl_2 Q_2 +$	$wl_3 Q_3 + \cdots +$	$wl_n Q_n$	$= \; wM$	
	$\pi_1 +$	$\pi_2 +$	$\pi_3 + \cdots +$	π_n	$= \; \pi$	
	$=$	$=$	$=$	$=$		$=$
Value of all Inputs $\hat{P}Q$	$p_1 Q_1 +$	$p_2 Q_2 +$	$p_3 Q_3 + \cdots +$	$p_n Q_n$		$= \; \hat{P}Q$

where p_i is the price of the ith good produced; a_{ij} is a technical coefficient defined as q_{ij}/Q_j where q_{ij} is the quantity of the ith industry's output used as an input in the jth industry and Q_j is the total output of the jth industry; X_i is the final output produced in the ith industry; w is the money wage rate, I_j is the jth industry's labor technical coefficient defined as the quantity of labor in manhours used in the jth industry relative to the output of the jth industry; M is the total quantity of labor in manhours; π_j is the residual, or margin above costs, earned in the jth industry, and π is the total residual.

a value greater than two, the sterility of one-commodity models, in which there can be no markets strictly speaking, and even of two-commodity models, in which there is no plausible role for money, is avoided. The open Leontief model, with the enterprise sector disaggregated into a complete set of separate industries, makes it possible to analyze, not just the flow of goods and services between business firms and households but also, what is far more important in understanding market activity, the inter-industry flow of goods among firms. These inter-industry flows are represented, empirically, by an input-output table.

At the heart of the open Leontief model, and uniquely defining this type of model, is a set of labor and other technical coefficients—what *are* commonly denoted as the **L** vector and **A** matrix. The technical coefficients for each industry indicate the fixed quantities of labor and material inputs required to produce a given unit of output. Delineated into vertical columns, these technical coefficients represent each industry's technology and, at the same time, its production function. Unlike a neoclassical production function, the capital inputs are only implicit, not explicit. [1] It is the particular configuration of capital goods presently in place—the plant and equipment delimiting each industry's productive capacity—that gives rise to a particular set of technical coefficients for that industry and, when all the technical coefficients are combined as in the **L** vector and **A** matrix, for the production system as a whole.

There are several things about these technical coefficients that are especially important from a theoretical point of view. One is that the coefficients can be assumed to exist independently of any particular set of prices, representing as they do, a given state of technology that has a logically prior existence. Indeed, in the model, it is the technology represented by the **A** matrix that determines the set of relative prices and not, as in a Walrasian model, the reverse. A second important thing about these technical coefficients is that they imply that the output of the industries can be produced only by using fixed combinations of all the various inputs, labor, and material. However, with a sufficient supply of the required inputs available in those fixed combinations, output can then be expanded indefinitely. The model is therefore consistent with the empirical evidence that production, in the short period at least in the industrial sector of the economy, is characterized both by fixed technical coefficients and by constant returns to scale.

The **A** matrix is the key to any analysis based on this type of production model. The inverse of the **A** matrix, when combined with a vector of final demand, makes it possible to determine the output of each of the industries that comprise the production system. The same Leontief inverse, when combined with a value added vector (or, with wages equal to subsistence or some other predetermined amount, when combined with a profit or residual income vector), leads to the dual price solution. This is the set of relative prices that must be charged if the production system is to cover all the costs of production.

The open Leontief model can be modified and/or extended in a number of important ways. Pasinetti (1981) has shown how, using the same Leontief inverse, a vertically integrated version of the model can be constructed, with labor as the only input. The vertically integrated version of the model makes it possible to examine the effect technical progress has on productivity, defined as the increase in output per worker over time. A slightly different version of the same vertically integrated model can be constructed, with natural resources along with labor as the only inputs. This version of the model can be used to examine both the natural resource constraints on economic expansion and, with the model extended to a global scale as Leontief *et al.* (1978) have done, the terms of trade between primary producers and industrial countries.

Pasinetti has also shown how the same type of open Leontief model can be extended so that it includes technical progress as an integral part of the analysis. The open Leontief model can be further modified to allow for a different choice of techniques before any new capacity is added and the technical coefficients again become fixed. This involves adding features of the somewhat more intricate von Neumann model to the basic Leontief model, the result being what is referred to in the growth literature as a ''putty-clay'' model with a capital stock that is at least partly vintage in nature.

It is this type of production theory, based on a set of fixed technical coefficients, or **A** matrix, that underlies the post-Keynesian model of the American economy Dr. Forman and I are attempting to construct. Block II of the model, which explains the growth of aggregate output and employment, assumes a set of fixed labor coefficients so that the cyclical movement of aggregate employment depends solely on the cyclical movement of aggregate output—with wage rates or any other factor reflecting the relative price of labor playing no significant role. The trend in the growth of employment, meanwhile, depends on the change in the labor coefficients taking place over time, both as a result of technical progress and, especially important in recent years, the shift toward a service economy.

In the model we are constructing, the notion basic to an open Leontief model—that the final demand vector, together with the inverse of the A matrix, determines the output of each of the n industries—is taken a step further in the direction Keynes (1936) pointed to by making the final demand vector itself, and thus the national product, depend on a particular subcomponent of that final demand vector. The subcomponent consists of the durable goods which flow to, and hence are purchased by, all the different sectors—government, household, and the rest-of-the-world as well as the production units, or business firms, which comprise the enterprise sector itself (see Exhibit 2). Indeed, this is the basis for the relationship traced out in the model between Blocks I and II (see Exhibit 3). Block I explains the growth of durable goods purchases by each of the sectors—what, because of their greater postponability and hence volatility, are referred to as discretionary expenditures—and this growth of durable goods purchases by each of the sectors is then the basis for explaining, via the multiplier effect, the growth of output and employment in Block II. Moreover, since the cyclical movement of durable goods purchases, or discretionary expenditures, in each of the sectors depends, among other factors, on the level of aggregate demand, the two blocks together give rise to a combined multiplier-accelerator process as the underlying basis for the economy's cyclical movements.

In explaining this growth of durable goods purchases in Block I, a second element of post-Keynesian theory becomes important. This is the theory of household expenditures.

The post-Keynesian theory of household expenditures

In place of the metaphysical indifference curves that underlie the neoclassical theory of demand, post-Keynesian theory starts with the price and income elasticities of demand which economists are actually able to estimate. Based on a substantial body of research going back to Engels' work in the nineteenth century, post-Keynesian economists generally

Exhibit 2

Decomposition of the Final Demand Vector

Final Output $\hat{P}D$		Households ND	D		Business D		Government ND	D		Foreign ND	D		Non-Durables H	G	F		Durables H	B	G	F
$p_1 X_1$	=	$p_1 X_1$	0	+	0	+	0	0	=	0	0	+	$p_1 X_1$	0	0	+	0	0	0	0
$p_2 X_2$	=	0	$p_2 X_2$	+	0	+	0	0	=	0	0	+	0	0	0	+	$p_2 X_2$	0	0	0
$p_3 X_3$	=	0	0	+	$p_3 X_3$	+	0	0	=	0	0	+	0	0	0	+	0	$p_3 X_3$	0	0
$p_4 X_4$	=	0	0	+	0	+	$p_4 X_4$	0	=	0	0	+	0	$p_4 X_4$	0	+	0	0	0	0
$p_5 X_5$	=	0	0	+	0	+	0	$p_5 X_5$	=	0	0	+	0	0	0	+	0	0	$p_5 X_5$	0
$p_6 X_6$	=	0	0	+	0	+	0	0	=	$p_6 X_6$	0	+	0	0	$p_6 X_6$	+	0	0	0	0
$p_7 X_7$	=	0	0	+	0	+	0	0	=	0	$p_7 X_7$	+	0	0	0	+	0	0	0	$p_7 X_7$

159

Exhibit 3

Flow Diagram

Blocks I and II of the CEAR Model

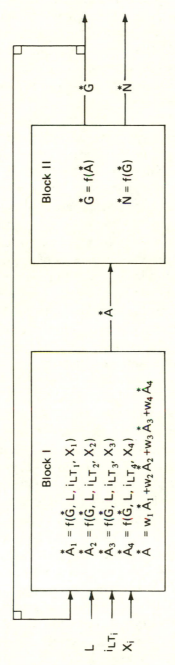

where A_1 is X_2, A_2 is X_3, A_3 is X_5 and A_4 is X_7

G is A plus X_1, X_4 and X_6

L is a measure of liquidity pressure

i_{LT_i} is the long-term interest rate that influences durable goods purchases in the ith sector

X_i is a set of exogenous factors that influences durable goods purchases in the ith sector

and N is aggregate employment

The star (*) over a variable, denotes the cyclical movement of the variable, that is, the current growth rate less the trend value.

assume that, in an economy that is expanding over time (though not necessarily at a constant rate), it is the income effect that will predominate over the relative price, or substitution, effects. Indeed, any substitution, based on a change in relative prices, is likely to be of only minor importance and, if ignored altogether, will be less disastrous to the argument than if, as in the typical neoclassical model, the income effects are ignored instead.

This lack of substitutability reflects two factors. One is the set of discrete consumption categories into which household expenditures are divided. The fact is that the major types of consumption goods purchased—food, clothing, housing, personal care, transport, recreation, other services, and durables—serve quite different physical needs so that an item under one category cannot readily be substituted for an item under another category. In choosing any particular basket of consumption goods, households must include items under each of the major categories—the subsistence categories of food, clothing, housing, and personal care in particular.[2] Substitution can take place only within fairly narrow subcategories. Consumer preferences are, in this sense, lexicographically ordered (Canterbery, 1979a; Earl, 1983). The second factor limiting the possibilities of substitution is the critical role played by social convention, and thus of acquired tastes, in determining each household's normal consumption patterns within those subcategories.

In a line of reasoning that can be traced back to Veblen (1899), Mitchell (1937), Duesenberry (1949), and other institutionalists, consumer preferences are seen as being the result of learned social behavior rather than being innate at birth or in some other sense given. These preferences are likely to be modified over time, not just by advertising and other forms of social conditioning but also, even more significantly, by the growth of income levels within each of the social groups, or classes, which comprise the household sector as an increasingly affluent lifestyle comes to be viewed as normal. A household's consumption pattern, at any given point in time, thus reflects the lifestyle of the other households that constitute its social reference group. What must be purchased is that basket of goods which, going beyond any subsistence needs, is required to maintain the household's relative position in society. This basket of goods can be reduced to a standardized shopping list that changes but slowly over time, and then for reasons that have little to do with relative prices.[3]

This theory of household expenditure is reflected in the equations included in Block I of the model to explain the growth of durable goods purchases, including structures, by the household sector. The trend growth rate depends on the income and price elasticities for the various types of consumer durables, while the cyclical movements around that trend line depend on a set of factors that reflect the cumulative body of empirical research that has been done on the Keynesian consumption function. Where Block I breaks new ground is in assuming that consumer durable goods purchases are but one component of the total durable goods purchases which have a short-period multiplier effect. The more important distinction, then, at least insofar as the cyclical movements of the economy are concerned, is between durable and nondurable goods purchases rather than between expenditures by households and expenditures by the other sectors. Insofar as capital formation and the increase in productive capacity are concerned, the matter is quite different. Only the durable goods purchased by the enterprise sector, i.e., any new plant and equipment, and that portion of government outlays that represent an investment in infrastructure are important. This leads to the third element of post-Keynesian theory.

The post-Keynesian theory of growth and distribution

The post-Keynesian theory of growth and distribution is based on the pioneering work of Harrod (1939, 1948) and Kalecki (1938)—two separate lines of analysis which were first synthesized by Joan Robinson in a book (1956) that marks the beginning of a distinctly different post-Keynesian body of theory. More recently Pasinetti (1981), by combining the same long-period analysis of steady-state expansion with a fixed-coefficient model of production encompassing technical progress, has produced an even broader synthesis. What links these various models is the key role played by investment, or the rate of accumulation, in simultaneously determining the secular growth of the economy, any cyclical fluctuations in economic activity, and the resulting distribution of income. A distinguishing feature of this theory is that the distribution of income, both in the long period and in the short, is explained by a set of macroeconomic conditions rather than by the microeconomic factors emphasized in neoclassical theory.

   The most important of these macroeconomic factors is the growth of output per worker, itself largely the result of the technical progress made possible by the application of science and other forms of knowledge to the problem of satisfying the material needs of society. The greater the growth of output per worker, the more rapid can be the secular increase in per capita consumption by workers, and hence the more rapid the secular growth of real wages. Still, the growth of real wages does not depend solely on the growth of output per worker. It also depends on the rate of investment, or accumulation.

Other things, including the rate of technical progress, remaining constant, it can be shown that the greater the rate of investment, and thus the more rapid the pace of economic expansion, the lower will be the relative share of income going to workers at a given rate of capacity utilization. This is because wages will need to be depressed, at least relative to profits, so that resources can be diverted from consumption into capital formation. Of course, the real wage need not fall in absolute terms. The growth of the real wage merely has to be less than the growth of profits so that the disproportionate increase in investment can be financed, both in money and in real terms. Moreover, the rate of technical progress will not necessarily be unaffected by the rate of investment. With technical progress to a significant extent capital-embodied, that is, dependent on the introduction of new types of capital goods, an increase in investment can be expected to lead to a higher rate of technical progress as measured by the growth of output per worker. It is just that, in the absence of any offsetting factors, an increase in the level of economic activity, as induced by a higher rate of investment or some other form of discretionary spending, can be expected to lead to a decline in labor's relative share. This can be observed both in the long period and in the short (Eichner and Kregel, 1975).

The growth of the real wage depends on one other factor: the amount of consumption out of profits, that is, the share of profits that is used for other than private investment purposes. An increase in the amount of consumption out of profits will, like an increase in investment, serve to reduce the share of national income going to workers. Only, in contrast to an increase in investment, it will not have the additional effect of at least increasing the future income of workers by expanding the productive capacity of the economic system. While it might seem that the amount of consumption out of profits is limited to the dividends paid out and other forms of rentier income that are not reinvested, it actually encompasses a much broader range of income flows. The government, through the taxes it collects from business, receives a share of all profits. Moreover, the foreign suppliers of raw materials, through any increase in the prices they are able to charge, can also siphon off a share of the profits being earned domestically. Thus, the share of national income that goes to workers will be reduced, not just by a more rapid rate of investment but also by an increase in the size of the public sector and by an adverse shift in the terms of trade.

This theory of income distribution is reflected in Block III of the model being constructed. In this block the cyclical movement of the discretionary funds, or net cash inflow, of the various sectors is explained—as distinct from the cyclical movement of discretionary expenditures explained in Block I. This net cash inflow consists of each sector's total revenue—its sales volume, disposable income or tax yields—less any outlays on nondurable goods and services. The cyclical movement of these discretionary expenditures depends on the cyclical movement in aggregate economic activity—holding prices, wages, tax rates, and other inter-sectoral compensation rates constant. It is the latter which determine the longer run, or noncyclical, distribution of income.

The discretionary funds for each sector can be compared with the sector's discretionary expenditures in nominal terms. The difference is the sector's net cash deficit, and this net cash deficit for each of the sectors has two separate effects. One is a monetary effect since the deficit will have to be financed in some manner. More will be said about this linkage shortly. The other effect is what can be termed the cash-flow feedback effect. While in an equilibrium model total discretionary funds will necessarily be equal to total discretionary expenditures, in the real world of persistent monetary disequilibrium this need not be the case. Indeed, with total discretionary expenditures greater than total discretionary funds, the economy will be further stimulated—as in a simple Keynesian model with investment greater than savings—while in the opposite case the expansion of the economy will be dampened. This is the cash-flow feedback effect which any model of an economy based on money transactions must incorporate (see Exhibit 4).

With Block III added to Blocks I and II, and with the cash-flow feedback effect thus modifying the results of the more basic multiplier-accelerator process, the analysis of the real flows in the model is complete. Block III, however, assumes the existence of a set of monetary institutions—including prices which are not simply notational but instead represent actual money transfers. Otherwise there would be no net cash inflow, or discretionary funds. It is therefore necessary to supplement the analysis of the real flows based

Exhibit 4

Flow Diagram

Blocks I, II and III of the CEAR Model

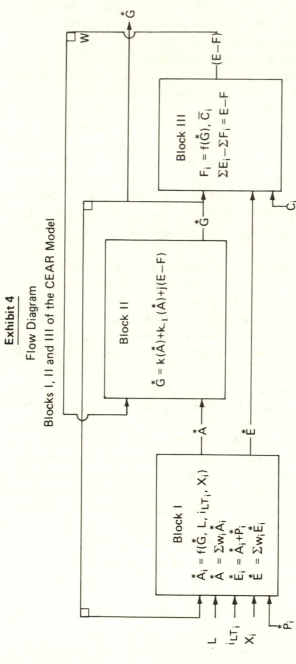

Block I

$$\overset{*}{A}_i = f(\overset{*}{G}, L, i_{LT_i}, X_i)$$
$$\overset{*}{A} = \Sigma w_i \overset{*}{A}_i$$
$$\overset{*}{E}_i = \overset{*}{A}_i + \overset{*}{P}_i$$
$$\overset{*}{E} = \Sigma w_i \overset{*}{E}_i$$

Block II

$$\overset{*}{G} = k(\overset{*}{A}) + k_{-1}(\overset{*}{A}) + j(E - F)$$

Block III

$$F_i = f(\overset{*}{G}), \bar{C}_i$$
$$\Sigma E_i - \Sigma F_i = E - F$$

where E_i is durable goods purchases by the ith sector in nominal terms,

E is total durable goods in nominal terms,

P_i is the price deflator, for durable goods purchases by the ith sector,

k and k_{-1} are the first and second round impact multipliers,

j is the cash-flow feedback effect,

F_i is discretionary funds in the ith sector, that is, total income or revenue earned by the sector less all expenditures on non-durable goods and services,

and C is the set of relevant inter-sectoral compensation rates, e.g. wages, taxes, etc., for the ith sector.

on an extension and elaboration of the open Leontief production model with a parallel analysis of the accompanying money flows. This leads to the next important element of post-Keynesian theory, the theory of prices and pricing in a monetarized, non-Walrasian economy.

The post-Keynesian theory of prices and pricing

The open Leontief model's dual price solution produces a price vector, or set of relative prices, which, interpreted in a Sraffaian or neo-Ricardian framework as a set of cost-of-production prices, becomes the post-Keynesian theory of relative prices. This dual price solution requires only that a wage bill and the amount of residual income, or profit, be specified for each industry. The wage bill and the residual income together constitute the value added vector, and this value added vector together with the Leontief inverse produces the set of relative prices that must prevail in the long period if all the costs of production are to be covered. To explain the set of relative prices, it is therefore necessary to explain only what determines the wage bill and residual income for each industry. The former will depend on the wage rate and the labor coefficients for each industry. Leaving aside for the moment what determines the wage rate and taking the labor coefficients as given, the set of relative prices will depend on the residual income, or mark-up, established in each industry. In an economy that is expanding over time, as in a von Neumann version of the open Leontief model, this mark-up will depend on the rate of investment and hence on the rate of expansion itself.

The theory of relative prices just outlined becomes a theory of pricing when the manner in which firms and/or industries act to establish those prices is specified. The basis for this theory of pricing (as distinct from a theory of relative prices) is one or more of the mark-up pricing models that follow from the work of Means (1962) and the Brookings Institution (Kaplan et al., 1958) in the United States and the Oxford Pricing Group in England (Wilson and Andrews, 1951; Andrews, 1964). These models, based on the mark-up that is added to wages and other unit costs of production at some standard, or expected, operating rate, make it possible to explain the actual level of prices that can be observed at any given point in time. In a line of theoretical development that can be traced back to Kalecki (1954), the mark-up itself is explained not by short-run demand conditions as emphasized in the orthodox pricing models (see Coutts *et al.*, 1978; Eckstein and

Fromm, 1968) but rather by the long-term financing needs of business enterprise relative to the degree of market, or "monopoly," power that individual firms and/or industries are able to exercise (Steindl, 1952; Sylos-Labini, 1962, 1974; Wood, 1975; Eichner, 1973a, 1976). What this model of pricing implies is that, to the extent an industry supply curve can even be said to exist (Wiles, 1956; R. Robinson, 1961), it is, within the observable range, perfectly elastic rather than positively sloped. A change in the industry price is produced only by a change in costs, and thus by a shift of the supply curve itself.

This mark-up model can then be generalized for the industrial sector as a whole. Indeed, it serves as the basis for the price equations which constitute Block IV of the model we are constructing. In that block, industrial prices are assumed to depend on unit labor and raw material prices, with the mark-up that is added to those unit costs changing only to the extent there is a perceived change in the secular rate of expansion for the economy as a whole. Unit labor costs depend on the growth of money wages relative to the growth of output per worker while unit raw material prices depend on the terms of trade and/or the exchange rate with the countries that supply oil and other primary products. It is the movement of industrial prices which is then used to explain both any change in the aggregate price level and any change in the various price deflators used in Block I of the model (see Exhibit 5).

The aggregate price level is assumed to be independent of the money supply. Indeed, the line of causation runs from the price level to the money supply, that is, in the opposite direction from that assumed in monetarist models. This leads to the next element of post-Keynesian theory, the treatment of money, credit, and finance.

The post-Keynesian theory of money, credit, and finance

The post-Keynesian theory of money, credit, and finance focuses on the availability of credit, and the fragility of the financial system rather than on the supply of what is usually defined as the money stock. It is the demand for and the availability of credit that is viewed as the critical link between the real and monetary sectors of a modern economy. This approach to money, which is only imminent in Keynes (1930, 1936), has been further developed in the writings of Davidson (1972) and Minsky (1975, 1982) among others, and it leads to the argument that not only the money stock, but also the monetary base itself (including

Exhibit 5

Flow Diagram

Block IV of the CEAR Model

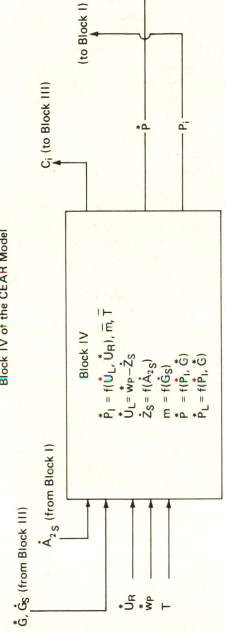

$\dot{\ast G}, \dot{G}_S$ (from Block III)

$\dot{A}_{2S}$ (from Block I)

$\ast U_R$
$\ast w_P$
T

Block IV

$\ast \dot{P}_I = f(\ast U_L, U_R), \bar{m}, \bar{T}$

$\ast U_L = \ast w_P - \dot{\ast Z}_S$

$\dot{Z}_S = f(\dot{A}_{2S})$

$m = f(\dot{G}_S)$

$\ast \dot{P} = f(P_I, \ast G)$

$\ast \dot{P}_L = f(P_I, \ast G)$

C_i (to Block III)

$\ast P$

P_i

(to Block I)

where P_I is an index of industrial prices

U_L is unit labour costs

U_R is unit raw material prices

m is the average mark-up

T is a vector of business tax rates

w_P is the pattern, or norm, established for the money wage rate

Z is output per worker

P is the aggregate price level

and a dot ($\dot{\ }$) over the variable together with an s subscript, denotes the secular growth rate especially bank reserves) is endogenously determined (Moore, 1979, 1983, as well as essay five above). In this view, it is the growth of money wages and any cash deficits from that or other sources that determines the demand for credit and hence the endogenous response of the banking system. The demand for credit thus creates its own supply—at least up to the limit set by existing bank reserves. If, in an effort to control inflation, the monetary authorities should attempt to limit the growth of bank reserves, the effect will be to reduce liquidity throughout the economy, creating a shortage of credit that will slow the growth of externally financed durable goods purchases, particularly within the private sector. The result will be, not a decline in the price level as hoped, but rather, a decline in real output. Indeed, if the effort is pushed too far, it may even produce a liquidity crisis.

This view of money is reflected in Block V of the model we are constructing (see Exhibit 6). The model assumes that the monetary base, consisting of bank reserves and currency in circulation, is to a significant extent endogenously determined. This is because, to maintain orderly financial markets, the monetary authorities are forced to offset or neutralize through open-market operations any flows into or out of the banking system as a result of any change in bank float, U.S. Treasury holdings of cash, the gold stock, or any of the other factors that either absorb or free up bank reserve funds. For much the same reason, the monetary authorities are forced to see to it that bank reserves expand or contract, again through their open-market operations, in response to any change in the demand for currency or bank loans. The net change in the Federal Reserve System's holdings of government securities that is associated with either of these two sets of factors, the one deriving from the central bank's neutralizing role and the other its accommodating role, is then defined in Block V as the Federal Reserve's endogenous policy response. It is the difference between the total purchase of government securities by the Federal Reserve System and this endogenous response which represents the discretionary, or nonendogenous, component of monetary policy.

A change in the discretionary component of monetary policy, measured by the difference between total open-market purchases of government securities by the Federal Reserve System and the neutralizing and/or accommodating amount of purchases, will have several effects, some more immediate than others. The most immediate, and most significant, effect will be on the degree of liquidity pressure throughout the economy. This is measured in Block V by the ratio of bank loans (on

Exhibit 6

Flow Diagram

Block V of the CEAR Model

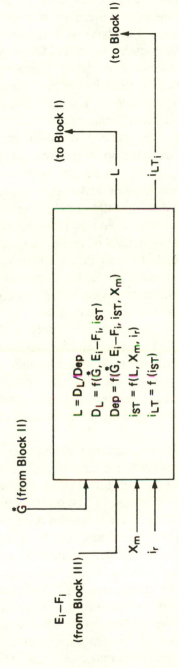

$E_i - F_i$
(from Block III)

X_m

i_r

$\overset{*}{G}$ (from Block II)

$L = D_L / Dep$
$D_L = f(\overset{*}{G}, E_i - F_i, i_{ST})$
$Dep = f(\overset{*}{G}, E_i - F_i, i_{ST}, X_m)$
$i_{ST} = f(L, X_m, i_r)$
$i_{LT} = f(i_{ST})$

(to Block I)

L

i_{LT_i}

(to Block I)

where D_L is the demand for bank loans,
Dep is the amount of bank deposits,
i_{ST} is the disturbance in the term structure of short-term interest rates,
X_m is the central bank's non-accommodating open-market operations,
and i_r is the rediscount rate.

the asset side of the bank's balance sheets) to bank deposits (on the liability side). A restrictive monetary policy, by reducing bank deposits and thus the denominator, will mean an increase in the liquidity pressure ratio. The capacity of the banking system to meet the credit needs of business firms and households will, in this way, be reduced relative to the demand for loans, or credit. While some of the shortfall in required reserves may be offset by the banks borrowing reserves, the banking system will nonetheless be under pressure to cut back on the amount of short-term credit being extended. An expansionary monetary policy, by increasing bank deposits and thus reducing the liquidity pressure ratio, will have the opposite effect, banks then being free to expand their lending activity at current interest rates.

There are thus two separate influences on the degree of liquidity pressure, as measured by the ratio of bank loans to bank deposits. One influence is the level of real and nominal economic activity. To the extent that a change in the level of real economic activity, either positive or negative, leads to cash deficits that must be financed, the demand for bank loans will rise and the numerator of the liquidity ratio will become larger. Similarly, to the extent that higher prices, and thus an increase in nominal economic activity, leads to the need for additional working capital, the same result will follow. These are the endogenous factors determining the demand for credit, and hence the numerator of the liquidity pressure ratio. The other influence on the degree of liquidity pressure is from the discretionary component of the monetary policy being pursued by the central bank. Whether the policy is a restrictive or expansionary one, it will affect the denominator of the liquidity ratio.

A restrictive policy will also reduce the banking system's free reserves (that is, its reserves in excess of the legally required amount) and, in this way, put further pressure on the banks to curtail their lending activity. The reduction in free reserves will, at the same time and even more directly than the increased pressure on the commercial banking system's liquidity position, lead to an increase in short-term interest rates. Indeed, it is primarily through the effect on the free reserve position of the banking system that a restrictive policy affects the entire spectrum of interest rates. Still, the liquidity pressure ratio is the most important of the several monetary-financial variables explained in Block V. First, it is a significant determinant of the cyclical movement of durable goods purchases, or discretionary expenditures, within many of the sectors. Its importance, in this respect, is considerably greater than that of the long-term interest rates also explained in Block V (Forman and Eichner, 1981). Second, it plays an independent role in determining any change in the spectrum of short-term interest rates which, with a further time lag, influences the level of long-term interest rates—especially the yield on high-grade corporate securities and the mortgage rate which, in turn, influence the cyclical movement of durable goods purchases.

With the monetary base for the most part endogenously determined, the money supply will for the most part itself be endogenous. This means that the monetary authorities cannot control either the money supply or even the monetary base directly. When they apply a strict monetarist rule and thereby, in a period of secular inflation, impose a restrictive, or nonaccommodating, monetary policy, they will only succeed in increasing the degree of liquidity pressure throughout the economy and in this way, through both the direct and indirect effect on durable goods purchases, reduce the growth of real output and employment (the indirect effect being through interest rates). Since the secular and cyclical growth of prices does not depend on any of the monetary-financial variables explained in Block V, the monetary authorities cannot do much about the problem of inflation. They can only make the problem worse by superimposing a cyclical downturn in real output and employment on the secular rise in the price level. (The exception is the cyclical movement of prices outside the industrial sector, and even within the nonoligopolistic component of the industrial sector, which depends in part on aggregate demand conditions and which the monetary authorities can therefore influence through a more or less restrictive monetary policy.)

But if inflation is not just a monetary phenomenon which the central bank can bring under control through the power it exercises over certain variables, then how is the secular rise in the price level, which has led to the widespread loss of faith in orthodox Keynesian models, to be explained? For an answer to this question, it is necessary to turn to the sixth and final element of post-Keynesian theory. This is the theory of money wage determination and inflation.

The post-Keynesian theory of money wage determination and inflation

The wage rate, rather than being just another price as in a Walrasian general equilibrium analysis, plays the key role in determining all the other value relationships within the stipulated model of a monetarized production system (see Exhibit 5). Here post-Keynesian theory is careful to distinguish between the real wage—which consists of the actual basket of consumption goods workers are able to purchase with the income they earn—and the money wage. The latter is simply a nominal rate of compensation and, as opposed to the real wage, depends on the socio-political and other noneconomic factors that determine the bargaining strength of workers. In other words, the money wage rate is at least partially exogenous and must be taken as given in modeling the economy—as distinct from the stock of money which is endogenously determined. This explanation represents a synthesis of the neo-Ricardian arguments of Sraffa (1960), the post-Keynesian theory of income distribution, and the labor market analysis of certain institutionalist economists, such as Dunlop (1950), and Piore (1979); see also Eichner (1979c).

The point is that, based on the bargaining power of workers, the money wage can take almost any value the monetary authorities are prepared to accommodate through their open-market operations. Indeed, this argument is the basis for the post-Keynesian theory of inflation, it being the growth of money wages in excess of the real wage that necessarily leads to an offsetting rise in the price level (Weintraub, 1959, 1966; Eichner, 1976, 1980a). To the extent the monetary authorities are not prepared to accommodate the rise in money wages, the economy will, as just explained, become less liquid, with a resulting decline in durable goods purchases and thus a decline in real output and employment, transforming the annoying problem of inflation into the far more serious problem of stagflation.

What is significant about this theory of inflation is that it does not rest on the presumed existence of an excess-demand condition, either in final product or factor markets. It therefore does not depend on the assumption that supply curves, especially in the industrial sector, are positively sloped or that the growth of money wages is primarily a function of the unemployment rate. The theory, in other words, does not assume a Phillipsian trade-off between price stability and economic expansion.

This theory of money wage determination and inflation is reflected in Block IV of the model we are constructing. The trend in the growth of money wages depends on the national incremental wage pattern established either through the ''key'' bargain in some bellwether industry or through an official incomes policy. This wage standard can be identified by following press reports of collective bargaining in the unionized sector of the economy. Taking into account the multi-year duration of many labor contracts, the wage standard can then be used to explain the observed movement of money wages in the unionized sector, which largely corresponds to the oligopolistic component of the industrial sector plus the public sector. The alternative Phillips curve hypothesis is rejected by showing that, once the national incremental wage pattern is correctly identified and then properly incorporated into the money wage equation, the unemployment rate no longer has any explanatory power. The exception is again in the unorganized, or small business, sector where a change in the unemployment rate will partly affect the differential that normally exists between wages in that sector and wages throughout the rest of the economy.

This is not to argue that the national incremental wage pattern, though socio-politically determined and therefore exogenous to the economic system, will necessarily be immune to all economic influences. Indeed, it can be shown that any change in the socio-politically determined wage standard is likely to reflect a change in the growth of business profits and/or a change in the growth of consumer prices. Moreover, the political authorities may even opt for a free market incomes policy, meaning they hope a deliberately induced high unemployment rate will persuade the unionized work force to accept a lower rate of growth of money wages—in which case the national incremental wage pattern may itself be influenced by the unemployment rate, especially if the free market policy is pushed with sufficient abandon. The point is rather that, whatever may be the socio-political factors, economic or otherwise, shaping the national incremental wage pattern, that wage standard is not itself a variable uniquely determined by economic factors and therefore endogenous to the model. The distinction is an important one because it raises the possibility that, through some form of incomes policy other than a "free market" one, a national incremental wage pattern can be established which is noninflationary and in this way economic expansion, together with price stability, can be achieved.

Conclusions

This discussion of the several key elements of post-Keynesian theory and the econometric model of the American economy being constructed based on those elements has necessarily had to be somewhat attenuated (but see Eichner and Kregel, 1975; Eichner, 1979b). Nonetheless, it is hoped that the discussion has served to provide a better understanding of what post-Keynesian theory is as distinct from what it is not. Moreover, it is hoped that the discussion has made clear that there exists a model that can explain the process of inflation for a growing economy in terms other than the existence of excess demand, either because there is "too much money" chasing too few goods or because of "irresponsible" government deficits—a model that, at the same time, does not present public officials with the cruel choice of either permitting prices to continue rising unchecked or of slamming on the monetary and fiscal brakes in a vain effort to bring the inflationary process under control. It is, one could argue, a model that avoids the conceptual and empirical as well as the policy limitations of the orthodox Keynesian models, based on the neoclassical synthesis, and of their monetarist counterparts.

Afterword

This essay was originally published as one of the *Thames Papers in Political Economy* (Eichner, 1983b). The macrodynamic model described in the essay represents an effort to integrate the theory discussed in the preceding essays with the type of empirical research called for in the next essay so that economics can thereby be placed on a more scientific foundation. The results obtained so far in estimating the parameters of this model are reported in Forman and Eichner, 1981; Forman, Groves, and Eichner, 1984. See also Eichner, 1979a; Eichner, Forman, and Groves, 1982; Arestis, Driver, and Jones, 1984.

Notes

1. Some post-Keynesians prefer to make the capital inputs explicit by including them in the production function. This can be done, at least formally, based on the von Neumann extension of the Leontief model, by treating any produced goods not completely consumed during the period of production as both a direct material input and as a joint output of the system. The produced goods that are not completely consumed during the period of production then become capital inputs which, at the end of that time, are one period older—and as such are an output of the system just like the goods those capital inputs make it possible to produce (see Pasinetti, 1980, especially the essays by Baldone and Schefold). The better approach, I would argue, is the one subsequently adopted by Pasinetti (1981), in which for each of the n industries a parallel capital goods industry is delineated. (The capital goods industry may, in fact, exist only notionally, an industry being compelled, in reality, to construct any new facilities on its own. Indeed, this will necessarily have to be the case for at

least one of the n industries.) Relying on this approach, it is possible to determine, on the basis of the technical coefficients for the parallel capital goods industry, the mix of heterogeneous goods required for any expansion of capacity and thus it is possible to determine, after introducing the relevant set of prices so that the combination of goods used as the capital input can be described in value terms, the incremental capital-output ratio.

2. It is for this reason that the behavior assumed in the more orthodox theory of household demand is unlikely to be actually observed. The point is that households must choose, not between alternative individual goods but rather, between alternative sets of all items. That is, they must choose between complete consumption baskets. If households were then to behave as the orthodox theory of demand assumes they do—first determining the various alternative sets of all consumption items to which they are indifferent before proceeding to use the governing set of relative prices to select an optimal consumption basket—it would impose such a burden on the information-processing capability of households as to make this method of decision making impractical. Households would have to draw up not a single, comprehensive budget on which they could then act but instead large numbers of such budgets only to have all but one rejected as suboptimal.

3. Following up on the earlier point, while a household may opt for an alternative consumption basket, one that replaces one item under a given subcategory of consumption for another, the choice is more likely to reflect the influence of social norms of consumption and changing income levels than a shift in relative prices. Indeed, those other factors may be entirely sufficient to account for the observed pattern of household demand over time.

8
Post-Keynesian Theory and Empirical Research

The movement to replace neoclassical theory with an alternative body of post-Keynesian (and post-Marxian) theory has now entered its third, and decisive, stage.

The first stage, extending almost from the moment the neoclassical theory emerged in the 1870s down through the immediate post–World War II period, or for nearly 100 years, was concerned with pointing out the fallacies of that approach. Marx, Veblen, Keynes, and others all contributed in important ways to the ensuing critique (Seligman, 1962). Still, the most striking blows, at least to the logic of the system, were struck by Piero Sraffa, first in his 1926 article on increasing returns and then, even more tellingly, in his 1960 book, *Production of Commodities by Means of Commodities*, and by Joan Robinson in her 1953 article, "The Production Function and the Theory of Capital," which marked the onset of the Cambridge controversy in capital theory.

Today, neoclassical theory stands totally discredited on intellectual grounds—whether the theory takes the form of Marshallian partial equilibrium analysis, a neo-Walrasian general equilibrium model, the microeconomic half of the Samuelson-Solow "neoclassical synthesis," or a Clarkian steady-state growth model. Whatever the form, neoclassical theory can be shown to be either logically flawed or empirically irrelevant. No less important, the inability of the theory to suggest effective policies for dealing with the world's economic problems—whether they be the widespread unemployment of the 1930s or the double-digit inflation of the 1970s—has shown neoclassical economics to be politically as well as intellectually bankrupt.

The second stage in the shift of economics away from the neoclassical paradigm, covering the years from the publication of Joan Robinson's great work of synthesis, *The Accumulation of Capital*, in 1956 down to the present, has been taken up with developing a comprehensive alternative. This effort has drawn on the three major dissident traditions in economics: Marxian, institutionalist, and Keynesian. Still, the core of the new approach that has emerged during this period is distinctly post-Keynesian (and post-Marxian), combining as it does the growth dynamics of Roy Harrod, the production theory of Wassily Leontief, the value theory of Sraffa, and the distribution and pricing models of Michal Kalecki—along with the monetary ideas of Keynes himself—into a single coherent view of a capitalist economy that is expanding unevenly over time (Eichner and Kregel, 1975, Eichner, 1979b).

Although much work still remains to be done in filling in the details, the broad outlines of the new theoretical approach are clear: it encompasses production rather than just distribution, income effects rather than just substitution effects, a monetarized rather than just a barter economy. The key to the dynamics of the system is the rate of accumulation, which in turn determines both the distribution of income and, in conjunction with the growth of real wages, the set of relative prices. In each of the areas touched upon by this alternative approach—production, distribution, pricing, labor, tax incidence, international trade, natural resources, and money—the conclusions are strikingly different from those of neoclassical theory. It is the economics of a real economy, moving forward in historical time, with the system almost certain to be "out-of-equilibrium" (Eichner, 1979b).

Still, the specification of this alternative theoretical system is not enough. A third, and final stage, is needed. This third, and final, stage involves the empirical validation of the theory that has been developed as an alternative to the neoclassical model. Unless this third stage can be carried out, there remains the danger that post-Keynesian theory, no matter how great its triumph in other respects, will simply lead to the establishment of a new orthodoxy, one that will be no more successful than the neoclassical approach has been in placing economics on a scientific footing. To understand this last point, one needs to examine the role of empirical research in a discipline which, like economics, would aspire to be a science. Only then can one fully appreciate why the neoclassical paradigm has become intellectually bankrupt and what role empirical research must play in the further development of post-Keynesian theory.

Economics and epistemology

It is a common error to think of science as being characterized by a particular methodology, or prescribed way of acquiring knowledge. However, a moment's reflection on the diverse methodologies pursued by scientists, ranging from the highly abstract mathematical models of the theoretical physicists to the carefully controlled laboratory experiments of the biologists and the painstaking field work of the geologists, should suffice to disabuse anyone of this notion. Instead what uniquely characterizes a scientific approach is a certain epistemology, or way of validating ideas. The modern world is qualitatively different from all previous civilizations, not because a certain group of savants identified as scientists has discovered a new way of adding to knowledge (though it has, indeed, developed an impressive array of new instruments for accumulating data), but rather because the members of that confraternity have evolved a set of rules for discerning what is false and thereby avoiding nonproductive lines of research. The set of rules for eschewing what is false is the epistemology of science, and it involves applying a series of tests to what anyone may assert to be true.

One of these tests is the test of coherence. This test consists of determining whether the conclusions adduced follow logically from the assumptions that have been made and thus whether the arguments are internally consistent. At one time, following Descartes, it had been believed that this test was sufficient to establish the validity of any proposition. Economists, especially those esteemed by their colleagues as theorists, by and large still believe this test to be sufficient. That is why they tend to favor the exclusive use of mathematics, a language especially suited to logical analysis, along with mathematical "proofs." However, in the wake of Hume's arguments as a skeptic on behalf of empiricism, scientists and philosophers (they were not then differentiated) came to recognize that the coherence test was only necessary, not sufficient. In addition, a series of further empirical tests was required to validate any proposition. These empirical tests are threefold in nature.

There is, first, the correspondence test. This test consists of determining whether the conclusions that follow from a theory are confirmed by what can be observed empirically of the real world. The greater the ability of a theory to anticipate what can be observed empirically, the greater is the basis for believing that the theory actually corresponds in some way to what happens in the real world. A classic example is provided by Eddington's observations of the solar eclipse in 1919, which confirmed Einstein's prediction, based on his theories of relativity, that the gravitational field of a large mass such as the sun would cause light to bend. Popper (1959), among others, has placed particular emphasis on this test as distinguishing science from other types of intellectual activity, and the classic laboratory experiments associated with science are actually efforts to apply this test.

Then there is the comprehensiveness test. This test consists of determining whether the theory is able to encompass all the known facts pertaining to the class of phenomena under study. The more of these facts the theory is able to account for, the greater the confidence one can have that the theory is comprehensive in nature. The Ptolemaic model of the universe, for example, was able to account for the observable movements of the sun and moon around the earth. But it was less successful in explaining the movements of the planets Venus and Mars. Even more critically, it could not account for the moons around Jupiter which Galileo was able to observe through his telescope. It was therefore eventually judged to be less comprehensive a theory than the alternative Copernican model of the universe. Similarly, Newtonian physics would have been unable to account for the bending of the sun's rays observed by Eddington, and for this reason—as well as for its inability to explain why gravity is proportional to inertia—it, too, was subsequently judged to be less comprehensive than Einstein's theory of relativity.

A theory may fail to meet the comprehensiveness test for either of two reasons: 1) because the theory provides no explanation for certain empirically observable phenomena (such as the bending of the sun's rays which can be seen during an eclipse); or 2) because what is empirically observed is, under certain circumstances, different from what the theory would lead one to expect. An example of the latter is when, because of air resistance, two bodies of unequal weight do not fall at the same speed—as classical mechanics would lead one to expect. A theory which, for either of these reasons, is unable to meet the comprehensiveness test is less likely to be rejected outright than to be relegated to the category of a special case—with the importance of that special case depending on how commonly encountered are the conditions, or assumptions, under which the theory holds. In that event, the comprehensiveness test consists of determining under what circumstances the theory remains valid.

Finally, there is the parsimony test. This test consists of determining whether any particular element in the construction of a theory, including one of its underlying assumptions, is necessary to account for what can be empirically observed. To the extent that the element can be eliminated without reducing the theory's explanatory power, it should be dropped as being superfluous. It is in this way that a theory is purged of its metaphysical elements, and subsequent investigators are not misled into pursuing nonproductive lines of research.

All three of these tests are empirical in nature. This can be seen more clearly by viewing a theory as a system of interrelated ideas. The inputs into the system are the assumptions, or conditions, under which the ideas become operative, and the output consists of the conclusions, or observable effects, derived from the theory. The internal structure of the theory, meanwhile, is the series of steps by which the conclusions are obtained from the assumptions. The correspondence test, then, consists of checking the theory's output, or conclusions, against the observable reality to determine if they are isomorphic; the comprehensiveness test consists of checking to see whether there is not some part of the observable reality that is left unexplained by the theory, requiring additional inputs, or assumptions, which make the theory a special rather than a general one; and the parsimony test consists of checking whether there is not some element of the theory, often based on an input, or assumption, which can be dispensed with entirely in explaining the observable reality. (The coherence test, it should be noted, is merely a check on the logical consistency of the theory's internal structure and involves no empirical question at all.) It is only by meeting all three of these tests that a theory can be said to have been validated empirically.

Social scientists, in arguing that their theories should be accepted without necessarily having to meet all of these tests, point out how difficult it is for them to carry out empirical research. Many economists would be among their number, noting that their subject matter does not lend itself to laboratory experiments, in which other factors can be held constant, and that a reliance on statistical analysis, the only feasible alternative, seldom leads to conclusive results. These points, unfortunately all too true, are nonetheless not a reason for relaxing the insistence on empirical validation of theory. If anything, they are a reason to insist on an even more stringent test in the case of any social science theory. The theory must be shown to make a difference to society which, when translated into one or more public policies, will lead to certain clearly distinguishable results. The policies must then be adopted and the predicted effect confirmed. This is the praxis test of a social science theory. It is a form of the correspondence test, but with society itself as the test subject and with the body politic as both the intermediate (should the policy be adopted) and the final (has the policy been successful) arbiter. While it might be argued that this is much too rigorous a test to insist that any theory meet, especially in the social sciences, the present sorry state of economics is evidence of what is likely to be the consequence when, despite its not having been validated empirically in this or any of the other ways, a body of theory continues to remain at the core of a discipline.

Economic theory and empirical validation

The neoclassical core of orthodox economics has met only one of the tests that a body of theory, to be considered scientifically valid, must satisfy. That is the coherence test—although even this point, in light of the Sraffa and Cambridge critiques, need no longer be conceded. The neoclassical core of orthodox economics has, however, consistently failed to meet any of the empirical tests identified above. As a result, it has become suffused with certain elements, or theoretical constructs, which are either metaphysical or fatuous, and which therefore need to be purged from economics before it can claim to be a scientifically based discipline. Among the most important of the offending elements of orthodox theory are 1) indifference curves; 2) isoquants; 3) positively sloped supply curves for the industrial sector; 4) the marginal physical product, especially of "capital"; 5) the Hicks-Hansen LM-IS model; and 6) the Phillips curve. Anyone with only a passing knowledge of economics will recognize how central these elements are to the core of the received, or orthodox, theory in economics.

The indifference curves upon which the orthodox theory of consumer demand is based stand indicted because it has proven impossible to derive a set of these curves from the available empirical data, either for individuals or for groups of individuals (cf., Mishan, 1961; Blaug, 1980, ch. 6). The theoretical construct of indifference curves is therefore metaphysical in the same sense that unicorns, ghosts, and the "vital force" once thought to animate human beings are metaphysical: there is no empirical evidence that such things actually exist. Indeed, a skeptic would have to assume they do not exist. When an essential element of a theory has no empirical counterpart in the observable world, the theory itself becomes incapable of empirical validation.

Hence, the orthodox theory of consumer demand cannot meet the correspondence test, among the other empirical tests identified above. The evidence usually cited in support of the indifference curve analysis—namely, the negative coefficient often (but not always) observed for the price variable in a fully specified demand equation—only confirms the existence of a negatively sloped demand curve, not the convex indifference curves thought by a majority of economists to underlie that curve. The negative coefficient for the price variable in a demand function is, however, readily accounted for by a much simpler explanation, namely, the tendency of households to alter their speculative holdings, or inventory, of consumer goods as the price varies around the long-period "normal value." Indifference curves being unnecessary to explain what can be observed empirically, this element of demand theory should, based on the parsimony test, be abandoned.

The isoquants upon which the orthodox theory of production is based stand equally indicted and for the same reason: it has been proven impossible to derive these curves from the available empirical data on production by individual firms. The concept of an isoquant is no less metaphysical than that of indifference curves. Indeed, the case against isoquants is even stronger. The implication of isoquants—namely, that firms are able to produce a given quantity of output, even in the absence of technical progress, by employing varying combinations of labor and other inputs—is strongly contradicted by the available evidence. Empirical investigation in a number of manufacturing industries has shown that production requires the use of labor, material, and other inputs in relatively fixed combinations—until such a time as a new plant is built and/or new equipment is installed, at which point a new fixed combination of inputs will be employed. The role of relative prices in determining which combination of inputs will be employed over the long period, as distinct from the short run, is unclear, once the intervening role of technical progress is recognized; and in any case a far more complex set of relationships is involved than that implied by a continuous, or smooth, set of isoquants (Gold, 1971). This element in the orthodox theory of production having consistently failed to meet the correspondence test, and with other, more parsimonious explanations being available (e.g., the Leontief, Sraffa, and von Neumann fixed-technical-coefficient models), it can readily be dispensed with—if a nonnormative, empirically operational theory is all that is desired.

The purging of indifference curves and isoquants from the theoretical "tool kit" of economists, on the grounds that they are metaphysical concepts without empirical foundation, is fatal to any neo-Walrasian (actually Hicks-Arrow-Debreu) general equilibrium model. While this would still leave the Marshallian partial equilibrium theory untouched, this variant of neoclassical microeconomic theory, too, stands indicted once it is realized that there is no empirical support, at least outside of agriculture and mining, for the positively sloped supply curve which is an essential half of Marshall's famous scissors. The positively sloped supply curve is based on two assumptions: 1) that firms are price takers seeking to maximize their net revenue in the short run, and 2) that production is subject to variable and indeed, beyond a certain point, to decreasing returns to scale. The available evidence would seem to contradict both assumptions, at least insofar as the industrial sector is concerned (Blaug, 1980, ch. 7; Eichner, 1976, ch. 2). Firms in that sector are generally price-setters rather than price-takers, and long-term survival and expansion rather than short-run profit maximization would appear to be their goal. Moreover, constant and even increasing returns to scale, rather than decreasing returns, appear to be the rule. At least there is no evidence that industrial firms encounter higher unit costs as they expand output (Johnston, 1960; Walters, 1963).

To the extent that the concept of a supply curve is even applicable to the industrial sector, the curve would appear to be perfectly elastic, at least over the observable range, rather than being positively sloped. The evidence to this effect is the insensitivity of prices in the industrial sector to changes in the level of demand (Coutts, Godley, and Nordhaus, 1978; Eckstein and Fromm, 1968). The positing of a positively sloped supply curve and with it, the conventional supply and demand analysis, therefore fails the comprehensiveness test. The Marshallian partial equilibrium model applies, at most, only in the case of agricultural and other internationally traded commodities. For goods produced in the industrial sector an alternative, more general theory of output and price determination is needed.

The marginal productivity analysis, the basis for the neoclassical theory of income distribution, is immediately suspect because of the fixed technical coefficients which, the evidence indicates, characterize the production process in at least the technologically most advanced sectors of the economy. With fixed technical coefficients, inputs cannot be varied in the manner required to make the marginal productivity theory applicable. The theory invites further skepticism because "capital," the marginal productivity of which is central to the explanation offered by neoclassical theory for the distribution of income, turns out to be another metaphysical concept like indifference curves and isoquants. No one would deny the importance of produced goods used as inputs in the production process. The problem is that these capital inputs are heterogeneous, with no common physical measure such as tons, barrels, or BTUs. This means there can be no measure, in real terms, of the capital inputs used in the production process and that therefore, except in the case of a primitive technology such as agriculture using only seed, the marginal physical productivity of "capital" cannot be determined. It is not possible to aggregate the capital inputs in physical terms, and thus any argument based on either a firm's production function or on an aggregate production function in which an abstract "capital" variable, K, appears as an explanatory variable cannot be validated empirically. The K term, lacking any empirical counterpart, is metaphysical. For this reason, the argument cannot meet the correspondence or any other empirical test (Blaug, 1980, ch. 9: Harcourt, 1972).

The Hicks-Hansen LM-IS model and the Phillips curve, rather than being basic to neoclassical theory, are merely appendages which have been added to counter the Keynesian challenge. They constitute the macroeconomic component of the orthodox approach and, together with the four microeconomic concepts already identified as being without empirical validity, form the "neoclassical" synthesis developed by Samuelson and his colleagues at MIT. While the concepts underlying the Hicks-Hansen model and the Phillips curve are not metaphysical—unlike the several other components of the neoclassical synthesis—they must nonetheless be rejected as having failed to meet even the correspondence test—not to mention the praxis test.

The Hicks-Hansen model places the primary emphasis on the interest rate as the factor determining the level of macroeconomic activity. Not only will a change in the interest rate lead to a new monetary equilibrium, but, even more importantly, according to the model, it will, because of the effect on business investment, lead to a change in the level of national income. The latter proposition is a fairly easy one to test empirically and, as numerous studies have shown, is unsubstantiated by the available evidence. A change in the interest rate will, at most, have only a slight effect on the level of business investment (Nickell, 1978, pp. 299–300; Forman and Eichner, 1981). This being the case, there is no basis for positing, as the Hicks-Hansen model does, that the level of national income depends on the interest rate.

Indeed, governments that have formulated their macroeconomic policies on that premise have been uniformly disappointed in the results.

Moreover, there is reason to be skeptical as to whether monetary equilibrium depends on the interest rate or whether there is even such a thing as a monetary equilibrium one can observe empirically. The proposition that the interest rate determines monetary equilibrium has usually been assumed rather than justified by reference to any evidence. What evidence does exist—in the form of unsatisfied credit demand and flow-of-funds movements—would seem to suggest that it is monetary disequilibrium, and not equilibrium, that is the prevailing condition. Indeed, an empirically operational definition of monetary equilibrium has yet to be offered in connection with the Hicks-Hansen model. Once the notion of an LM curve representing all the points of possible monetary equilibrium is abandoned, the rest of the Hicks-Hansen model, and especially the notion of a uniquely determined level of income, Y, based on the balance between real and monetary factors, disappears with it. The Hicks-Hansen model, it turns out, is largely fatuous. This does not mean that large-scale macroeconomic models have not been constructed starting from a Hicks-Hansen framework (Klein and Burmeister, 1976). It merely means that, when the empirical work of constructing the models is complete, very little of the original theoretical framework is likely to remain.

The Phillips curve has been grafted on to the Hicks-Hansen model for much the same reason the Hicks-Hansen model has been added to the core of the orthodox neoclassical theory: to explain what cannot otherwise be accounted for. Just as it is not possible, within a neoclassical framework, to explain fluctuations in real output and employment without introducing the Hicks-Hansen model or some similar bastardization of Keynes' arguments, so, too, it is not possible, within the context of any of those orthodox Keynesian models, to explain the inflation which has bedeviled the world's economies since the end of World War II without positing an inverse relationship between the rate of growth of prices and the unemployment rate. Orthodox Keynesian models can only explain the level of income, Y, undifferentiated between price and quantity movements. To explain changes in the price level, separate from the movement of real output and employment, a Phillips curve must be added. Monetarist models, it should be noted, also need to posit a Phillips curve—if they are to distinguish a short-period change in real income from a short-period change in nominal income. These models, too, can only explain the level of income, Y, undifferentiated between price and quantity movements. The difference is that the monetarist models use the Phillips curve to convert the nominal magnitudes into real magnitudes rather than the reverse. Both the orthodox Keynesian and the monetarist models, then, must rely on the Phillips curve to separate out the price and quantity movements. The problem is that the Phillips curve, like the Hicks-Hansen model, has consistently failed to meet either the correspondence or the praxis test.

Although the unemployment rate is often specified as the principal factor determining the rate of growth of prices, it turns out, when the matter is investigated empirically, that other factors are actually more important. The predominant influence on the price level, by far, is the rise in labor and material costs. The unemployment rate, like the interest rate in the case of business investment, adds only marginally to the explanatory power of the price equations which econometricians have developed, and with the influence of rising labor and material costs properly taken into account, that variable can be all but ignored. It would seem to be merely a proxy, and a poor one at that, for the level of demand in certain commodity markets. Thus, when governments, acting on the assumption implicit in the Phillips curve that the unemployment rate can be used instrumentally, have attempted to curb the rise in prices by deliberately engineering a slowdown in the level of economic activity, they have only succeeded in transforming the troublesome problem of inflation into the even more serious problem of stagflation.

Moreover, the somewhat weak inverse relationship between the unemployment rate and the growth of prices which can be observed once the more important, other determinants of the price level have been taken into account would appear to be an unstable one—the presumed trade-off between unemployment and inflation having apparently become less favorable over time. More recent studies suggest that it now requires a higher rate of unemployment to prevent prices from rising by a certain percentage than it previously did. This evidence is, of course, consistent with the explanation frequently offered that the Phillips curve has shifted outwardly to the right over time. But the same evidence is also consistent with a quite different hypothesis, namely, that the Phillips curve is actually a figment of the economists' imagination, invented to fill a hole in the neoclassical line of argument. The Phillips curve, like the Hicks-Hansen model, would appear to be fatuous.

It will, of course, be argued in response that if all six of the key theoretical constructs just identified were to be purged from the economics textbooks on the grounds that they have not been validated empirically, very little would remain and what was left would lack coherence. This, however, is not a compelling argument for retaining the six key elements of the neoclassical synthesis but rather is a measure of how intellectually bankrupt the dominant orthodoxy has become. If economics is to establish itself as a scientifically based activity, it has no choice but to purge all six elements from the core of its discipline. This is an essential first step to revitalizing economics as a field of study—however painful an adjustment it may require in accustomed modes of thinking. As for what should be taught in the place of the above six theoretical constructs, the newly emergent body of post-Keynesian theory provides a ready answer. No less coherent than the alternative neoclassical paradigm, it has yet to be discredited empirically. Still, if this newly emergent body of post-Keynesian theory is not to leave economics in the same sorry state as the reigning orthodoxy, it is essential that certain methodological principles be observed. Hopefully, these will become the methodological principles of those who regard themselves as post-Keynesians working within the mainstream of modern science.

Methodological principles

The purpose of economics as a scientific discipline should be to develop cumulatively a body of theory to explain the *observable* behavior of economic systems over time. (Thus, modeling the unobservable behavior of nonexistent economic systems, as many welfare and general equilibrium theorists are content to do, falls outside the scope of economics as a scientific and socially useful activity.) The theory should be both coherent, that is, internally consistent in terms of the logic, and empirically valid, that is, in accord with all the available evidence. In adding any new element to the core previously developed and empirically validated, it is essential to distinguish the theory construction stage from the theory validation stage. Each stage needs to be governed by a different set of methodological principles.

At the theory construction stage, the primary emphasis should be on coherence and comprehensiveness. The object is to encompass as much of what is known about a given phenomenon as possible without doing violence to any logical principle. It is at this prevalidation stage of theory construction that both "formal" (i.e., mathematical) and historical modes of analysis come into their own. One can use the logic of mathematics to derive a most interesting theoretical proposition for subsequent empirical testing—as, for example, in the case of Samuelson's multiplier-accelerator model—just as one can try to fit all the historical evidence together into a thesis which similarly lends itself to later empirical validation. An example of the latter would be Gerschenkron's theory of relative backwardness (Gerschenkron, 1962). How the testable proposition is derived, whether through formal or historical methods, is less important than whether it will be able to meet the subsequent empirical test. Thus, at the theory construction stage the permissible methodology is more open. Whatever technique will enable one to extend the core body of theory in such a way that the whole can meet the correspondence, comprehensiveness, parsimony, and even praxis tests is acceptable. Even so, there are certain methodological pitfalls to avoid.

One pitfall is to insist that the theory cannot be developed except in a purely formal way, that is, deductively; or, alternatively, based on the historical method, that it cannot be developed except in a way that encompasses every known piece of evidence. This is to impose constraints on the construction of theories which not only will hamper creativity but, even more harmfully, are likely to keep the truth hidden. The error to which economists are particularly prone is the insistence that a theory be developed formally. Indeed, this is part of what Wiles (1979–80), following Schumpeter, has termed the Ricardian vice which infuses economics as a discipline. The fallacy here is in equating what may not be logical with what is illogical.

Certain empirically observable phenomena may not be deducible from simpler propositions, assumptions, or observable phenomena. This, it turns out, is a common result of moving from one resolution level to another, e.g., from physical atoms to chemical molecules. It does not mean the phenomena are illogical. It only means that they cannot be arrived at in a logical manner—or at least not by using the system of logic, mathematical or otherwise, which one has selected as the tool of analysis. There are many phenomena in economics that, by this definition, are nonlogical but still readily observable. They include the interdependent behavior of price leaders-price followers in oligopolistic industries, the commitment of workers to the quality of whatever good or service they are providing, and the unemployment created by excess private savings relative to investment. One may be able subsequently to "rationalize" the observable result, that is, to show it is not illogical within a certain theoretical framework, but one cannot obtain the result deductively as a necessary conclusion. Economics as a discipline has been greatly impoverished over the years by its insistence that all phenomena be explained by purely formal, that is, mathematical models. The entire real world of the nonlogical but observable has, as a consequence, escaped it.

No less crippling is the insistence that a theory be fully comprehensive, accounting for every known piece of evidence. This involves the fallacy that nothing is explained unless everything is explained at once. Economists, as a group, have not been prone to this error. They have been more than willing to develop simplified models which abstract from the complexity of the observable reality—even if they have then been reluctant to validate those models empirically. Still, there is a hint of this fallacy in the argument by some economists that an equilibrium, to be a true equilibrium, must be a general one with all markets clearing simultaneously. Even though the models based on this line of argument are not meant to explain any observable phenomena, and indeed are antiempirical and thus antiscientific in spirit for precisely that reason, still the antecedent question of whether every market throughout the economy must be shown to have cleared before the analysis of any one of those markets can be said to be complete needs to be addressed. The argument, it should be understood, is but a variation on the theme that nothing is explained unless everything is explained at once. Of course, if a disequilibrium in one market were to have a significant impact on another market, that would be another matter. But then the issue would be the empirical one to determine the impact of the one market on the other—not a matter of a priori insistence, whatever the evidence may be.

A second pitfall to avoid at the theory construction stage is that of developing a line of argument which, by the very nature of the factors identified, cannot be validated empirically—or which is at such variance with the observable reality that it is certain, once the theory has been fully worked out, not to pass any of the necessary empirical tests. To fall into this trap is to waste everyone's time, including one's own. It is a sign that one is not really serious about adding to the stock of knowledge. Unfortunately, this is precisely the trap into which the majority of economists have fallen repeatedly throughout the post–World War II Keynesian period, beginning with the diversion created by the emphasis on neoclassical growth models and continuing today with the excitement over "rational expectations" models. The former, based on the metaphysical concept of a "marginal productivity" associated with "capital," had little prospect of ever being validated empirically. The initial encouraging results from econometric tests were simply the result of an unchanging labor share of national income and the specification of a Cobb-Douglass production function; the same evidence was consistent with almost any other model of economic growth (see, for example, Shaikh, 1974; Davenport, 1981). As for the rational expectations models, it is hard to take seriously an argument based on both a one-commodity economy and price-adjusting Walrasian markets. The one-commodity assumption precludes any role for money, let alone the markets otherwise assumed, while the price-adjusting, Walrasian nature of the markets suggests the absence of an industrial sector. How a model with features such as these can be expected to meet the praxis test, let alone any other empirical test, is a mystery.

This second pitfall, then, is an especially important one for economists to avoid. It requires that economists adhere to a few simple rules.

First, the variables identified as either dependent variables or explanatory factors must be capable of being observed, in some manner, empirically. Metaphysical concepts are to be eschewed altogether. It is this rule which argues for abandoning the neoclassical theory of production, based on isoquants, and starting instead with the fixed-technical-coefficient models of Leontief, Sraffa, and von Neumann. (The same rule requires that indifference curves be replaced, in economic analysis, with empirically estimatable income and price elasticities and that the variable K, denoting the capital stock in real terms, be avoided throughout.)

Second, the assumptions underlying the model, and therefore the conditions under which the model holds, should be identified at the outset. Ordinarily, this would suffice to protect against either of two possible sources of later difficulty: 1) that the conditions under which the model holds are extreme ones unlikely to be encountered in practice and that therefore the model will be of no relevance to the real world; or, 2) that the model will be applied in circumstances other than those represented by the conditions under which the argument holds and that the model will therefore be used to draw the wrong conclusions. But many economists have been persuaded, by Friedman (1953) among others, that any assumption is permissible. Thus it is necessary to add two codicils to this second rule:

a. If the assumptions underlying the model represent conditions unlikely to ever be realized or observed in practice, abandon the model as worthless.

b. If the model holds only under certain conditions, do not use it to analyze a different set of conditions.

Unfortunately, there are more than enough examples of both strictures being flagrantly violated. The models that hold only under conditions unlikely ever to be observed in practice include not just the rational expectations ones but, indeed, the entire broader group of Hicks-Arrow-Debreu general equilibrium models. As for the models that have been applied to circumstances other than those under which they hold, these include all the models that rely on supply and demand curves to analyze pricing behavior in the industrial sector. The positively sloped supply curve—if not also the negatively sloped demand curve—applies only to the commodity sector of a modern market economy and even then only to the portion not controlled either by the government or by large industrial enterprises. This is why the excess-demand explanation for inflation has proved to be so misleading. It assumes that the supply curves in the industrial sector are for the most part positively sloped.

Yet a third pitfall to avoid is trying to extend or modify a body of theory that, experience has shown, cannot be empirically validated. The most that can be hoped for is that this latest extension or modification will not be immediately disconfirmed by the available evidence and thus that the proposition will, for the moment, satisfy the correspondence test (most likely because, as will be noted shortly, a weak form of the correspondence test has been applied). Whatever may be the evidence in support of the proposition, if it is logically linked to a more basic body of theory, one which, being inconsistent with other evidence, lacks empirical validity, the two together will still fail the comprehensiveness test. This is why the effort to improve neoclassical theory by adding more "realistic" features, such as money or fixed-price markets, is an exercise in futility. Progress cannot in fact be made until all of economic theory's neoclassical features, and not just some, have been eradicated. Building upon a false argument, no matter how sound the extension or modification itself may be, will still leave the argument false. Once the task of formulating an addition to some existing body of theory has been accomplished so that it satisfies both the coherence and comprehensiveness criteria, the steps that must then be taken are narrowly circumscribed. The methodological principles that need to be followed at the theory validation stage permit little latitude. The proposition being advanced must first be contrasted with each of the alternative formulations that are possible (including, but not limited to, the null hypothesis that no such relationship exists). The available empirical evidence (including, but not limited to, quantitative data) must then be examined to see which of the several alternatives the evidence is most consistent with. Finally, if the proposition that the available evidence is most consistent with is not the one that was initially advanced, one needs to retreat to the theory construction stage and rework the entire argument. Just as there are pitfalls one can fall into at the theory construction stage, so too there are pitfalls at the subsequent validation stage.

The first pitfall is that of failing to identify all the possible other arguments and thus failing to test the proposition being advanced against some explicit alternative. Indeed, this is one reason for being skeptical about much of the empirical work being done along neoclassical lines. It is seldom, if ever, that the proposition being advanced is tested against the explicit post-Keynesian or any other alternative, even when that alternative has long been a part of the economics literature. The usual practice is to test the proposition against the null hypothesis only—a notoriously weak test, one that engenders even less confidence when it is based on time series data. Since the serial correlation which occurs when time series data are used cannot be eliminated entirely, this type of test leads to an inflated R^2, and thus may give credence to an argument which in fact is false. Even if other types of data are used, however, a test against the null hypothesis, namely, that no such relationship exists, is a weak test.

To have greater confidence in the results, one must test a proposition, not just against the null hypothesis (as may be necessary initially) but also against each of the alternative arguments for which there is similar supporting evidence. In this way, one is less likely to be left with several explanations which, though seemingly at odds with one another, are all equally consistent with the available evidence. One can instead focus on what is the crucial difference between any two of the explanations: the result that one would expect to observe if the one explanation were correct but not if the other were correct. Once that crucial difference has been identified, a more rigorous test of the proposition being advanced can then be devised. To apply the correspondence test in this more rigorous form, it is, of course, essential that each of the possible alternative arguments first be identified. Indeed, unless this is done, and the investigation then centered on what is the crucial difference between that proposition and any alternative explanation, the test will be a flawed one.

A second pitfall to avoid at the theory validation stage is that of drawing too hard and fast a distinction between theoretical and empirical work. It is not just that a theory must be tested, either to be accepted or rejected. It is also that, when the results obtained from an empirical study are different from those expected, the theory must be revised so that it will be consistent with all the evidence, old as well as new. Unless this second step is taken, one can expect to continue observing the situation that prevails in economics today: the steady accrual of evidence against most, if not all, of the prevailing theories.

The necessary revision of theory in light of the empirical evidence is less likely to occur, when, as is the case in economics, such a sharp line is drawn between theoretical and empirical work. The theorists will continue to ignore the evidence, insisting that the formal proofs they provide are sufficient, while those engaged in empirical research will consider the revision of the theories they find wanting to be the responsibility of the theorists. This unfortunate situation will end only when economists begin, as a routine matter, to cross the line separating theoretical and empirical work. Theory construction and empirical validation are not two separate activities, to be pursued by two separate groups of economists. They are only separate steps in the same iterative process of trying to make the theory and the available evidence consistent with one another. Indeed, the sharp line that is drawn in economics between theoretical and empirical work is unknown in the natural and biological sciences. In those fields, no reputable scholar would present a new theory without at least some supporting evidence.

The integration of the theoretical and the empirical needs to be a part of every economist's normal mode of working. Theoretical arguments are likely to remain naive about the real world as long as those making the arguments have little or no feel for the empirical evidence because they do not themselves work with data. And empirical studies are likely to be of little value as long as those carrying out the studies remain unconcerned about the underlying theoretical issues. Indeed, this last point is illustrated by the great bulk of empirical work being done today which, rather than providing support for any of the key elements of neoclassical theory previously identified, merely use those theoretical contructs to draw certain conclusions from the evidence at hand. The conclusions are only as valid as the theoretical constructs upon which they are based—which means, in light of what has already been said, that very little confidence can be placed in them. Virtually all the studies of economic growth based on the neoclassical growth model, along with virtually all the studies of the returns to education and training based on the human capital model, fall in this category. What the above argument suggests is that theorists need to be more directly involved in empirical research and empirical researchers need to be more directly concerned with the ongoing, cumulative development of theory. While economists are still likely to continue specializing in one or the other type of work, depending on their particular bent, the two activities cannot be kept as separate as they have in the past—not if economics is to become a truly scientific endeavor.

Post-Keynesian economists do not have the same need to resist this integration of the theoretical and the empirical. Unlike those who rely on a neoclassical approach, they need not fear that the theory in which they have invested themselves cannot serve as the basis for successful empirical work. Still, since the largest number of post-Keynesian economists view themselves primarily as theorists, not feeling comfortable with the techniques required for empirical research, it will be all too easy for them to fall into the same methodological trap of keeping theory construction and empirical validation separate from one another. It is a temptation to be strongly resisted. The fact is that, at the present critical stage in the development of post-Keynesian theory, it is essential that an extensive program of empirical research be carried out. Only in this way will the prevailing neoclassical theory be replaced by an alternative which is more relevant to the real world and more useful to policymakers. It is this program of empirical research which constitutes the imminent research agenda for post-Keynesian economists.

The imminent research agenda

The development of a post-Keynesian alternative to the orthodox theory should prove a veritable boon to empirical research, both quantitative and historical. There is first the fact that what empirical researchers tend to observe in the real world—whether it be mark-up pricing, fixed technical coefficients of production, dual labor markets, or credit rationing—will no longer seem puzzling in light of the available theory. When the empirical results turn out to be anomalous, it creates doubts about the investigative techniques being employed, and it makes researchers reluctant to press on to exploit their finding—if they do not first succumb to the temptation to reinterpret the results so as to make them seem consistent with the theory. With the post-Keynesian body of theory against which to compare their findings, empirical researchers will no longer meet with the same discouragement. What they observe will tend to confirm, rather than contradict, the available theory. One of the first items on the research agenda, then, is to go back over the past accumulated body of empirical work to see whether most of the unsatisfactory results previously reported are not actually confirmation of the alternative post-Keynesian theory. In this way, a good deal of the earlier empirical work can be given the importance it deserves, and a new generation of researchers can be encouraged to follow up on those leads.

No less beneficial is the fact that post-Keynesian theory itself suggests a large number of testable hypotheses—whether it be the importance of fixed investment in determining both the growth of aggregate output and the growth of productivity, the effect of macroeconomic variables on the distribution of income, the relationship between the growth of money wages and inflation, or the endogenous nature of the money supply. While some evidence of each of these points is already in hand, a systematic test of these and the many other relationships suggested by post-Keynesian theory is needed. A specific program to test the key post-Keynesian propositions is, then, a second item on the research agenda.

In turning to this second item on the research agenda, one must recognize the two separate parts of post-Keynesian theory. There is the long-period analysis, based on a comparison of alternative steady-state expansion paths, and there is the short-period analysis, intended to explain the actual movement of economic systems through historical time. While it might be thought that, since steady-state rates of economic expansion can never actually be observed—only the second of these two parts lends itself to empirical validation—this is not true. However derived, whether mathematically or otherwise, the propositions that follow from a long-period analysis, no less than those that follow from a short-period analysis, can be tested empirically. Although steady-state rates of expansion may never actually be observed, the rate of growth of the economy over time, once any cyclical fluctuations have been taken into account, may serve as a reasonable approximation—at least reasonable enough to demonstrate the validity of the post-Keynesian long-period propositions. This means that the long-period theory can be tested in either of two ways: 1) by comparing the growth experience among a group of similarly developed countries, such as the OECD nations, or 2) by comparing the growth experience of the same country over different time intervals. While there are serious limitations to either approach, the two together should provide a sufficient basis for testing empirically the key points derived from a post-Keynesian long-period analysis. Cornwall (1977) and Wilson (1981) have already demonstrated how the first approach can be used to good effect, while Garrett (1981) has shown the use that can be made of the second approach.

It is, however, in testing the implications of the short-period model that empirical research based on post-Keynesian theory is most likely to flourish. Several elements of that short-period model, such as the fixed technical coefficients of production and the mark-up basis for price formation, have already been extensively tested empirically—with results that are almost without exception favorable to those arguments. Recently Moore (1979, 1983) has begun to provide evidence as to the endogeneity of the money supply. Still, there are certain elements, such as the disequilibrium properties of the model and the exogenous nature of the money wage rate, which have yet to be tested explicitly. Moreover, the model as a whole needs to be empirically validated. For this, as well as for several other reasons, the construction of large-scale macroeconomic models is likely to become the focal point for empirical research based on post-Keynesian theory, and in particular, for efforts to validate empirically the essential features of the post-Keynesian short-period analysis.

One of those other reasons has to do with the difficulty of testing a theory in economics. While statistical analysis can compensate somewhat for the near inability to carry out controlled laboratory experiments, econometric studies are not without their serious limitations. Because of serial correlation and other problems encountered, especially when the study must be based, as it often needs to be, on time series data, it is all too easy to reject the null hypothesis—even when the proposition being tested is a false one. Experienced econometricians have learned to distrust the R^2 and similar statistics. They have also learned to distrust the results of any single-equation model. While a multi-equation model may be just as invalid as any single-equation model, it at least must bring out more of the underlying relationships— and thus the likelihood is greater that, if incorrectly specified, a multi-equation model will fail the several empirical tests. Errors, rather than being concealed in aggregates, will tend to be compounded as the simulation of the model proceeds so that those errors will, by the end of the simulation exercise, be more readily apparent. One can therefore have a greater confidence in a multi-equation model that is consistent with the historical data, especially if the test is based on a simulation exercise, than one can have in a single-equation model. It is this logic for developing multi-equation models that argues for constructing a model for the economy as a whole, this being the ultimate limit, within a nationalistic framework, on the type of multi-equation model that can be developed.

There is the further advantage that a model constructed to explain the behavior of the economy as a whole can be used to obtain future estimates of precisely those variables that are of the greatest interest not just to economists but to public officials and other lay people as well. These variables are the growth of real output, the growth of the aggregate price level, and the growth of employment. The ability of the model to provide future estimates of these variables means not only that the model has greater potential social usefulness but also that it can be subjected to a further empirical test. When the estimates as to the future growth of real output, prices, and employment turn out to be consistently wrong, even after unanticipated changes in policy are taken into account, there is good reason to reject the model as being invalid. By being represented in a large-scale econometric model of the economy, then, it is easier to determine if a body of theory, such as the post-Keynesian short-period analysis, can meet the correspondence test and, to the extent that policy is subsequently based on that model, the praxis test as well.

It is for all of these reasons that efforts are now under way to construct large-scale econometric models of the economy, based on what can broadly be termed post-Keynesian theory, in a number of countries. These are models that can be sharply distinguished from the more conventional Keynesian and monetarist models. The model now being constructed at the Center for Economic Anthropogenic Research, the CEAR model of the American economy, is an example of such a model (see the preceding essay), though by no means the only one. The models being developed by the Cambridge Applied Economics Group and by Arestis and his colleagues at Thames Polytechnic in London, both models covering the British economy, should also be mentioned.[1] The CEAR model is being developed so that both the results and the underlying data base will be available to other researchers. This is being done not just so others can reproduce, and thereby check, the results. It is being done, in addition, so that others will have a common data base from which to start in pursuing empirical research of their own—especially empirical research which seeks to extend, in some important way, the same post-Keynesian model of the economy. Starting from a common data base is essential if the development of economics along post-Keynesian lines is to be cumulative.

This common data base does not preclude the possibility that different versions of the same basic model will emerge as others join the task of empirically validating post-Keynesian theory. Indeed, differences have already arisen in the way the several large-scale econometric models now being constructed are specified, and further differences can be expected to arise as other investigators attempt to enlarge upon or extend those models. It only means that, whatever the different versions, the models should not be at odds with one another on any fundamental point, as the post-Keynesian and more orthodox neoclassical models now are. If they are at odds, it is a sign that the program of empirical research has omitted an important step along the way. That step is to make sure that when two or more opposing arguments emerge within the broader post-Keynesian framework—each interpretation equally defensible in light of the available evidence—a concerted effort is then made to determine which argument has the greater empirical validity. This systematic attempt to reconcile, through further empirical research, any points of difference within the post-Keynesian body of literature itself is the third item on the imminent research agenda. It is yet another way in which the development of economics along post-Keynesian lines is likely to prove a boon to empirical research.

The research agenda just outlined should go far to establish economics as a scientifically based discipline, with a body of theory that has been empirically validated and which can, at the same time, provide the understanding of economic phenomena needed to solve pressing social problems. If the theory that can thereby meet all the required empirical tests turns out to be post-Keynesian, then that emerging new paradigm in economics will have passed the third, and most critical, stage in its development. But even if that body of theory will need to be significantly modified, in addition to being considerably expanded, it will nonetheless have served the important historical purpose of rescuing economics from the intellectual and political bankruptcy into which it has now sunk, demonstrating the more constructive lines that empirical research can take if fully supported by a more appropriate theoretical foundation. In this way, post-Keynesian theory and empirical research will each have served the other well. More importantly, economics will have finally become a science, with its theoretical core merely the starting point for further empirical research rather than a body of settled doctrine to be defended against the observations of the real world.

Afterword

This essay was originally a paper prepared for the Conference on Keynes and Sraffa at Ottawa University, March 1981, and was subsequently published in a French translation in *L'Actualité Economique* (Eichner, 1982), along with the other papers given at the conference. It has not previously been published in English, however. The essay was initially prompted by the disagreement among the faculty at Rutgers University over the content of the graduate economic program's core curriculum. The essay is, in effect, an argument against basing the core curriculum in economics on the neoclassical synthesis exclusively, as is almost without exception the case in English-speaking universities, on the ground that the theory has failed to meet the necessary empirical tests. Many of the same arguments will be found in the title essay of *Why Economics Is Not Yet a Science* (Eichner, 1983), a collection of papers by various authors criticizing the prevailing analytical methods in economics.

Note

1. Earlier examples are Cornwall, 1972, and Sylos-Labini, 1974.

9

Reflections
on Social Democracy

A certain vision has guided the policies of the developed nations of the West since the end of World War II. It is a vision rooted in the philosophical speculations of past centuries, drawing sustenance from the humanism of the Renaissance, the rationalism of the Enlightenment, and the optimism of the nineteenth century. But it is a vision even more directly shaped by the experience of the interwar years and the desire, based on that experience, to avoid the twin calamities of worldwide depression and global war. The vision is one of societies organized politically as democracies, pursuing Keynesian policies at home to assure full employment while competing peacefully among themselves for foreign markets under a beneficent regime of free trade and fixed exchange rates—with a nuclear shield provided by the United States to protect against the expansionism of an antithetical Soviet communism. This explicitly conceived alternative to centrally planned totalitarianism might be called Keynesian social democracy. It is Keynesian in that it views government as being responsible for maintaining high levels of aggregate demand. It is social democratic in that it conceives of government as offering solutions to a whole range of social problems as well. The trouble is that this vision of the ''good society'' now seems to provide an increasingly faltering and unreliable guide for public policy in the United States and the other Western countries.

The growing inadequacy of this vision, it should be noted, stems at least in part from its triumph. Given the goals of the postwar planners in 1945, Keynesian social democracy has been extraordinarily successful. Political democracy has been established as the norm in all the developed countries of the West. The Axis powers of World War II—West Germany, Austria, Italy, and Japan—as well as the late-developing countries of Southern Europe—Spain, Portugal, and Greece—now seem firmly in the democratic camp, and there is little doubt as to the direction in which the East European countries would move if ever the threat of Soviet intervention were removed. Economically, the gains have been no less impressive. Although the pattern of development has been uneven, per capita levels of income have risen throughout the entire OECD community of nations, with a number of countries—France, Germany, Sweden, and Japan—enjoying a standard of living that nearly matches, if it does not in some cases exceed, that of the United States. Sharp and prolonged downturns in economic activity have been avoided while the growing volume of world trade, as tariff and other barriers have fallen, has helped sustain the period of unprecedented prosperity. Finally, but by no means unimportant, the advance of Soviet communism seems to have been halted without a mutually destructive World War III. In light of this success, it is hardly surprising that the older generation of social philosophers and political activists should be reluctant to abandon Keynesian social democracy as their vision of the best society that can reasonably be achieved.

Nor is it surprising that a new generation should find that vision less and less adequate—and not, as some claim, because its very success would seem to leave the members of that generation with insufficient challenge. The fact is that the post–World War II period has seen the emergence of problems which policies based on Keynesian social democracy seem incapable of solving. The continued threat of nuclear annihilation, the persistence of secular inflation, and the unequal distribution of income, both within nations and across the divide between developed and underdeveloped countries, are only the most ominous of the seemingly intractable problems the current generation has inherited.

The malaise is not just intergenerational, however. It is felt with particular intensity in the United States. Many here have held the largely ethnocentric but still somewhat justified belief that the success of Keynesian social democracy has been due mostly to the enlightened leadership of the United States in the period following World War II. It was the United States that served as the counterweight to Soviet expansionism while providing the long-term credits needed to rebuild a war-devastated Europe; and it was the United States that rallied its allies under the NATO banner while encouraging the formation of the Common Market and the other cooperative efforts which, as successors to the Marshall Plan, have helped produce the postwar economic "miracle." The troubling question, and the source of uneasiness, is how the United States, no longer the dominant nation it once was, can continue to provide the leadership the Western countries need and at the same time cope with the new realities at home. It is of little comfort to realize that the relative decline of the United States is but one mark of the success of Keynesian social democracy—in Europe, if not around the world.

We are indeed in a new era—one that might be called post-Keynesian. And the new era requires a new type of leadership by the United States, based not on the disproportionate power of that country—a historical accident of the two world wars—but rather on example. That is the kind of leadership which the United States at its best has provided during its 200 years of existence. This new leadership requires, in turn, a new vision of how a nation-state—and, more than that, a world community—can be structured to best serve people's needs. It is a vision that would build on, not just replace, the older vision of Keynesian social democracy.

The tasks of this new American leadership are threefold:

1. to help establish a new international order to supersede the one created at the end of World War II;

2. to resolve certain issues in political economy at the national level which still impede policymaking here in the United States; and

3. to redefine the goals of a modern, progressive state. This implies a new vision of the good society, and what it can be expected to achieve.

A new international order

The most important task that the United States faces as a world leader is to see to it that civilization as we know it does not end in a nuclear "big bang." The conventional view is that the greatest danger of this arises from a possible confrontation between the United States and the Soviet Union. This view, however, ignores the growing number of countries in unstable regions of the world that have achieved a nuclear military capability—though not nearly, of course, on so large a scale as the two superpowers. It also ignores the tremendous buildup in conventional arms among the so-called non-aligned nations. World War I, it should be remembered, began in the Balkans and not on the border between the British and German spheres of influence. Today there are too many of the world's regions with degrees of political instability once associated only with the Balkans—and this includes even the East European countries. It may well be that the United States and the other OECD nations need to think of their mutual security in terms that transcend an outmoded cold war mentality.

Only a vulgar Marxist would assert that World War III will necessarily begin because of a conflict in economic interest among nations. The passions most likely to drive one country into war with another, and even to condone the use of nuclear weapons, are those that derive from racial, religious, and other ethnic differences. Still, the economic arrangements among nations can well play a key role in keeping those passions within noncombustible limits. That was the idea behind the international economic order created at the end of World War II, and that is the reason for considering what kind of new international arrangement is now needed to take its place.

The international economic order that was created in the aftermath of World War II can also be termed Keynesian in honor of its principal architect. True, Keynes' vision was not fully realized (just as it was not fully realized on the domestic front, either); and true, the free-trade orientation that gave rise to the General Agreement on Tariffs and Trade (GATT) and its supporting set of institutions owed little of its inspiration to the British Treasury advisor. (The impetus came from Cordell Hull's disciples in the American State Department, though Keynes, it should be noted, was not opposed to free trade, provided it was compatible with full employment.) Still, at the core of the international economic system that was created in the 1940s lay the monetary arrangements that Keynes and Harry Dexter White, the American Under Secretary of the Treasury, worked out at Bretton Woods.

The International Monetary Fund (IMF) and the World Bank were the most tangible outcomes of the Bretton Woods conference. The former, though falling short of Keynes' plan to create an institution with the power to act as a world central bank, did at least provide for the pooling of whatever international monetary reserves, especially gold, existed then. The IMF also bound its member countries, which soon included all the non-Communist nations, to maintain a fixed exchange rate between their own currencies and gold. The World Bank, meanwhile, was created to provide long-term financing for economic development projects in countries that lacked the necessary foreign exchange earnings. Even more important, however, was the pledge Keynes obtained from the Americans—it was his price for giving in on the other matters—that they would continue to redeem dollars in gold. With the United States then in possession of almost the entire world's supply of gold, the pledge meant that the dollar would become as good as gold—and enable other countries, including Great Britain, to hold dollars instead of gold. In this way, though not all the consequences were fully foreseen, even by Keynes himself, the dollar was established as a reserve currency under a system of fixed exchange rates. It was that arrangement more than any other feature that defined the new international order, and especially the pivotal role that was to be played by the United States.

Like Keynesian social democracy on the domestic front, which it complemented, this international economic order was enormously successful—while it lasted. The absence of competitive devaluations, the rapid expansion of trade, and the steady growth of national income within the OECD community between 1945 and 1971 all attest to the effectiveness of the system which Keynes had helped to fashion in the recognition that it was the best that could be achieved under the circumstances of 1945. Still, even before 1971, it was clear that the system was only a second-best solution. There was already the dispute over the favored status which the dollar's role as a reserve currency gave the United States and the corresponding refusal of the French to continue playing by the old rules. Less firmly impressed upon the consciousness of the more advanced nations, but hardly a matter of indifference to the rest of the world, was the failure of the system to give any special consideration to the needs of developing nations—those countries seeking to escape from being simply exporters of raw materials. The international economic order was one that only already industrialized countries could be comfortable with.

What finally did in the Bretton Woods system was the failure to devise an acceptable substitute for the dollar as the underlying basis for monetary expansion on a worldwide scale. To be sure, the immediate precipitating factor was the huge American deficit in the balance of payments and the refusal of the Nixon administration in 1971 to acquiesce to a contraction of the domestic economy when European patience with the deficit was finally at an end. And even then the hope was that, by a massive devaluation of the American dollar and a corresponding upward evaluation of American gold stocks, the clock could be turned back to 1945 and the Bretton Woods system thereby resurrected. Of course, the actual result was not so much to preserve the dollar's unique status as a reserve currency as to replace fixed exchange rates with flexible exchange rates, thereby scuttling the Bretton Woods system. These misunderstandings and miscalculations aside, however, the fact remains that, had the world's central banks been willing to continue supporting the dollar or, bowing to French sensitivities, had they been able to agree on some alternative form of monetary reserve which would automatically expand or contract with the volume of world trade, the Bretton Woods accomplishment of relative fixed exchange rates and a somewhat elastic medium of international exchange need not have been lost.

The shift to flexible exchange rates, it must now be recognized, was a step backward. Exchange rates are still, to a certain extent, "pegged," while at the same time there has been a substantial increase in the risks of engaging in foreign trade as the result of some unforeseeable decline in the value of a particular country's currency. Even more to the point, the growth of international money and credit is no more under the control of a responsible world body than when global expansion was being fueled by American deficits. The only thing that can be said for the change is that the United States enjoys slightly less of a special advantage because of the role played by the dollar. In the meantime, the chaos engendered by the demise of the Bretton Woods system and the resulting realignment of world currencies created an opportunity that at least one group of less developed countries was able to exploit.

Enter OPEC

For years exporters of basic commodities had complained that the system worked to their disadvantage. While the price of the raw materials they sold abroad either remained constant or fell, the price of the manufacturing goods they imported, especially the capital equipment, rose. As a result, they found themselves falling further behind in the race to industrialize as the terms of trade moved against them. Western countries might argue that this was simply the blind working of the marketplace, but the less developed countries strongly suspected that the oligopolistic structure of the industries supplying them with manufactured goods had a lot to do with the situation. When the less developed countries called for long-term commodity agreements to stabilize the relative price of raw materials, the Western countries balked, invoking Smithian principles against interfering with the market. But then, through a combination of unique historical events—not the least important of which was the slide of the American dollar following the scuttling of the Bretton Woods system—the oil-exporting nations suddenly found themselves able to redress the long-standing grievance.

The periodic spurts in OPEC prices, reinforcing the effect of flexible exchange rates, were a significant factor in producing the double-digit inflation of the 1970s. Because of the feedback effects on their domestic economies, not even the OPEC countries themselves were immune from the rise in domestic price levels. The double-digit inflation, in turn, has been the principal reason for the slowdown in the growth rates of the Western countries, turning the optimism of the previous period into the present pessimism. The Western countries, knowing of no other way to contain the inflationary contagion, have resorted to the deliberate weakening of their domestic economies, and this has only transformed the problem of secular inflation into the problem of world-wide stagflation. It is this situation that calls for the creation of a new international order.

From the historical causes of the present difficulties, at least two essential features of the required new economic order can be discerned. One is an international monetary system which, instead of turning backward from Bretton Woods, moves the world forward. The new international monetary system must allow for some adjustment in exchange rates over time while still offering the security of fixed exchange rates in the short period. This means it must provide for some type of "crawling peg," at least between the currencies of major trading blocks such as the North American continent, the Common Market of Europe, and the market economies of the Far East. This would restore greater stability to international trading relationships without imposing the straitjacket of completely fixed exchange rates. Even more important, the new international monetary system must provide an assured source of short-time liquidity to countries that, as a consequence of increased domestic economic activity, incur a temporary balance of payments deficit. In this way, countries would be spared the agony of "stop-and-go" policies while the growth of an international medium of exchange over the long run would be assured. The new type of world bank at the center of the system would have to be able to cope not only with the central banks of individual countries but also with multinational corporations and their banking counterparts. To arrange all this in a satisfactory way will present quite a challenge to those who would improve on Keynes' earlier work. For it is not merely a question of hammering out technical details; it is also a matter of reconciling conflicting national interests.

The other essential feature of the new international order would have to be an understanding between the developed Western countries and the other, less developed nations. On their part, the commodity exporters, particularly the OPEC countries, would have to agree to freeze the prices of certain key raw materials. In return, they would have to be given certain long-term credits, in excess of the prices they receive, enabling them to purchase capital goods in the future at similarly fixed prices. In addition, tariff and other barriers to the importation of manufactured goods from the less developed countries would have to be gradually lowered, giving those countries a growing share of the markets in the West even as the advanced industrial nations increased their exports of capital goods to the less developed countries. In this way, the present potent source of double-digit inflation would be avoided while the legitimate needs of the less developed countries for the means to achieve their own industrialization would be met.

It should not be thought, however, that these two arrangements alone will suffice to establish the new economic order that will carry the world forward with prosperity into the twenty-first century. A new set of international monetary institutions and a new trading relationship between the developed and less developed countries are merely the items at the top of the agenda. Among the other types of international institutional rejuvenation required are:

1. New security arrangements to protect the Western countries themselves from Soviet expansionism and, even more important in light of likely developments, to prevent any instability within the Third World from escalating into a major world conflict.

2. Strengthening the Organization for Economic Cooperation and Development so that matters of policy no longer within the control of any one member nation can be effectively dealt with, while at the same time ensuring that the interests of vitally affected groups are effectively represented within the councils of the OECD.

The United States will have to exert a special kind of leadership to help bring this new international order into being. At the very least it must have a clear view of what is to be accomplished and then work patiently with its allies, as "the first among equals," to reach that goal.

Issues of political economy

The Keynesian revolution in domestic economic policy was the principal means by which the century-old faith in a *laissez-faire* approach was finally broken. If massive unemployment could be avoided only through an activist fiscal and monetary policy, then the basis for arguing against government intervention in the economy was seriously undermined. Indeed, once the need for high levels of government spending was conceded, together with other forms of intervention to assure rapid and sustained economic growth, it was difficult to draw the line as to where the government's intervention in the economy should end. It is hardly surprising, therefore, that as faith in the Keynesian remedies for controlling inflation, if not unemployment, has waned, the fundamental issue in political economy—what, ideally, should be the role of the government in the economy—has again moved to the center of public debate. Since the issue was largely pushed to one side with the heady success of, first, Keynesian countercyclical policy, then the Great Society initiatives, and finally the populist movements of the 1970s, it is a question in serious need of rethinking. So far, as an examination of the best-selling titles among economic books would indicate, the platform has been commandeered primarily by those who would revive the *laissez-faire* philosophy of the nineteenth century. Yet it hardly seems likely that the issue can be effectively dealt with on the basis of the simplistic belief that the market generally provides the best solution to economic problems.

Indeed, the question of what the government's role in the economy should be needs to be broken down into three different questions, each requiring its own separate answer. First, what role must the government play if inflation, along with unemployment, is to be brought under effective control? The answer, as will be seen, goes beyond the monetary, fiscal, and other demand-management policies usually argued for it. It thus means giving up the simple-minded notion that prices can be stabilized merely by avoiding an undue increase in the money supply and/or by avoiding government deficits. Second, what types of government expenditures can be justified and at what levels? Again, the easy answer that it would be enough simply to reduce (or, for that matter, to increase) government expenditures will not suffice. The issue here is how the public sector can be made to work more effectively to meet the need for public goods and services. Third, what forms of regulation, and thus what legal constraints, should the government as the principal rule-making body impose on private parties? The maxim that the government that is best is the one that regulates the least flies in the face of the complex reality historical experience reveals.

The secular rise in prices

Perhaps no factor has contributed more to the loss of faith in Keynesian social democracy, at least in the developed nations, than the inability of governments to bring a halt to the secular rise in prices. The culprit here, however, is not Keynes' own theory but rather the misrepresentation of that theory by other economists, especially in the United States. It is they who have taken a theory intended to explain how an economy can be rescued from widespread unemployment and tried to use it as a guide for dealing with the quite different problem of inflation. True, Keynes might have better anticipated and warned against the type of problem most likely to arise as the economy recovered from the Great Depression—as did Michal Kalecki, who actually anticipated Keynes by earlier presenting (in Polish) the ideas found in *The General Theory*. Still, Keynes himself did not suggest that the cure for inflation was simply the reversal of the policies required to cure unemployment.

Indeed, by insisting that his arguments held only on the assumption that money wages remained constant, Keynes provided the key to understanding why the post–World War II period has been one marked by a secular rise in prices. As part of the shift to Keynesian social democracy, the very conditions that once assured that money wages would remain unchanged have been fundamentally altered. The development of strong trade unions, together with the government's commitment to full employment policies, has meant that money wages, instead of remaining constant, have risen steadily during the postwar period, not just in the United States but throughout the OECD community of nations. Not that the economies of these countries would have been better off if money wages had remained at the same level. Quite the contrary. It has been largely the growth of money wages which has fostered the postwar economic prosperity. With prices unlikely to fall because of the concentrated market power of firms, there was no other way besides the rise in money wages to translate the gains from technical progress into a higher standard of living for the great majority of citizens.

The problem is, rather, that money wages cannot rise by more than a certain percentage each year without the higher rates of compensation becoming inflationary. What that percentage is will depend on the circumstances—how great the growth of labor productivity has been, what shifts in the composition of final demand are to occur simultaneously, and other considerations. Still, there is a maximum growth of wages which will still be noninflationary, and it is this fact that requires that the more conventional fiscal and monetary policy instruments be supplemented by an incomes policy if inflation is to be brought under control. Most countries, including the United States at various points in its recent history, have learned this lesson. The question, then, is not whether an incomes policy should be implemented but instead how such a policy can be made to work successfully.

The mistake, it seems clear in retrospect, has been to attempt to implement an incomes policy in a political and social vacuum. An incomes policy strikes at the most sensitive of all political issues: How shall income be distributed between workers and other groups in society? The government is ill-suited to tackle this question head-on by itself; it must instead approach it in a roundabout manner, acting as the conciliating force among a larger body of contending interest groups. But there is an antecedent question: What shall the long-term rate of economic expansion be and, as a corollary, what types of investment, private as well as public, are needed to achieve that goal? Once that antecedent question has been answered, it will be found that only one rate of growth of money wages and other forms of household income will be consistent with a stable price level. It is that rate of growth upon which an incomes policy should be based. In other words, a successful incomes policy can only be an extension of a more general planning process for the economy as a whole.

What this means is that the United States must finally develop the political maturity needed to accept the idea of national planning—and thus join the ranks of the world's other successful industrialized countries which have recognized that without planning, future economic growth cannot be assured. The belief that markets alone will solve a nation's economic problems is dangerously naive—and likely to lead to the further slippage of the United States behind other OECD countries.

A bloated public sector

The secular rise in prices is not the only source of dissatisfaction with Keynesian social democracy. There is another: a bloated public sector. Initially, it was the cold war that provided the rationale for the government's commanding one-fifth of the nation's entire economic output. Unable to persuade the political leadership to fund other types of programs, social democrats were content to see the Defense Department budget grow fat. At least in that way sufficiently high levels of aggregate demand, in keeping with Keynesian principles, could be maintained. Later, as the cold war partly thawed and not even the race to outer space could provide a sufficiently powerful equivalent way to maintain economic prosperity, the political leadership was persuaded to draw up plans for a domestic war on poverty—only to have those plans overtaken by an actual hot war in Southeast Asia. Still, the Vietnam adventure, as a war fought largely out of inventory, was only a minor epicycle on the growth curve of government expenditures. It was domestic social programs—community development, education and training, health, and income security—which grew from 25 percent of the federal budget and 4.5 percent of GNP in 1965 to 50 percent of the federal budget and 11.4 percent of GNP by the end of the Carter administration in 1980. It was in this way that the hopes of social democrats were finally realized—that the squalor of the public sector which John Kenneth Galbraith had so eloquently pointed to in *The Affluent Society* could be ended.

And yet the average citizen, rather than feeling enriched by the expansion of the public sector, feels only the pain of the higher taxes required to support both the new programs and the greatly expanded coverage of the older programs. It turned out that, just as it was a mistake to assume that inflation could be controlled simply by reversing the policies needed to prevent unemployment, so too it was a mistake to assume that the squalor of the public sector could be ended simply by pouring more money into it. This error, which would be the undoing of public sector programs despite the best intentions of the nation, had two sources. One was the mistaken belief that enough was known about the dynamics of human behavior for the government to be successful when it intervened to interrupt the cycle of poverty in which one-fifth of the society—including a disproportionate number of blacks—found itself trapped. After all, it was reasoned, the government had learned how to interrupt the cycle of economic booms and busts—why could it not end poverty as well? This was a conceit of the behavioral scientists for which the rest of the society would pay dearly. The other source of error was the failure to recognize the challenge which the vast expansion of the public sector would pose to effective administration. As would soon be learned, neither management techniques borrowed from the private sector nor ''maximum feasible participation'' by the poor could guarantee that the billions of dollars appropriated for domestic social programs would translate into more and better public services. This was the myopia of the political scientists which then compounded the cost of the behavioral scientists' conceit.

To be sure, the problem of poverty will not solve itself. There is a cycle of deprivation, extending from one generation to the next, which only the intervention of the government can interrupt. Even more generally, there are certain services that only the government can provide. Still, we have passed beyond the point of innocence where we can honestly believe that public monies alone will solve the nation's social problems. What we need, then, is a better sense of the areas where the government can play a constructive role, and where the expenditure of public funds will bring the highest social return. We can no longer fall back on the excuse that, whatever the waste, at least more jobs are being created. This argument applies with equal force to the expensive and largely useless new weapons systems which, under the Reagan administration, have replaced the Great Society programs as the government's preferred form of largesse. What we need, in other words, is a clear demonstration that the public sector, whatever its size, can be managed more effectively in the public interest. If the squalor of the public sector is to be ended, if indeed there is to be a significant public sector at all, then the majority of citizens will have to be convinced that they can get more from the taxes they pay than if they were to spend the money themselves. (On this point, see Eichner and Brecher, 1979.)

Too much regulation

The third and final source of dissatisfaction with Keynesian social democracy, at least on the domestic front, is the belief that it has led to too much regulation of the economy. The irony here is that it was primarily the ostensible foes of bigger government, in particular key officials in the Nixon and Ford administrations, who were responsible for the policies that have produced this feeling. It was the Nixon administration that acted to impose wage and price controls when its prior economic policies portended disaster, and it was under the Nixon and succeeding Ford administrations that businesses became subject to a set of rules and regulations about product quality, worker safety, and environmental protection far more comprehensive and detailed in nature than any previous Democratic administration would have dared to propose. It should be recognized, furthermore, that many of the cries heard in protest are simply the self-serving pleas of those who would shift the costs of production, which rightfully should be theirs, onto the backs of others. Still, the belief that ours is an economy which has become overregulated—with the government playing much too obtrusive a role—is not entirely without foundation.

The mistake here was the failure to recognize how crude and limited a social instrument government is—and how easily the public purposes of government can be perverted to serve private ends. It was as though, in reaction to the nation's overly long and too steadfast commitment to *laissez-faire*, all the reasons why social philosophers had once been distrustful of government power were forgotten. People failed to ask: What are the least steps the government can take to achieve its social objectives? Indeed, the limits on what could be accomplished through the actions of the state seemed to have been lost sight of altogether. Instead, the solution to each problem that presented itself seemed to be just to write another set of government regulations—whether the problem was a shortage of oil or discrimination on the job. In this way, the minimalist state was replaced by the maximalist state. But the problems the maximalist state was supposed to solve still did not show any signs of diminishing.

It may seem contradictory, if not actually dishonest, to argue for both national planning and a minimalist state. The contradiction arises, however, only when national planning is conceived of as a detailed set of instructions emanating from a single governmental body to which all firms and industries must then adhere. This is planning as it is practiced in totalitarian societies like the Soviet Union. It is not national planning as it is carried out in democratic societies like France, Sweden, Austria, and even Japan—or as it would be carried out in the United States if the ideological bias against any effort by government to develop a long-term growth strategy in cooperation with private groups could be overcome. The key to this type of democratic, or indicative, planning is agreement beforehand as to what types of investment, both public and private, are required over the next five to ten years to achieve a given set of economic goals. Under this form of planning, the market system, along with the long-range strategic planning now engaged in by almost every large corporation, would be retained. The difference would be that those private plans would be better articulated with a set of national economic objectives, the latter emerging out of discussions among leaders of business, labor, government, and other groups and reflected in the choice among several possible alternatives of a specific capital expenditures program for the nation as a whole.

Indeed, except for the public part of the capital expenditure program and the other fiscal and monetary instruments it already commands, the government would have no power to implement the plan on its own. It would have to count on voluntary adherence by all the private groups affected, especially the members of certain key industries. Still, the enlightened self-interest of the private groups, together with the tax and other incentives the government is able to provide, should be sufficient to make the plan work. And since the plan would grow out of quasi-public discussions among the various major interest groups, and since any action the government might take to implement its part of the plan would require Congressional approval, the planning process itself would be fully consistent with democratic principles.

Once a consensus developed in support of a particular investment program for the nation as a whole, other issues could more easily be dealt with. There would then be a basis for determining priorities within the public sector, for example. The government's own budget, and especially the capital component, would have to be consistent with the overall national plan for that year, with preference given to those public expenditures required if private spending plans were to be realized. The consensus on a national investment plan would also provide the prerequisite for an effective incomes policy. Finally, with agreement as to the socially optimal rate and composition of investment in each industry, most other forms of regulation could be relaxed, if not eliminated altogether. There would be no need to control prices directly, whether by a regulatory commission or otherwise. The social control over investment implicit in the way the capital spending plans were developed would mean that prices themselves were being controlled— albeit indirectly. Indeed, one could be certain that in this same way, that is, by the types of investment projects being sanctioned in each of the industries, environmental and other types of social needs were being met. A system of indicative planning is therefore a means of replacing the present excess regulation of business activity so that, while the government can still protect the general public interest, its role in the economy can be kept to a minimum. It is only in this way that we can ever hope to see a return to the minimalist state.

The good society

The democratic society which the United States has enjoyed for at least 200 years and which all the other OECD countries can now be said to have attained has brought the citizens of those countries a certain amount of civil liberty and produced a certain degree of government responsiveness. The political goals of a good society, then, can be said to have now been minimally achieved. Similarly, in the post-World War II period, the rising per capita income and avoidance of widespread unemployment has given the citizens of those same countries a relatively comfortable standard of living. The economic goals of a good society, too, can be said to have now been minimally achieved. If this still leaves room for widespread ennui, if not actual dissatisfaction, it is because there are still minimal goals of a good society yet to be achieved. Those goals are not political or economic; rather they are anthropogenic—having to do with human development. Just as it is necessary to assure everyone a certain amount of political liberty, along with the power to influence the policies of government, and a certain minimal standard of living, along with the means to influence the types of goods and services to be provided, so too it is necessary to assure everyone the opportunity to lead a productive and meaningful life. To realize the anthropogenic goals of post-Keynesian social democracy, it is necessary that the United States adopt policies that would, among other things:

1. Complete the democratization of education by making the years spent in high school and college a truly liberating experience, with each individual learning not only to think critically and incisively but also to enjoy the process of learning itself.

2. Enable each individual to realize more fully his or her innate potential by removing as many of the barriers to personal development as possible—and in this way achieve greater equality of opportunity.

Still, the key to realizing the anthropogenic goals of post-Keynesian social democracy are the types of aggregate demand policies that would make the declared goal of "full employment" a reality by insuring that all people, for at least a portion of their lives, have a job that is intrinsically satisfying, and not just a source of income.

The declared Keynesian goal of full employment has been compromised throughout the post–World War II period by the fear that the high levels of aggregate demand that would be required would exacerbate the problem of inflation. This is why an incomes policy as part of a broader indicative planning process is so essential. It is needed not just to assure price stability but also to obviate the need for the restrictive aggregate demand policies that have periodically led to a rise in the unemployment rate. However, even if an effective incomes policy were to be implemented and the specter of inflation thereby dispelled, the United States would still be likely to fall far short of being able to provide intrinsically satisfying jobs to all who would like them. The fact is that, at whatever happens to be the present level of technology, only a certain number of individuals need to be employed in order to produce most efficiently the goods that constitute the current standard of living—and among those employed only a certain number are likely to hold jobs which they find intrinsically satisfying. While more individuals can always be put to work, by being put on the government payroll if by no other means, this cannot be done, beyond a certain point, without its leading to a decline in output per worker for the labor force as a whole, and thus without its lowering the standard of living, at least for those who were previously employed.

Thus if the goal of full employment is to be realized in the sense of providing everyone with an intrinsically satisfying job for at least a portion of life without this leading to a decline in the standard of living for those previously employed, two further steps will have to be taken—besides ending the fear of inflation through the successful implementation of an incomes policy. The first is to distribute the society's workload, and thus the available employment opportunities, more evenly among those who are of working age. The other step is to make the kinds of employment opportunities that are to be provided, along with the amount of intrinsic satisfaction they offer, an integral part of the design in formulating aggregate demand policies. The extent to which either of these two steps is taken will depend on what use is made of the growing social surplus which technical progress makes possible.

Up to now, the gains in output per worker have been used primarily to increase the supply of goods and services and, when the private demand has proven inadequate, to support a larger public sector—even if this has meant that a significant portion of the social surplus has been wasted on military and other boondoggles. Individuals have then had to fit themselves into the employment opportunities that this use of the growing social surplus has created. There are, however, two other ways to make use of the growing social surplus that technical progress makes possible.

One is to reduce the number of hours that have to be spent in paid employment. This is the leisure option, and it can be realized through a reduction in the work week, a reduction in the work year (through increased vacation time), or a reduction in the work lifetime itself (through paid sabbaticals, earlier retirement, etc.). Under this option, real income in the form of more goods and services is sacrificed for increased time that can be spent on other activities besides paid employment. The other possibility is to reverse the relationship that presently exists between aggregate demand and employment by starting with the types of jobs that individuals are likely to find intrinsically satisfying and then, with public expenditures supplementing the private demand, create that set of employment opportunities. This is the work satisfaction option, and it involves the sacrifice of real income for greater satisfaction on the job.

Either of the two options, were they to be included as part of a full employment policy, would seem likely to require that Americans accept a slower rate of growth—if not an actual decline—in real income. Both involve the use of the growing social surplus which technical progress makes possible, not to increase the supply of goods and services but rather to enable people to spend more time doing what they like to do, whether they are compensated for their time or not. Fear that the growth of real income might be slowed, however, ignores the effect that increased leisure and greater work satisfaction are likely to have on technical progress and the growth of output per worker—if they are the result of a consciously implemented full employment policy.

With individuals assured of being able to obtain another job, or at least of still receiving adequate income, should technical progress eliminate their present position, they are less likely to resist the changes that lead to increasing output per worker. Moreover, with individuals in a better position to do what they want to do, either because they have more leisure time or because the jobs they hold give them that greater freedom, the pace of technical progress is likely to be accelerated as more people engage in the types of activities that contribute to the growth of knowledge and the development of better techniques, both on the job and within the other spheres of everyday life. Indeed, all that would be needed to insure that the leisure and work satisfaction options would have this more positive effect on the growth of real income would be two further measures: 1) a more liberal system of transfer payments for those who lose their jobs as a result of technological developments, and 2) the types of pedagogical reforms that would complete the democratization of education in the United States. Only the latter measure need be discussed further.

The great danger, as the United States and the other OECD countries continue to reap the benefits of the technological advance the computer revolution holds in store, is that these societies will become increasingly polarized between those who, by virtue of the skills they have acquired, can easily be incorporated into the labor force and those who, because of the various types of deprivation they have suffered, cannot. If the existence of social democratic institutions is not to be threatened, then it is essential that the size of the latter group be kept as small as possible. Although lack of access to the types of educational institutions that prepare one for a professional career is not the only type of deprivation that makes it difficult to obtain a good job, still it is an important reason why some individuals are likely to find themselves excluded from all but the most menial of occupations. It is for this reason that completing the democratization of education and taking other steps to insure greater equality of opportunity is so important to realizing the anthropogenic goals of society. To the extent that any significant number of persons are unable to acquire the skills that a technologically advanced society requires, not only will their potential as human beings not be fully realized but, in addition, the continued viability of social democratic institutions will be threatened.

It is not being suggested here that all of these programs—political and economic as well as anthropogenic—can be implemented in the near future. Rather the purpose is to suggest the direction social democracy will need to take as a follow-up to the earlier, but now increasingly limited, success of Keynesian policies if every individual is to realize his or her full potential as a human being. It is a vision of the "good society" that will take at least several decades to achieve—and thus can challenge this and succeeding generations for many years to come.

Afterword

This essay originally appeared in *Challenge* magazine (March 1982), though with the final section, covering the anthropogenic aspects of the good society, less fully developed.

References

Ackoff, Russel L., and Fred E. Emery. 1972. *On Purposeful Systems*, Chicago: Aldine.

Anderson, W. Locke. 1964. *Corporate Finance and Fixed Investment: An Econometric Study*, Boston: Harvard Business School.

Andrews, P. W. S. 1949. *Manufacturing Business*, London: Macmillan.

——. 1964. *On Competition in Economic Theory*, London: Macmillan.

Andrews, P. W. S., and Elizabeth Brunner. 1975. *Studies in Pricing*, London: Macmillan.

Appelbaum, Eileen. 1979. "The Labor Market," in *A Guide to Post Keynesian Theory*, Alfred S. Eichner, ed., White Plains, N.Y.: M. E. Sharpe.

Arestis, Philip, Ciaran Driver, and P. I. H. Jones. 1984. "The Monetary Sector of a Post-Keynesian Model of the U.K. Economy," London: Economics Division, School of Social Sciences, Thames Polytechnic, unpublished, December.

Arrow, Kenneth J., and Gerhard Debreu. 1954. "Existence of an Equilibrium for a Competitive Economy," *Econometrica*, July, pp. 265–90.

Arrow, Kenneth J., and Frank H. Hahn. 1971. *General Competitive Analysis*, Edinburgh: Oliver and Boyd.

Asimakopulos, A., and John Burbridge. 1974. "The Short-Period Incidence of Taxation," *Economic Journal*, June, pp. 267–88.

Bain, Joe S. 1956. *Barriers to New Competition*, Cambridge, Mass.: Harvard University Press.

Baumol, William J. 1967. *Business Behavior, Value and Growth*, New York: Harcourt, Brace and World (lst ed., 1959, New York: Macmillan).

Becker, Gary S. 1957. *The Economics of Discrimination*, Chicago: University of Chicago Press.

——. 1964. *Human Capital*, Princeton, N.J.: Princeton University Press.

——. 1968. "Crime and Punishment: An Economic Approach," *Journal of Political Economy*, March, pp. 169–217.

Bell, Daniel, and Irving Kristol. 1980. *The Crisis in Economic Theory*, New York: Basic Books.

Berg, Ivar M. 1970. *Education and Jobs, The Great Training Robbery*, New York: Praeger.

——. 1972. *Human Resources and Economic Welfare, Essays in Honor of Eli Ginzberg*, New York: Columbia University Press.

Berger, Peter L. 1963. *Invitation to Sociology: A Humanistic Perspective*, New York: Anchor Books.

Bershady, Harold J. 1973. *Ideology and Social Knowledge*, New York: Wiley.

Black, Max, ed. 1961. *The Social Theories of Talcott Parsons*, Englewood Cliffs, N.J.: Prentice-Hall.

Blair, John M. 1972. *Economic Concentration*, New York: Harcourt, Brace Jovanovich.

Blatt, John. 1983. *Dynamic Economic Systems, A Post-Keynesian Approach*, Armonk, N.Y.: M. E. Sharpe, Inc.

Blaug, Mark. 1974. *The Cambridge Revolution*, London: Institute of Economic Affairs.

————. 1976. "The Empirical Status of Human Capital Theory: A Slightly Jaundiced Survey," *Journal of Economic Literature*, September, pp. 827–55.

————. 1980. *The Methodology of Economics, Or How Economists Think*, London: Cambridge University Press.

Boulding, Kenneth E. 1970. *A Primer on Social Dynamics; History as Dialectics and Development*, New York: Free Press.

Bosworth, Barry. 1971. "Patterns of Corporate External Financing," *Brookings Papers on Economic Activity*, no. 2, pp. 253–79.

Brems, Hans. 1977. "Reality and Neoclassical Theory," *Journal of Economic Literature*, March, pp. 72–83.

Brenner, M. Harvey. 1973. *Mental Illness and the Economy*, Cambridge, Mass.: Harvard University Press.

Cain, Glen C. 1976. "The Challenge of Segmented Labor Market Theories to Orthodox Theory: A Survey," *Journal of Economic Literature*, December, pp. 1215–57.

Canterbery, Ray. 1979a. "Inflation, Necessities and Distributive Efficiency," in J. H. Gapinski and C. E. Rockwood, eds., *Essays in Post-Keynesian Inflation*, Cambridge, Mass.: Ballinger.

————. 1979b. "A Vita Theory of the Personal Income Distribution," *Southern Economic Journal*, July, pp. 12–48.

Chandler, Alfred D. Jr. 1962. *Strategy and Structure: Chapters in the History of Industrial Enterprise*. Cambridge, Mass.: MIT Press.

————. 1965. "The Railroads: Pioneers in Modern Corporate Management," *Business History Review*, spring, pp. 16–40.

————. 1971. *Pierre S. du Pont and the Making of the Modern Corporation*, New York: Harper.

————. 1977. *The Visible Hand, The Managerial Revolution in American Business*, Cambridge, Mass.: Harvard University Press.

Chandler, Alfred D. Jr., and Stephen Salsbury. 1965. "The Railroads: Innovators in Modern Business Administration," in *The Railroads and the Space Program*, Bruce Maydish, ed., Cambridge, Mass.: MIT Press.

Chapman, Stanley D. 1974. "The Textile Factory Before Arkwright: A Typology of Factory Development," *Business History Review*, winter, pp. 451–78.

Chick, Victoria. 1983. *Macroeconomics After Keynes, A Reconsideration of The General Theory*, Cambridge, Mass.: MIT Press.

Christianson, Paul, and Richard G. Fritz. 1981. "Environmental Resources in a Post-Keynesian Model," *Review of Regional Studies*, fall.

Clark, John M. 1961. *Competition as a Dynamic Process*, Washington: Brookings Institution.

Commons, John R. 1934. *Institutional Economics*, New York: Macmillan, 2 vols.

————. 1957. *The Legal Foundations of Capitalism*, Madison: University of Wisconsin Press.

Cooley, Thomas F., and Stephen F. LeRoy. 1981. "Identification and Estimation of Money Demand," *American Economic Review*, December, pp. 825–44.

Cornwall, John. 1972. *Growth and Stability in a Mature Economy*, New York: Halstad Press.

————. 1977. *Modern Capitalism*, New York: St. Martin's Press.

Coutts, Kenneth, Wynne Godley, and William Nordhaus. 1978. *Pricing in the United Kingdom*, London: Cambridge University Press.

Cuff, Robert D., and Melvin I. Urofsky. 1970. "The Steel Industry and Price Fixing During World War I," *Business History Review*, autumn, pp. 291–306.

Cuthberston, Keith. 1979. *Macroeconomic Policy, The New Cambridge, Keynesian and Monetarist Controversies*, New York: Wiley.

Cyert, Richard M., and Morris H. DeGroot. 1971. "Interfirm Learning and the Kinked Demand Curve," *Journal of Economic Theory*, September, pp. 272–87.

Cyert, Richard M., and J. G. March. 1963. *A Behavioral Theory of the Firm*, Englewood, N.J.: Prentice-Hall.

Davenport, Paul. 1981. "Investment, Technical Change, and Economic Growth," a paper presented at a conference on Keynes and Sraffa, Ottawa University, March (reprinted in *L'Actualité Economique*, Janvier-Juin, 1982).

————. 1983. "Embodied Technical Change: A New Approach," *Canadian Journal of Economics*, February, pp. 139–49.

Davidson, Paul. 1972. *Money and the Real World*, London: Macmillan.

————. 1980. "Post Keynesian Economics: Solving the Crisis in Economic Theory," in *The Crisis in Economic Theory*, Daniel Bell and Irving Kristol, eds., New York: Basic Books.

Day, Richard H., and E. Herbert Tinney. 1968. "How to Co-operate in Business Without Really Trying: A Learning Model of Decentralized Decision Making," *Journal of Political Economy*, July, pp. 583–600.

Debreu, Gerhard. 1959. *Theory of Value*, New York: Wiley.

Deutsch, Karl. 1966. *The Nerves of Government*, New York: Free Press.

Dewey, Donald. 1959. *Monopoly in Economics and Law*, Chicago: Rand McNally.

Dewing, Arthur S. 1913. *A History of the National Cordage Company*, Cambridge, Mass.: Harvard University Press.

————. 1914. *Corporate Promotion and Reorganization*, Cambridge, Mass.: Harvard University Press.

Didrichsen, Jon. 1972. "The Development of Diversified and Conglomerate Firms in the United States, 1920–1970," *Business History Review*, summer, pp. 202–19.

Doeringer, Peter B., and Michael J. Piore. 1971. *Internal Labor Markets and Manpower Analysis*, Lexington, Mass.: Heath.

Domar, Evsey D. 1946. "Capital Expansion, Rate of Growth, and Employment," *American Economic Review*, April, pp. 137–47.

————. 1947. "Expansion and Employment," *American Economic Review*, March, pp. 34–55.

————. 1957. *Essays in the Theory of Growth*, London: Oxford University Press.

Dorfman, Robert, ed. 1965. *Measuring the Benefits of Government Investments*, Washington: Brookings Institution.

Downie, Jack. 1958. *The Competitive Process*, London: Duckworth.

Duesenberry, James S. 1949. *Income, Saving and the Theory of Consumer Behavior*, Cambridge, Mass.: Harvard University Press.

Dunlop, J. T. 1950. *Wage Determination Under Trade Unions*, New York: A. Kelley.

Earl, T. E. 1983. *The Economic Imagination*, Armonk, N.Y.: M. E. Sharpe.

Easton, David. 1964. *A Systems Analysis of Political Life*, New York: Wiley.

Eckstein, Otto, and Gary Fromm. 1968. "The Price Equation," *American Economic Review*, December, pp. 1159–83.

Eichner, Alfred S. 1969. *The Emergence of Oligopoly, Sugar Refining as a Case Study*, Johns Hopkins Press (reprinted by Greenwood Press, 1978).

————. 1973a. "A Theory of the Determination of the Mark-up under Oligopoly," *Economic Journal*, December, pp. 1184–1200.

————. 1973b. "Human Resources Planning," in *New York Is Very Much Alive*, Eli Ginzberg, ed., New York: McGraw-Hill.

————. 1973c. "Manpower Planning and Economic Planning: The Two Prerequisites," in *The Localization of Federal Manpower*, Robert L. Aronson, ed., Ithaca, N.Y.: New York State School of Industrial and Labor Relations.

————. 1974. "Pricing Policies of Oligopolistic Companies: The Larger Dynamic," in Regional Trade Union Seminar, *Final Report*, Paris: Organization for Economic Cooperation and Development.

————. 1976. *The Megacorp and Oligopoly, Micro Foundations of Macro Dynamics*, London: Cambridge University Press (reprinted by M. E. Sharpe, 1980).

————. 1977a. "The Geometry of Macrodynamic Balance," *Australian Economic Papers*, June, pp. 53–71.

————. 1977b. "Inflation: The International Dimensions," paper presented at Conference on Post-Keynesian Theory, Rutgers University, April, unpublished.

————. 1979a. "A Post-Keynesian Short-Period Model," *Journal of Post Keynesian Economics*, summer, pp. 38–63.

————. 1979b. *A Guide to Post-Keynesian Economics*, White Plains, N.Y.: M. E. Sharpe.

————. 1979c. "An Anthropogenic Model of the Labor Market," *Eastern Economic Journal*, October, pp. 349–66 (reprinted here as essay four).

————. 1980a. "A Post-Keynesian Interpretation of Stagflation: Changing Theory to Fit the Reality," U.S. Congress, Joint Economic Committee, *Stagflation: The Causes, Effects and Solutions, Special Study on Economic Change*, Washington: Government Printing Office (reprinted here as essay six).

————. 1980b. "A General Model of Investment and Pricing," in *Growth, Profits and Property, Essays in the Revival of Political Economy*, Edwin J. Nell, ed., London: Cambridge University Press.

————. 1980c. "A Post-Keynesian Interpretation of Stagflation: Changing Theory to Fit the Reality," U.S. Congress, Joint Economic Committee, *Stagflation: The Causes, Effects and Solution*, Special Study on Economic Change, Washington: Government Printing Office (reprinted here as essay six).

————. 1981. "Post-Keynesian Theory and Empirical Research," a paper presented at a conference on Keynes and Sraffa, Ottawa University, March. CEAR working paper no. 6 (reprinted here as essay eight and in *L'Actualité Economique*, Janvier-Juin, 1982).

————. 1983a. *Why Economics Is Not Yet a Science*, Armonk, N.Y.: M. E. Sharpe.

————. 1983b. "The Post-Keynesian Paradigm and Macrodynamic Modeling," *Thames Papers in Political Economy*, summer (reprinted here as essay seven).

————. 1983c. "The Micro Foundations of the Corporate Economy," *Managerial and Decision Economics*, November, pp. 136–52 (reprinted here as essay three).

————. Forthcoming. *Money: Exogenous or Endogenous?* Armonk, N.Y.: M. E. Sharpe.

Eichner, Alfred S., and Charles Brecher. 1979. *Controlling Social Expenditures: The Search for Output Measures*, Montclair, N.J.: Allanheld, Osmun & Co.

Eichner, Alfred S., Leonard Forman, and Miles Groves. 1982. "Profits and Investment in a Post-Keynesian Short-Period Model," CEAR working paper no. 10, unpublished.

Eichner, Alfred S., and J. A. Kregel. 1975. "An Essay on Post-Keynesian Theory: A New Paradigm in Economics," *Journal of Economic Literature*, December, pp. 1293–1314.

Etzioni, Amitai. 1968. *The Active Society*, New York: Free Press.

Feiwel, George. 1975. *The Intellectual Capital of Michal Kalecki*, Knoxville, Tenn.: University of Tennessee Press.

Forman, Leonard, and Alfred S. Eichner. 1981. "A Post-Keynesian Short-Period Model: Some Preliminary Econometric Results," *Journal of Post Keynesian Economics*, autumn, pp. 117–35.

Forman, Leonard, Miles Groves, and Alfred S. Eichner. 1983. "Modeling the Monetary-Financial Block of a Post-Keynesian Short-Period Model," in *Money: Exogenous or Endogenous?* Alfred S. Eichner, ed., Armonk, N.Y.: M. E. Sharpe, forthcoming.

————. 1984. "The Monetary-Financial Block of a Post-Keynesian Short-Period Model," *British Review of Economic Issues*, autumn.

Freedman, Marcia. 1969. *The Process of Work Establishment*, New York: Columbia University Press.

————. 1976. *Labor Markets: Segments and Shelters*, Montclair, N.J.: Allanheld, Osmun & Co.

Freeman, C. 1982. *Unemployment and Technological Innovation*, Westport, Conn.: Greenwood Press.

Friedlander, Stanley. 1972. *Unemployment in the Urban Core*, New York: Praeger.

Friedman, Milton. 1953. "The Methodology of Positive Economics," in *Essays in Positive Economics*, Chicago: University of Chicago Press.

————. 1976. *Price Theory, A Provisional Text*, Chicago: University of Chicago Press.

Galbraith, John Kenneth. 1955. *The Great Crash*, Boston: Houghton Mifflin.

Garner, Paul S. 1968. "Highlights in the Development of Cost Accounting," in *Contemporary Studies in the Development of Accounting Thought*, Michael Chatfield, ed., Belmont, Cal.: Dickinson.

Garrett, Richard. 1981. "Variations in the Rate of Growth of the U.S. Economy since 1953," unpublished.

Gerschenkron, Alexander. 1961. *Economic Backwardness in Historical Perspective*, Cambridge, Mass.: Harvard University Press.

Ginzberg, Eli. 1966. *The Development of Human Resources*, New York: McGraw-Hill.

————. 1971. *Manpower for Development, Perspectives on Five Continents*, New York: Praeger.

————. 1976. *The Human Economy*, New York: McGraw-Hill.

Ginzberg, Eli, and Ivar Berg. 1963. *Democratic Values and the Rights of Management*, New York: Columbia University Press.

Ginzberg, Eli, and John L. Herma. 1964. *Talent and Performance*, New York: Columbia University Press.

Ginzberg, Eli, Sol W. Ginsburg, Sidney Axelron, and John L. Herma. 1951. *Occupational Choice: An Approach to a General Theory*, New York: Columbia University Press.

Ginzberg, Eli, and Ewing W. Reilley. 1957. *Effecting Change in Large Organizations*, New York: Columbia University Press.

Gold, Bela. 1971. *Explorations in Managerial Economics, Productivity, Costs, Technology and Growth*, New York: Basic Books.

Gordon, David M. 1972. *Theories of Poverty and Underemployment: Orthodox, Radical and Dual Labor Market Perspectives*, Lexington, Mass.: Heath.

Gordon, Robert A. 1945. *Business Leadership in the Large Corporation*, Washington: Brookings Institution.

Graebner, William. 1974. "Great Expectations: The Search for Order in Bituminous Coal, 1890–1917," *Business History Review*, spring, pp. 49–72.

Gruchy, Allan C. 1947. *Modern Economic Thought, The American Contribution*, New York: Prentice-Hall.

Guttentag, Jack. 1966. "The Strategy of Open Market Operations," *Quarterly Journal of Economics*, February, pp. 486–90.

Harcourt, Geoffrey C. 1972. *Some Cambridge Controversies in the Theory of Capital*, London: Cambridge University Press.

Harris, Donald J. 1974. "The Price Policy of Firms, the Level of Employment and the Distribution of Income in the Short Run," *Australian Economic Papers*, June, pp. 144–51.

Harris, Marvin. 1979. *Cultural Materialism, The Struggle for a Science of Culture*, New York: Random House.

Harrod, Roy. 1939. "An Essay in Dynamic Theory," *Economic Journal*, March, pp. 14–33.

————. 1948. *Towards a Dynamic Economics*, London: Macmillan.

Hendershott, Patric. 1968. *The Neutralized Money Stock: An Unbiased Measure of Federal Reserve Actions*, Homewood, Ill.: Irwin.

Hicks, John. 1939. *Value and Capital*, New York: Oxford University Press.

————. 1965. *Capital and Growth*, Oxford: Clarendon Press.

————. 1974. *The Crisis in Keynesian Economics*, New York: Basic Books.

Hidy, Ralph, and Muriel Hidy. 1955. *Pioneering in Big Business, 1882–1911*, 2 vols, New York: Harper.

Hofstadter, Richard. 1955. *The Age of Reform*, New York: Knopf.

Jencks, Christopher et al. 1979. *Who Gets Ahead? The Determinants of Economic Success in America*, New York: Basic Books.

Johnson, Thomas H. 1972. "Early Cost Accounting for Management Control: Lyman Mills in the 1850's," *Business History Review*, winter, pp. 466–74.

Johnston, John. 1960. *Statistical Cost Analysis*, New York: McGraw-Hill.

Jones, Eliot. 1914. *The Anthracite Coal Combination in the United States*, Cambridge, Mass.: Harvard University Press.

Judd, John P., and John L. Scadding. 1982. "The Search for a Stable Money Demand Function: A Survey of the Post-1973 Literature," *Journal of Economic Literature*, September, pp. 993–1023.

Kaldor, Nicholas. 1956. "Alternative Theories of Distribution," *Review of Economic Studies*, no. 2, pp. 83–100, reprinted in Kaldor, 1960a.

————. 1960a. *Essays on Value and Distribution*, Glencoe, Ill.: Free Press.

————. 1960b. *Essays on Economic Stability and Growth*, Glencoe, Ill.: Free Press.

————. 1961. "Capital Accumulation and Economic Growth," in *The Theory of Capital*, F. A. Lutz and D. C. Hague, eds., London: Macmillan.

————. 1983. *The Scourge of Monetarism*, New York: Oxford University Press.

Kaldor, Nicholas, and James A. Mirrlees. 1962. "A New Model of Economic Growth," *Review of Economic Studies*, June, pp. 174–92.

Kalecki, Michal. 1939. *Essays in the Theory of Economic Fluctuations*, London: Allen and Unwin.

————. 1943. "Political Aspects of Full Employment," *Political Quarterly*, no. 4, reprinted in Kalecki, 1971.

————. 1954a. *Theory of Economic Dynamics*, New York: Rinehart.

————. 1954b. *Selected Essays on the Dynamics of the Capital Economy, 1933–1970*, London: Cambridge University Press.

————. 1971. *Selected Essays on the Dynamics of the Capitalist Economy, 1933–1970*, London: Cambridge University Press.

Kaplan, A. D. H., Joel B. Dirlam and Robert F. Lanzilotti. 1958. *Pricing in Big Business: A Case Approach*, Washington: Brookings Institution.

Kenyon, Peter. 1978. "Post-Keynesian Theory: Pricing," *Challenge*, July.

————. 1979. "Pricing," in *A Guide to Post-Keynesian Theory*, Alfred S. Eichner, ed., White Plains, N.Y.: M. E. Sharpe.

Kessler, William C. 1948. "Incorporation in New England: A Statistical Study, 1800–1875," *Journal of Economic History*, May, pp. 43–62.

Keynes, John Maynard. 1930. *A Treatise on Money*, London: Macmillan. 2 vols.

————. 1936. *The General Theory of Employment, Interest and Money*, London: Macmillan, p. 375.

Kiker, B. F. 1968. *Human Capital in Retrospect*, Columbia, S.C.: University of South Carolina, Bureau of Business and Economic Research.

Klein, Lawrence R., and Edwin Burmeister. 1976. *Econometric Model Performance*, Philadelphia: University of Pennsylvania Press.

Klir, Jir, and Miroslav Valach. 1967. *Cybernetic Modelling*, London: Iliffe.

Kolko, Gabriel. 1963. *The Triumph of Conservatism*, New York: Free Press.

Kregel, J. A. 1971. *Rate of Profit, Distribution and Growth: Two Views*, Chicago: Aldine.

————. 1973. *The Reconstruction of Political Economy: An Introduction to Post-Keynesian Economics*, New York: Wiley.

————. 1980. "Economic Dynamics and the Theory of Steady Growth: An Historical Essay on Harrod's 'Knife-edge,' " *History of Political Economy*, spring, pp. 97–123.

Kuhn, Alfred. 1963. *The Study of Society: A Unified Approach*, Homewood, Ill.: Irwin.

Kuhn, Thomas S. 1962. *The Structure of Scientific Revolutions*, Chicago: University of Chicago Press.

Laszlo, Ervin. 1972. *Introduction to Systems Philosophy, Towards a New Paradigm of Contemporary Thought*, New York: Gordon and Breach.

Lee, Frederick S. 1982. "Full-Cost Pricing: An Historical and Theoretical Analysis," unpublished doctoral dissertation, Rutgers University.

Leibenstein, Harvey. 1966. "Allocative Efficiency vs. 'X-Efficiency,' " *American Economic Review*, June, pp. 392–415.

Leontief, Wassily. 1951. *The Structure of the American Economy, 1919–1939*, New York: Oxford University Press.

Leontief, Wassily *et al.* 1954. *Studies in the Structure of the American Economy*, New York: Oxford University Press.

Leontief, Wassily, Ann P. Carter, and P. A. Petri. 1978. *The Future of the World Economy, A United Nations Study*. New York: Oxford University Press.

Letwin, William. 1965. *Law and Economic Policy in America: The Evolution of the Sherman Act*, New York: Random House.

Lewin, David, Raymond Horton, Robert Schick, and Charles Brecher. 1974. *The Urban Labor Market, Institutions, Information, Linkages*, New York: Praeger.

Lichtenstein, Peter M. 1983. *An Introduction to Post-Keynesian and Marxian Theories of Value and Price*, Armonk, N.Y.: M. E. Sharpe.

Livermore, Shaw. 1935. "The Success of Industrial Mergers," *Quarterly Journal of Economics*, November, pp. 68–96.

Livernash, E. Robert. 1957. "The Internal Wage Structure," in *New Concepts in Wage Determination*, George W. Taylor and Frank C. Pierson, eds., New York: McGraw-Hill.

Loasby, Brian J. 1976. *Choice, Complexity and Ignorance*, London: Cambridge University Press.

Lombra, Raymond E. 1981. "Financial Innovation, Deregulation and the Effectiveness of Monetary Policy: A Graphical Approach," unpublished.

Lombra, Raymond E., and Raymond G. Torto. 1973. "Federal Reserve 'Defensive' Behavior and the Reverse Causation Argument," *Southern Economic Journal*, July, pp. 45–55.

Lombra, Raymond E., and Herbert M. Kaufman. 1982. "The Money Supply Process: Stability and Simultaneity," unpublished.

Luce, Robert D., and Howard Raiffa. 1957. *Games and Decisions*, New York: Wiley, pp. 95–96.

Marris, Robin. 1963. *The Economic Theory of "Managerial" Capitalism*, New York: Free Press.

Marris, Robin, and Adrian Wood, eds. 1971. *The Corporate Economy*, Cambridge, Mass.: Harvard University Press.

Marshall, Alfred. 1920. *Principles of Economics*, London: Macmillan.

Martin, Albro. 1971. *Enterprise Denied: Origins of the Decline of American Railroads, 1879–1917*, New York: Columbia University Press.

Maruyama, Magorah. 1963. "The Second Cybernetics: Deviation-Amplifying Mutual Causal Processes," *American Scientist*, June, pp. 164–79.

Maybee, Rolland. 1940. *Railroad Competition and the Oil Trade, 1855–1873*, Mt. Pleasant, Mich.: Extension Press.

McNeil, William. 1963. *The Rise of the West, A History of the Human Community*, Chicago: University of Chicago Press.

Means, Gardiner C. 1962. *The Corporate Revolution in America*, New York: Crowell-Collier.

Metzler, Lloyd. 1947. "Factors Governing the Length of Inventory Cycles," *Review of Economics and Statistics*, February.

Miller, William. 1940. "A Note on the History of Business Corporations in Pennsylvania, 1800–1860," *Quarterly Journal of Economics*, November, pp. 150–60.

Minsky, Hyman P. 1975. *John Maynard Keynes*, Columbia University Press.

————. 1978. "The Financial Instability Hypothesis: A Restatement," *Thames Papers in Political Economy*, autumn, reprinted in Minsky, 1982.

————. 1982. *Can "It" Happen Again?* Armonk, N.Y.: M. E. Sharpe.

Mishan, Edward. 1961. "Theories of Consumers' Behaviour: A Cynical View," *Economica*, February, pp. 1–11.

Mitchell, Wesley C. 1937. *The Backward Art of Spending Money and Other Essays*, New York: McGraw-Hill.

Mitchell, William. 1967. *Sociological Analysis and Politics, The Theories of Talcott Parsons*, Englewood Cliffs, N.J.: Prentice-Hall.

Monsen, R. J. Jr., and Anthony Downs. 1965. "A Theory of Large Managerial Firms," *Journal of Political Economy*, June, pp. 221–36.

Moore, B. J. 1979. "The Endogenous Money Supply," *Journal of Post Keynesian Economics*, fall, pp. 49–70.

————. 1983. "Unpacking the Post-Keynesian Black Box: Bank Lending and the Money Supply," *Journal of Post Keynesian Economics*, autumn, pp. 537–556.

————. Forthcoming. *Verticalists and Horizontalists*.

Morse, Dean. 1969. *The Peripheral Worker*, New York: Columbia University Press.

Moggridge, Donald. 1973. *The Collected Writings of John Maynard Keynes*, vol. XIII, London: Macmillan.

Myrdal, Gunnar. 1939. *Monetary Equilibrium*, London: William Hodge.

Navin, T. R., and M. V. Sears. 1955. "The Rise of a Market for Industrial Securities, 1887-1902," *Business History Review*, June, pp. 105-38.

Nell, Edward J., ed. 1980. *Growth, Profits and Property, Essays in the Revival of Political Economy*, New York: Cambridge University Press.

Nevins, Allan. 1953. *Study in Power: John D. Rockefeller, Industrialist and Philanthropist*, 2 vols., New York: Scribner.

Nickell, S. J. 1978. *The Investment Decision of Firms*, London: Cambridge University Press.

Ong, Nai-Pew. 1981. "Target Pricing, Competition and Growth," *Journal of Post Keynesian Economics*, fall, pp. 101-16.

Ostow, Miriam, and Anna Dutka. 1975. *Work and Welfare in New York City*, Baltimore: Johns Hopkins University Press.

Parsons, Talcott. 1951. *The Social System*, New York: Free Press.

————. 1954. *Toward a General Theory of Action*, New York: Free Press.

————. 1970. "On Building Social System Theory: A Personal History," *Daedalus*, fall, pp. 826-81.

Parsons, Talcott, and Neil J.Smelser. 1956. *Economy and Society*, New York: Free Press.

Pasinetti, Luigi L. 1962. "Rate of Profit and Income Distribution in Relation to the Rate of Economic Growth," *Review of Economic Studies*, October, pp. 267-79.

————. 1974. *Growth and Income Distribution: Essays in Economic Theory*, London: Cambridge University Press.

————. 1980. "The Notion of Vertical Integration in Economic Analysis," in *Essays on the Theory of Joint Production*, Pasinetti, ed., New York: Columbia University Press.

————. 1981. *Structural Change and Economic Growth, A Theoretical Essay on the Dynamics of the Wealth of Nations*, London: Cambridge University Press.

Penrose, Edith T. 1959. *The Theory of the Growth of the Firm*, Oxford: Basil Blackwell.

Phelps, Edmund S. 1970. *Microeconomic Foundations of Employment and Inflation Theory*, New York: Norton.

Piore, Michael J. ed. 1979. *Unemployment and Inflation, Institutional and Structuralist Views*, Armonk, N.Y.: M. E. Sharpe.

Popper, Karl. 1959. *The Logic of Scientific Discovery*, New York: Basic Books.

Porter, Glenn. 1973. *The Rise of Big Business, 1860-1910*. New York: Crowell.

Porter, Patrick G. 1969. "Origins of the American Tobacco Company," *Business History Review*, spring, pp. 59-79.

Rakowski, James J. "Income Conflicts, Inflation and Controls," *Journal of Post Keynesian Economics*, summer, pp. 590-602.

Rapoport, Anatol, and Albert M. Chammah. 1965. *Prisoners' Dilemma*, Ann Arbor: University of Michigan Press.

Reubens, Beatrice. 1977. *Bridges to Work: International Comparisons of Transitional Services*, Montclair, N.J.: Allanheld, Osmun & Co.

Rivlin, Alice. 1971. *Systematic Thinking for Social Action*, Washington: Brookings Institution.

Robinson, Joan. 1953-54. "The Production Function and the Theory of Capital," *Review of Economic Studies*, no. 1, pp. 81-106.

—————. 1956. *The Accumulation of Capital*, London: Macmillan.

—————. 1962a. "The Basic Theory of Normal Price," *Quarterly Journal of Economics*, February, pp. 1–19.

—————. 1962b. *Essays in the Theory of Economic Growth*, London: Macmillan.

—————. 1972. "The Second Crisis of Economic Theory," *American Economic Review*, May, pp. 1–10, reprinted in Robinson, 1981.

—————. 1981. *What Are the Questions?* Armonk, N.Y.: M. E. Sharpe, Inc.

Robinson, Romney. 1961. "The Economics of Disequilibrium Price," *Quarterly Journal of Economics*, May, pp. 199–233.

Rosenberg, Nathan. 1972. *Technology and American Economic Growth*, New York: Harper.

Samuelson, Paul. 1948. *Foundations of Economic Analysis*, Cambridge, Mass.: Harvard University Press.

Schultz, Theodore W. 1961. "Investment in Human Capital," *American Economic Review*, March, pp. 1–17.

Schultze, Charles L. 1968. *The Politics and Economics of Public Spending*, Washington: Brookings Institution.

Seligman, Ben. 1962. *Main Currents in Modern Economics*, New York: Free Press.

Shaikh, Anwar. 1974. "The Laws of Production and Laws of Algebra: The Humbug Production Function," *Review of Economics and Statistics*, February, pp. 115–20, reprinted in Nell, 1980.

Shapiro, Nina. 1977. "The Revolutionary Character of Post-Keynesian Economics," *Journal of Economic Issues*, September, pp. 541–60.

—————. 1981. "Pricing and the Growth of the Firm," *Journal of Post Keynesian Economics*, fall, pp. 85–100.

Shepherd, William G. 1970. *Market Power and Economic Welfare: An Introduction*, New York: Random House.

Simon, Herbert A. 1955. "A Behavioral Model of Rational Choice," *Quarterly Journal of Economics*, February, pp. 99–118.

Solow, Robert. 1956. "A Contribution to the Theory of Economic Growth," *Quarterly Journal of Economics*, February, pp. 65–94.

Soule, Robert. 1947. *Prosperity Decade, From War to Depression: 1919–1929*, New York: Harper & Row.

Sraffa, Piero. 1926. "The Laws of Returns under Competitive Conditions," *Economic Journal*, December, pp. 535–50.

—————. 1960. *Production of Commodities by Means of Commodities*, London: Cambridge University Press.

Steedman, Ian. 1979. *Trade Amongst Growing Economics*, Cambridge University Press.

Steindl, J. 1952. *Maturity and Stagnation in American Capitalism*, Oxford: Basil Blackwell.

Stoke, Harold. 1930. "Economic Influence upon the Corporation Laws of New Jersey," *Journal of Political Economy*, October, pp. 551–79.

Swan, T. W. 1956. "Economic Growth and Capital Accumulation," *Economic Record*, November, pp. 334–61.

Sylos-Labini, Paolo. 1962. *Oligopoly and Technical Progress*, Cambridge, Mass.: Harvard University Press.

—————. 1974. *Trade Unions, Inflation and Productivity*, Lexington, Mass.: Lexington Books.

Taylor, George Rogers. 1951. *The Transportation Revolution, 1815–1860*, New York: Holt.

Tennant, Richard. 1950. *The American Cigarette Industry*, New Haven: Yale University Press.

Thorelli, Hans B. 1955. *The Federal Anti-Trust Policy*, Baltimore: Johns Hopkins Press.

Thurow, Lester C. 1975. *Generating Inequality: Mechanisms of Distribution in the U.S. Economy*, New York: Basic Books.

————. 1983. *Dangerous Currents*, New York: Random House.

Veblen, Thorstein. 1898. "Why Is Economics Not an Evolutionary Science?" *Quarterly Journal of Economics,* July, pp. 373–97, reprinted in Veblen, *The Place of Science in Modern Civilization,* Huebsch, 1919.

————. 1899. *The Theory of the Leisure Class*, New York: Modern Library edition, 1961.

Vernon, Raymond. 1971. *Sovereignty at Bay, The Multinational Spread of U.S. Enterprises*, New York: Basic Books.

Vickers, Douglas. 1968. *The Theory of the Firm, Production, Capital and Finance*, New York: McGraw-Hill.

von Neumann, John. 1945. "A Model of General Economic Equilibrium," *Review of Economic Studies*, no. 1, pp. 1–9.

Wachter, Michael. 1974. "Primary and Secondary Labor Markets: A Critique of the Dual Approach," *Brookings Papers in Economic Activity*, no. 3, pp. 637–80.

Wallerstein, Immanuel. 1976. *The Modern World-System*. New York: Academic Press.

Walters, Alan A. 1963. "Production and Cost, An Econometric Survey," *Econometrica*, January, pp. 1–66.

Ward, Benjamin. 1972. *What's Wrong with Economics?* New York: Basic Books.

Weintraub, Sidney. 1959. *A General Theory of the Price Level, Output, Income Distribution, and Economic Growth*, Philadelphia: Chilton.

————. 1966. *A Keynesian Theory of Employment, Growth and Income Distribution*, Philadelphia: Chilton.

Whipple, D. 1973. "A Generalized Theory of Job Search," *Journal of Political Economy*, September-October, pp. 1170–88.

Wiebe, Robert H. 1967. *The Search for Order, 1877–1920*, New York: Hill and Wang.

Wiles, Peter J. 1956. *Prices, Cost and Output*, Oxford: Basil Blackwell.

————. 1979–80. "Ideology, Methodology and Neoclassical Economics," *Journal of Post Keynesian Economics*, winter, pp. 155–80, reprinted in Eichner, 1983a.

Wilkins, Mira. 1974. *The Maturing of Multinational Enterprise*, Cambridge, Mass.: Harvard University Press.

Williamson, Harold F., and Arnold Daum. 1959. *The American Petroleum Industry*, Evanston, Ill.: Northwestern University Press.

Williamson, J. 1966. "Profit, Growth and Sales Maximization," *Econometrica*, February, pp. 1–16.

Williamson, Oliver E. 1964. *Economics of Discretionary Behavior*, Englewood Cliffs, N.J.: Prentice-Hall.

Wilson, Bryan. 1981. "The Effect of Compositional Changes in Government Expenditures on Economic Growth," unpublished.

Wilson, T., and P. W. S. Andrews. 1951. *Oxford Studies in the Price Mechanism*, Oxford: Clarendon Press.

Wood, Adrian. 1975. *A Theory of Profits*, London: Cambridge University Press.

Yavitz, Boris, and Dean Morse. 1973. *The Labor Market, An Information System*, New York: Praeger.

Index

Accommodation, degree of, by monetary authorities, 99–104, 106–07, 109–10, 122, 168–72

Accumulation, process, 114, 118–19, 122–23; rate of, 61, 125, 133, 135, 161–62, 177. *See also* Investment

Activeness, degree of within markets, 76, 79–80

Advertising, 33, 46, 66, 160

Affiliation, 15, 78–79, 82–84, 94

Aggregate demand, 20, 48, 71–72, 115–16, 119, 200, 210; influence of, on rate of inflation, 133–35; level of (*see* Economic activity, level of)

Aggregate demand condition, for continuous growth, 55–56, 60, 62, 73

Aggregate income, growth of real, 48, 53, 55–56, 62, 73, 132, 135, 138; nominal, 99, 184–86

Aggregate output, 156, 171–72

Aggregate supply, 62, 115–16, 119

Agriculture, 29, 134, 183–84

Anthropogenic dimension, 11, 14–16, 77–78

Anthropogenic goals, 215

Anthropogenic model, 75–97

Anthropogenic system, 78, 87, 94

Assumptions, 11, 57, 63, 179–80, 188, 190–91

Attachment, of workers to jobs, 83–84, 94

Autonomy, of workers, 83

Axiomatic reasoning, 188

Backwardness, country's relative, 118

Balance of payments, 206

Bank deposits, 6

Banking system, 99–101, 106, 108, 121–23, 168

Barriers, to entry. *See* Entry of new firms

Behavioralist theory, 28

Bellwether industry, 91, 127, 145, 172

Bretton Woods, 8, 132, 203–6

Brookings Institution, 165

Business firms, 122

Business sector. *See* Enterprise sector

Capacity, 6, 20, 29, 115–16, 118–20, 130, 132, 155; engineer-rated, 36, 39; expansion of, 32–34, 50, 55, 59, 62, 71, 161–62; reserve, 31–32, 36

Capital, expropriation of, 20, 125; marginal efficiency of, 6

Capital budget, 30, 33–35, 37, 44, 69–70

Capital funds markets, 22, 33, 40, 42

Capital goods, 119, 155; sector, 29–30, 32, 48

Capital inputs, 50, 59, 88, 152, 155, 184

Capital intensity of production, 20

Capital stock, 184, 190. *See also* Capacity

Capital theory, Cambridge controversy in, 176, 181

Capital-output ratio, incremental, 49–52, 55, 59

Career path, 78, 84–85, 87, 93

Cartels, international, 138

Cash balances, 106

Cash flow, of firm, 33, 35, 37–39, 41–44, 50, 68–69, 71; average rate of, 36, 39, 50; net (*see* Discretionary funds)

Cash-flow feedback effect, 72, 121, 163

Causal sequence, 100, 107–8

Causation, direction of, 63

Central bank, 70, 99; world, 203, 206. *See also* Monetary authorities; Federal Reserve system

Chandler, Alfred, 22

Choice, social, 77
Circular flow, 71
Civil liberty, 214
Coalition formation, 13, 77–78
Coherence, of theory, 151, 178, 180–81, 187, 191
Collective bargaining, 56, 91, 126–27, 173
Commodity agreements, 205–07
Commodity approach, to labor economics, 75–76, 79–80
Commodity exports. See Exports, of commodities
Commodity markets, 6, 8, 77, 110, 138–39, 183, 186, 190–91
Common Market, 210
Communism, 200–201
Compensation, of employees, 30, 34, 44, 82–83, 90–92
Competences, 14–16, 75, 78, 83–84, 92, 95
Competition, 51, 123–24; atomistic, 23; Golden Age of, 20; inter-firm, 48, 64–67; for jobs, 93; nature of under oligopolistic conditions, 33–34, 70; nonprice, 48; "ruinous," 20
Comprehensiveness, of theories, 63, 151, 179–80, 183, 187–89, 191
Constancy, of firm's costs, 36
Constraints, on macrodynamic model, 60–61
Consume, propensity to out of non-wage income, 120, 130–33, 138, 162
Consumer interest, 81
Consumer purchasing power, 48, 126, 173
Consumption, 29–30, 48–49, 55–57, 60, 67, 123, 130–32, 138, 162, 181
Consumption goods, 119, 160, 172
Contractual arrangements, 82–83
Control, of firm, 19, 31, 40
Controls, wage and price, 145–48, 212, 214
Conventional theory. See Orthodox theory; Neoclassical theory
Cornwall, John, 196
Corporate economy, 28–74
Corporate law, 21–22
Corporate revolution, 21–26
Correspondence test, 178–82, 184, 186, 188, 191
Cost, of external funds, 40; of internal funds, 33, 37–39, 66

Cost-of-production prices, 165
Costs, 20–21, 31–33, 35–37, 44–45, 110, 123, 127–28, 166, 183, 186; reduction in, 66
Credit, availability of, 72, 109, 123, 166–70; demand for, 99, 102, 106, 108, 122, 166–70; theory of money and, 120–22, 152, 166–71
Credit markets. See Money markets
Credit money, 3, 8, 70, 72
Credit rationing, 107, 109, 194
Crime, 77, 95
Currency, 98–101, 107, 109, 168; devaluation of, 132, 138–39, 204
Cybernetic theory, 18–19
Cyclical behavior, of the economy, 107, 118; of firm, 31
Cyclical fluctuations, 21, 31, 36, 64, 68, 71, 116–18, 126, 129, 142–43, 153, 156–57, 161, 167, 170–71, 185, 195

Davidson, Paul, 166
Debt, firm's, 30, 33, 50; government, 67
Debt-equity ratio, 40
Decision-making, by the firm, 35, 42, 44
Decisions, societal, 78
Defense, national, 120, 211–12
Deficit, cash, 71–72, 121, 163, 168, 170
Deficit spending, by government, 131
Demand, aggregate (see Aggregate demand); for credit, 99, 102, 106, 108; as determinant of supply, 6, 95, 168; effective, 115; for labor, 75, 87, 95; for money, 98, 105, 110
Demand condition. See Aggregate demand condition
Demand conditions, effect of, on prices, 165–66, 171, 186
Demand curve, industry, 62, 182; for investment funds, 39–44; for labor, 88, 91; for loans (see Loan demand); for money, 98, 105
Demand and supply, for labor, 75, 95; for money, 98–99, 105, 110, 166–68; for savings, 4
Demand and supply conditions, 37
Demand and supply framework, 4–9, 57, 62, 75, 77, 85–88, 98, 183, 191
Democracy, 200, 213–15, 217
Deposits, bank, 98–99, 102, 105–9, 170
Depressions, economic, 115, 125, 200–1. See also Cyclical fluctuations

Descartes, Rene, 178
Developmental institutions, 15, 78, 96, 215
Developmental path, 15
Dialectical process, 77
Differentials, in development opportunities, 82; in income, 92
Discount window, Fed's, 102, 107
Discretionary expenditures, 107, 118, 121, 124, 157, 163, 170; by government, 73, 157
Discretionary funds, 109, 121, 163; of business firms, 123, 126
Discrimination, 77
Disequilibrium, 177; of the economy, 122, 163; within individual markets, 189; monetary, 99, 108-9, 121
Distribution, 48, 82, 92, 95, 114, 119-20, 122-23, 125-29, 135-36, 161, 177, 201, 210; neoclassical theory of, 183-84; post-Keynesian theory of, 119-20, 152, 161-63, 172, 177
Distributional variables, 60-61
Diversification, 26, 30, 34-35, 66, 68
Dividends, 30-31, 48, 60, 63, 130, 136, 141, 162
Domar, Evsey, 115
Dominant firm, 30, 32-33, 36, 43
Dual labor markets, 194
Duesenberry, James S., 160
Durable goods industries, 31, 36
Durable goods purchases, 71-73, 99, 107, 121, 157, 161, 168, 170-72; by enterprises (*see* Investment, business); by households, 106, 118, 157, 161
Dynamic analysis, in economics, 116; of society, 17, 78-79

Econometric issues, 98, 192, 196-97
Econometric model, of U.K. economy, 99-100, 107, 197; of U.S. economy, 99-100, 107, 153, 156, 185, 197-98
Economic activity, level of, 99-100, 102, 105, 108-10, 124, 170, 184, 186; monetary-financial determinants of, 105-06, 184-85
Economic dimension, 11, 13-14, 78
Economic organization, 19
Economic system, 87, 94
Economics, as a discipline, 177, 181, 187-88

Education, 75, 77, 92-93, 95, 194, 215, 217
Elasticity of demand. *See* Income elasticity of demand; Price elasticity of demand
Empirical basis, of neoclassical theory, 181-86; of theory, 151-52, 177-80
Empirical evidence, 98-100, 102-5, 107-8, 110, 182-84, 190, 193
Empirical research, 7, 110, 145, 177, 180, 194-99
Empirical tests, 7, 153, 177-82, 184-92, 195-96, 198
Employing organization, 15, 78, 87, 96
Employment, aggregate, 28, 64, 68, 78, 156, 171-72, 215-18; growth of, 157; of the individual, 76, 88, 94
Employment opportunities, 78, 81, 87, 94-96, 216
Enlightenment, the, 200
Enterprise sector, 29, 48, 121
Entry of new firms, 25, 30, 32-33, 37-39, 45-46, 66, 124
Entry level jobs, 93
Epistemology, 178
Equilibrium, monetary, 184-85; nature of, 116, 121; necessary conditions for, 5-6, 51, 75
Equity issues, 81
Exchange, 14, 76-78
Exchange rates, 8, 132, 166, 200, 203-6
Executive group, 22, 30-31, 35-36, 41, 44
Exogenous nature, of money supply, 98-99, 105, 168-70, 172; of money wages, 59-60, 172-73, 196; open market operations, 100, 102
Expectations, 67, 73
Experiments, controlled, 178, 180, 196
Exports, 47, 132; of commodities, 204-7
External financing, 22, 35, 40, 42, 44, 50-51

Family, 14-15, 78, 95
Federal Reserve system, 100-5, 108-10, 122, 145-46
Federal funds, 102; rate, 107-8
Feedback mechanisms, 18-19
Final demand vector, 6, 49, 57-58, 62, 72, 156-57
Finance, 28-29, 31, 34; theory of money and, 120-22, 152, 166-71

Financial crises, 102, 122, 168
Financial institutions, 72, 106
Financial markets, 21–22, 168
Financial system. *See* Monetary-financial system
Firm, representative type of, 45
Firm, theory of. *See* Price theory
Fiscal policy, 67, 113, 119, 135, 137–38, 141, 174, 207–9, 213
Fixed costs, 20–21, 36. *See also* Overhead costs
Fixed nature, of technical coefficients (factor inputs), 88, 155–56, 182–83, 194, 196
Float, 100–1, 168
Flow of funds, 101, 109, 121
Food, cost of, 69, 134
Formal proofs, 178, 188–89, 193
Forward market, 86
Friedman, Milton, 190

Galbraith, John Kenneth, 23, 211
General equilibrium model, 5, 8, 57, 63, 183, 187–88, 191
General Theory of Employment Interest and Money, The, 4–5, 85–86, 95, 110, 115–16, 136, 209
Gerschenkron, Alexander, 188
Ginzberg, Eli, 10, 14–15
Goals, conflict between those of individual and those of the organization, 89–90; of firm, 30, 45, 90; of individual worker, 80–81; of macroeconomic policy, 100
Gold, 100–1, 168, 203–4
Goods markets, 5–6
Government, 12, 17, 67, 69, 162; budget, 60, 67–68, 214; budget deficit, 68, 72, 174; demand by, for goods and services, 47, 67, 115, 120, 122, 130, 207–8; destabilizing effect of, 68, 135; intervention by, in collective bargaining, 127; intervention by, within a particular industry, 33, 38–39, 66; role of, in the economy, 207–14; use of resources by, 120. *See also* Policy, government
Government sector, 122
Government securities, 99–106, 168
Great Britain, 203
Growth, balanced steady-state, 64, 116,

118–19, 126–27, 153, 161, 195; dynamics, 114–16, 177; process, 123; secular, 29, 48–50, 55–57, 60, 62, 64–65, 67–69, 73, 129, 161, 166; theory of, 115–16, 152, 161–62; of world's economies, 201, 204, 206; uneven, 67–68
Growth path, 128; change in, 127–29, 131, 133, 135; choice of, 138, 210; non-inflationary, 136, 143; sustainable, 48, 70–73, 119, 126
Growth rate, of the economy, 119, 128, 143; firm's, 30, 33–34; industry, 48–53, 55, 59, 64–65; warranted, 116–17
Growth vector, 57, 59
Guideposts, Presidential, 127, 137, 146

Harrod, Roy, 4–6, 9, 57, 114–16, 119, 161, 177
Harrod-Domar formula, 116, 118
Hicks-Hansen model. *See* LM-IS model
History, 10, 12–16, 18–26, 125–26
Historical method, 188
Household demand, theory of, 152, 157–61, 181–82. *See also* Consumption
Household sector, 48, 71, 73, 121
Households, 122; compensation of, 136, 141; inventory holdings of, 182
Housing. *See* Residential construction
Hull, Cordell, 203
Human capital approach, to labor, 75, 194
Human developmental dimension. *See* Anthropogenic dimension
Human resource inputs, 88–89, 93–94, 152, 155–56
Human resources, 76, 88, 120
Humanism, 200
Hume, David, 178

Income, aggregate (*see* Aggregate income); division of, 119–20, 125–32; need for, 91–94
Income distribution. *See* Distribution
Income effect, 58, 160, 177; of wage cuts, 86
Income elasticity of demand, 49, 53, 58, 60, 63, 157, 161, 190
Income shares, 119–20, 124
Incomes policy, 91, 110, 113, 136–37, 142–43, 209, 214–15; types of, 145–48, 172

Indifference curves, 151, 157, 181–82, 184, 190
Industrial prices, 166, 205
Industrial revolution, 20
Industrial sector, 6, 134, 166, 171–72, 183, 190–91
Industrialists, 20–21
Industries, emergence of new, 64, 67; life cycle of, 64–66; number of, 29–30, 53–54, 155
Inflation, 5, 7, 29, 55–57, 64, 70, 73, 96, 110, 113, 127, 133, 135–36, 141, 143, 152, 171–74, 185–86, 201, 205–11, 215; excess-demand theory of, 5, 67–68, 96, 135, 172, 174, 191; rate of, 68. *See also* Wage-price spiral
Infrastructure, 120, 130, 161
Innovation, institutional, 8, 10, 18; process, 60; product, 29, 32, 47–49, 52, 60, 62, 64–67
Input-output relationships, 29, 37, 44, 155
Inputs, 152, 182
Institutional dimensions, of society, 11–18
Institutionalist theory, 3, 28, 76, 160, 172, 177
Institutions, economic, 8, 93–94, 96, 113, 124, 137–43; social, 10–16, 75, 93–94, 96
Interest income, 120
Interest rate, 4, 6, 98–99, 105–09, 122, 170–71, 184–86; implicit, on internally generated funds, 38–39, 41–44
Interfirm rivalry, 29
Inter-industry flow. *See* Input-output relationships
Intermediate output, 30
International Monetary Fund, 203
International monetary system, pre-1971, 203–4; reform of, 139, 206
International relationships, 8, 202–4, 206–7
Inventory, stock of, 31–32, 44
Investment, aggregate, 5, 28–29, 55–56, 121–22, 124, 161–63, 188; business, 107, 115–16, 118, 121, 123–24, 126, 135, 161, 184; corporate, 71; by the firm, 30, 33–34, 44, 46; in human beings, 75; within an industry, 50, 55, 65–66; by the megacorp, 70–73; rate

of, 119–20, 125, 127, 138, 141, 162; rate of growth of, 61–62, 116, 118; social control over, 214; social rate of return on, 116
Investment funds, 33, 39, 69, 122–24, 129, 166; demand for, 37, 39; internally generated, 123; supply cost of, 37–39
Investment goods. *See* capital goods
Isoquants, 63, 152, 181–82, 184, 190

Job slots, 88–89, 93
Jobs, access to, 87, 95–96

Kalecki, Michal, 114, 119, 122–24, 135, 161, 165, 177, 209
Key bargain, 91, 127, 172
Keynes, John Maynard, 3–5, 24, 85–86, 113–16, 119, 121–22, 145, 157, 166, 176, 203–4, 209
Keynesian policy, 70, 73, 200, 207
Keynesian theory, 119, 121, 163, 177; orthodox, 98–99, 107, 113, 115, 151, 174, 185–86
Knife-edge problem, 57

LM-IS curves, 152
LM-IS model, 8, 110, 181, 184–85
Labor, cost of, 32, 37, 51–55, 69, 123, 157, 166, 186; nature of, 75
Labor coefficients, 32, 49, 51–54, 58–59, 155–57, 165
Labor economics, 5–6, 75–76, 78, 177
Labor force. *See* Work force
Labor force participation rate, 94
Labor inputs. *See* Human resources
Labor markets, 5–6, 76, 85–87, 93, 172
Labor-output ratio, 32, 49
Laissez-faire, 207–8, 213
Law, role of, in corporate revolution, 21–22
Leisure, 91, 216–17
Lending capacity, of banking system, 99, 106, 108, 170
Leontief, Wassily, 177, 190
Leontief inverse, 51–52, 54, 57–58, 156–57, 165
Leontief model of production, 54, 153–57, 165, 190
Less developed countries, 201, 204–5, 207

Liquidity, 121, 168, 172; international, 206; of monetary-financial system, 99, 102, 106, 170

Liquidity pressure, degree of, 99, 105, 107-9, 168-71

List price, 33, 36-37, 42-44, 46

Loan demand, 6, 99, 170

Loans, 102, 105-7, 109, 121-22, 167-68; to business, 99, 106; to consumers, 99, 106

Logical proofs. See Formal proofs; Mathematical models

Long period, 57, 116-18, 120, 155, 161-62, 182, 195-96

Macrodynamic model, 7-8, 28, 99-100, 106, 151-74; monetary-financial block of, 99-110

Macroeconomic analysis, 28, 108, 115, 184-86; separate from microeconomic analysis, 114

Management techniques, 21-22

Managerial class, 26

Managerial control, 19

Managerial structure, 30, 88

Managerial theory of the firm, 28

Marginal physical product, of capital, 63, 152, 181, 184

Marginal productivity, of capital, 183-84, 190; of labor, 88, 95, 152; theory, 183

Marginalist revolution in economics, 3

Market clearing, 85-87, 95, 189

Market mechanism, 14, 76-77, 85-87, 125, 136, 208

Market share, 30, 32, 34, 38; change in, 47, 66; stabilization of, 65-66

Markets, number of, 155, 190; types of, 5. See also Commodity markets

Mark-up, 29-30, 32-33, 35, 37-44, 46, 49-52, 54-55, 58-60, 65-66, 165-66; pricing model, 165-166, 194, 196

Marshall, Alfred, 183

Marshall plan, 201

Marshallian theory of the firm, 44-47, 176, 183

Marx, Karl, 20, 176

Marxian theory, 8, 27, 114, 177, 203

Material inputs, 30, 48, 155; cost of, 37, 186

Material needs, 78, 80-81, 92, 125, 162, 209

Mathematical models, 178, 188-89

Mathematics, 178, 188

Means, Gardiner C., 165

Means of payment. See Money

Megacorp, 8, 10, 14, 18-19, 21-26, 28-44, 66-67, 70-73, 88, 124-26, 129-31, 133, 136, 142-43

Mental illness, 95

Merchants, 20-21

Metaphysical categories, 63, 180; in economics, 181-84, 190

Methodology, 178, 187-94

Microfoundations, of corporate economy, 28-74; of neoclassical theory, 5, 8, 28, 44-47, 124; of post-Keynesian theory, 124

Mitchell, Wesley C., 160

Monetarism, 56

Monetarist models, 99, 107, 110, 113, 151, 166, 171, 185-86

Monetary authorities, 98, 168, 171-72. See also Central bank; Federal Reserve system

Monetary base, 99, 101, 106, 166, 168, 171

Monetary factors, 99-110, 163-71, 185

Monetary flows, 5, 121, 163-71

Monetary policy, 67, 104, 113, 119, 168, 174, 207-9, 213; accommodating, 47, 67, 102-4, 135, 137, 168-73

Monetary theory, 5-6, 98, 177

Monetary-financial system, 72, 99

Money, 6, 77, 109, 177, 190; international, 204-5; theory of, 120-122, 152, 166-171

Money markets, 5-6

Money supply, 56, 63, 68, 98-100, 105-10, 121, 166, 171, 174, 196

Moore, Basil, 196

Multinational corporation, 3, 8, 14, 26, 206. See also Megacorp

Multiple-plant operation, 31, 35-36

Multiplier, Keynesian, 118, 121, 157, 161

Multiplier-accelerator model, 157, 163, 188

Natural resources, 156, 177

Neoclassical growth models, 64, 176, 189-90, 194

Neoclassical synthesis, 3, 113-14, 151-53, 174, 176, 184, 187; microfoundations of, 5, 8, 28, 44-47, 124

Neoclassical theory, 4, 135, 145, 151–52, 160–61, 174, 176–77, 181–85, 190–91
Neo-Keynesian. *See* Post-Keynesian
Neo-Ricardian theory, 151, 165, 172
Neo-Walrasian, counter-revolution in economics, 5; model, 44, 57, 62–63, 155, 171, 176, 183
Nonwage share, of national income, 119–20, 122, 129–30
Nonworkers, 48, 131–32
Normative dimension, 11–17, 77
Norms, 78

Oil prices, 120, 132, 205
Oligopolistic sector, 30, 67, 71, 173
Oligopoly, 19, 23–24, 29–30, 126, 188
Open market operations, 99–102, 105, 109, 168, 172
Options, individual, 81, 94
Organizational factors, 30–31, 88–89
Orthodox theory, 6–7, 9, 28–29, 44–47, 51, 75, 88, 91–92, 94–95, 99, 113, 116, 118, 122–24, 144, 151–52, 165, 181. *See also* Neoclassical theory
Output, aggregate, 28, 56, 60, 62, 68; firm's standard rate of, 36, 39, 165; industry, 57, 156–57
Output decision, by firm, 28–29, 31, 45–46
Output per worker, 32–33, 37, 48–49, 52–58, 61–62, 68–69, 73, 110, 125–28, 132, 135, 141, 156, 161–62, 166, 216–17
Output vector, 57–58, 62
Overhead costs, 31, 36. *See also* Fixed costs
Oxford pricing group, 165

Parameters, of macrodynamic model, 60–61, 64, 105; of technical progress function, 62
Parsimony principle, 63, 179–80, 182, 188
Parsons, Talcott, 10, 27
Pasinetti, Luigi, 156, 161
Pattern bargaining. *See* Wage pattern
Payback period, 34–35
Pedagogical reform, 217
Peripheral labor force, 85, 93–94
Personnel policy, of megacorp, 31

Phillips curve, 110, 147, 152, 172–73, 181, 184–86
Planning, 210, 213; central, 200; indicative, 8, 146, 213–14
Plant and equipment. *See* Capacity; Investment
Plants, 31; number of, to be operated, 31–32, 44
Policy, coordination of, 142–43; economic, 67–70, 73, 113–14, 119; "full employment," 215–18; government, 129, 133–35, 141–43; public, 7–8, 29, 47–48, 64, 129, 209
Policy implications, of post-Keynesian theory, 135–45
Political dimension, of society, 11–18, 77
Political economy, issues in, 202, 207–8
Political goals, 214–15
Political system, 18
Political trade cycle, 68, 135
Popper, Karl, 179
Portfolio shifts, 106
Post-classical theory, 3, 151
Post-Keynesian theory, 3, 8, 28, 56, 99, 113–25, 127, 133, 135–36, 138, 140, 145, 151–53, 157–58, 161, 165–66, 171–73, 176–77, 187, 195, 197–99; analytical framework of, 153
Post-Marxist theory, 3, 176
Poverty, 211–12
Praxis test, 181, 186, 188
Preferences, consumer, 152, 160–61
Price, as determinant of business savings, 123; as determinant of quantity demanded, 182; as determinant of quantity supplied, 6–7, 62; vs. quantity movements, 184–85
Price-cutting, 20–21, 46
Price elasticity of demand, 37, 53, 58, 60, 63, 66, 157, 161, 190
Price flexibility, 72–73, 125, 183
Price leader. *See* Dominant firm
Price leadership, system of, 72, 188
Price level, 123; aggregate, 28, 54–57, 64, 68, 73, 110, 129, 166, 168–72, 185–86, 209; decline in, as means of distributing benefits of technical progress, 125–26; rise in, 127
Price theory, 5–7, 28; orthodox, 44–47
Price vector (relative prices), 51–54, 56–59, 62, 65, 72, 118, 122, 124, 155–56, 160, 165, 177, 182

Prices, role of, 163; sensitivity of, to change in demand, 183
Pricing, 28–29, 32–44, 114, 119, 152, 165–66, 177, 183; coordination of, by firms, 32–33, 36–37, 41–42; theory of, 165–66, 177
Pricing period, 33
Pricing power, 123, 127, 136, 166
Primary sector, 29, 47, 134, 166, 209
Prisoners' dilemma, 21
Producer welfare, 81
Product life cycle, 64
Product line, 31, 36, 48
Production, 177; model of, 161; neoclassical theory of, 190; post-Keynesian theory of, 152–57, 177, 190; system of, 153, 183. See also Output decision, by firm
Production function, 155; Cobb-Douglass, 190
Production possibility sets, 63
Production system. See Enterprise sector
Productivity, 96, 156. See also Marginal productivity; Output per worker
Products, new, 65
Profit margin, 29, 32, 50, 55–56, 122–29, 131, 133, 143
Profit maximization, 45–46, 152, 183
Profit share, of national income. See nonwage share, of national income
Profits, 36, 119–20, 123, 129–30, 143, 156, 162, 165, 173
Proprietary form of business organization, 19, 29, 45, 122
Public sector, size of, 131–33, 138, 163, 208, 210–12; wages within, 173
Purposeful activity, 92

Queues, labor, 82–84, 87, 93–94

Railroads, 22
Rate of return, on investment, 34, 37, 66, 116; target, 30, 33–35
Rational expectations, 190–91
Rationalism, 200
Raw materials, cost of, 37, 69, 132–34, 138–39, 162, 166, 205, 207; export of (see Exports, of commodities)
Real flows, 5, 121, 163, 185
Recruitment, of workers, 82–84
Regulation, of economic activity by government, 207, 212–14

Renaissance, 200
Rentiers, 60, 132, 162
Rents, 136
Research and development (R&D), 33, 46, 66
Reserves, bank, 99–102, 104–9, 122, 168–70
Residential construction, 29, 118
Residual income, 50, 165. See also Profits
Resource allocation, 95
Retail distribution, 29, 47
Returns to scale, 31, 45, 88, 156, 183
Ricardian vice, 188
Robinson, Joan, 114, 161, 176
Roosevelt, Theodore, 24

Sales, change in, 31–32, 37; expected level of, 39; growth of, 30, 32–34, 71, 123; level of, 43
Samuelson, Paul, 151, 184, 188
Save, propensity to, 116
Savings, aggregate, 4–5, 51, 55–56, 60, 121–22, 124, 163, 188; by business, 55, 122–24; household, 122; by workers, 119
Scarcity, relative, 122
Schools, 15, 78, 93, 96
Schumpeter, Joseph, 23, 65, 188
Science, 178–79, 193
Scientific status, of economics, 7, 178, 187, 194, 199
Search, for jobs, 82–83
Secondary labor force. See Peripheral labor force
Secretariat, of social and economic council, 139–41, 143–44
Security, mutual, 202–3, 207
Services, 157
Sheltering mechanisms, for labor, 90–91, 93
Short period, 116–18, 120–21, 153, 162, 182, 195–96
Skills, 78, 83–84, 95
Slumps. See Depressions, economic
Social class, 96, 160
Social contract, 141, 143, 146
Social democracy, 8, 200–202, 209–11, 215, 217
Social and economic council, 137–39, 142–44
Social milieu, of work, 83–84

Social organization, 62
Social sciences, 8, 180–81
Social security, 132
Social surplus, 17, 136, 216
Social systems framework, 76–79
Sociology, 10
Soviet Union, 200–202
Specification error, 99, 105
Speculation, 126, 139, 182
Speculative interest, within markets, 86
Sraffa, Piero, 165, 172, 176–77, 181, 190
Stability, of economic system, 51, 67, 70–74, 116
Stabilizers, 70–74
Stagflation, 7, 70, 113, 125–35, 145, 151, 172, 186, 206
State, minimalist vs. maximalist, 213–14
Static analysis, of society, 17–18
Static nature, of Keynesian theory, 115–16
Stockholders, 130, 132
Stylized facts, 118
Substitutability, lack of, among consumption goods, 160–61
Substitution effect, 33, 37–38, 53, 58, 160, 177; of wage cuts, 86
Supply, of labor, 75, 91–94
Supply bottlenecks, 138
Supply condition, for continuous growth, 55–56, 61–62, 71–72
Supply curve, for all investment funds, 40–44; firm's, 152; industry, 62, 152, 166, 172, 181–82, 191; for internally generated funds, 39–44; for labor, 6, 75, 91–94
Supply and demand. *See* Demand and supply
Supply function, independence of, from demand function, 5–8
Supply-offer curve, 43
Surplus, cash, 72, 121
Systems theory, 18

Tariff barriers, 200–201, 207
Tax, corporate profits, 34, 60
Tax incidence, 177
Tax policy, 47, 67
Tax rate, 60, 63, 67, 73, 211
Tax revenues, 60, 67, 115, 130, 162
Technical coefficients, 6, 31, 45, 54, 60, 88, 95, 155, 183

Technical progress, 49, 52, 60–62, 120, 125, 156–57, 161–62, 182, 209, 215, 217; capital-embodied nature of, 61, 63, 125–28, 130–32, 135–36, 162
Technique, choice of, 156
Technology, 20, 32, 60, 155, 215
Teleology, 80
Theoretical constructs, of neoclassical theory, 151–52, 181–87
Theory construction, 187–89, 192–93
Theory validation, 187, 192–93
Time, historical vs. logical, 153, 177
Totalitarianism, 200
Trade, between agricultural and industrial sectors, 134; between commodity producing and industrialized countries, 156, 205–7; free, 200; international, 177, 201, 203–6; terms of, 69, 120, 132–134, 162–163, 166
Trade unions, 3, 8, 56, 69–70, 73, 85, 91, 93, 124, 126–29, 131, 133, 136–37, 141–43, 173, 209
Training, on-the-job, 87, 92, 95
Transfer payments, 48, 94, 131, 138, 217
Transportation revolution, 20
Trends, long-run, 116–18, 153, 161. *See also* Long period

U.K. economy, model of, 99
U.S. dollar, reserve currency status of, 203–4
U.S. economy, model of, 99
U.S. leadership, 201–2, 207
USSR. *See* Soviet Union
Uncertainty, 29, 34, 47, 57, 64–70
Underdeveloped countries. *See* Less developed countries
Unemployment, 56, 86, 110, 113, 115, 136, 143, 172–73, 185–86, 188, 207–9, 211, 215; "natural rate" of, 56
Utility functions, 63, 152
Utilization, of labor, 76, 87

Value added vector, 51, 54, 58–59, 156, 165
Value condition, for continuous growth, 55–56, 58, 60, 72
Values, social, 11–18, 77. *See also* Normative dimension
Veblen, Thorstein, 160, 176
Vertically integrated model of produc-

tion, 54, 59, 156
Vintage capital stock, 31, 46
von Neumann model, 156, 165, 190

Wage bargain, 83
Wage bill, 55–56, 58, 94, 165
Wage cuts, 5–6, 85–86
Wage determination, theory of, 152, 171–73
Wage differentials, between organized and unorganized sectors, 173. *See also* Differentials, in income
Wage drift, 56
Wage norm, 56, 90–91, 172
Wage pattern, 127–128, 172–73
Wage rate, 165, 171
Wage share, of national income, 119–20, 122, 126–29, 131–32, 162, 190
Wage structure, internal, 90–91
Wage-price spiral, 68–70, 95, 129–136
Wages, annual increment, 30, 56; growth of, 59, 63, 68–69, 73, 83, 110, 141, 168, 172–73, 209–10; money, 32–33,

37, 51–57, 59–60, 63, 73, 94–95, 126–29, 131, 133–34, 136, 141–43, 156, 166, 172–73, 209; real, 56, 95, 119–20, 123, 126–28, 130–34, 138, 141–43, 162, 172; role of, 83
Walras, Leon, 114
Walrasian model. *See* Neo-Walrasian, model
War, 200–203; cold, 203, 210; nuclear, 201–2
White, Harry Dexter, 203
Wiles, Peter, 188
Work, disutility of, 76, 91
Work force, 6; permanent, 84, 94
Work satisfaction, 216–17
Workers, bargaining power of, 172; consumption by, 162; distribution of income to, 48, 69, 162; representation of by trade union, 70
Working capital, 106, 170
World Bank, 203

X-efficiency, 90